SYLVIA RAFAEL

Foreign Military Studies

History is replete with examples of notable military campaigns and exceptional military leaders and theorists. Military professionals and students of the art and science of war cannot afford to ignore these sources of knowledge or limit their studies to the history of the U.S. armed forces. This series features original works, translations, and reprints of classics outside the American canon that promote a deeper understanding of international military theory and practice.

The Institute for Advanced Military Thinking (IAMT) was formed by retired senior officers of the Israel Defense Forces to serve as a bridge between the theories and policies of the academic world and the doctrine, training, and other preparations required for field operations. The IAMT applies this approach across the full spectrum of future land warfare by:

- initiating and supporting joint discussions regarding the historical lessons offered by land warfare in the Middle East;
- encouraging innovative thinking and open debate about current critical defense issues;
- supporting decision makers as they prepare for future challenges.

Series editors: Roger Cirillo and Gideon Avidor

An AUSA Book

SYLVIA RAFAEL

The Life and Death of a Mossad Spy

RAM OREN AND MOTI KFIR

Translated and Annotated by
RONNA ENGLESBERG

Foreword by
MAJOR GENERAL SHLOMO GAZIT, IDF (RET.)

UNIVERSITY PRESS OF KENTUCKY

Published by The University Press of Kentucky

Scholarly publisher for the Commonwealth,
serving Bellarmine University, Berea College, Centre College of Kentucky, Eastern Kentucky University, The Filson Historical Society, Georgetown College, Kentucky Historical Society, Kentucky State University, Morehead State University, Murray State University, Northern Kentucky University, Transylvania University, University of Kentucky, University of Louisville, and Western Kentucky University.

Editorial and Sales Offices: The University Press of Kentucky
663 South Limestone Street, Lexington, Kentucky 40508-4008
www.kentuckypress.com

Library of Congress Cataloging-in-Publication Data

Oren, Ram, author.
  [Silviyah. English]
  Sylvia Rafael : the life and death of a Mossad spy / Ram Oren and Moti Kfir ; foreword by Major General Shlomo Gazit, IDF (Ret.).
      pages ; cm. — (Foreign military studies)
  Includes bibliographical references and index.
  ISBN 978-0-8131-4695-9 (hardcover : alk. paper) —
  ISBN 978-0-8131-4696-6 (pdf) — ISBN 978-0-8131-4697-3 (epub)
  1. Rafael, Sylvia, 1937-2005. 2. Spies—Israel—Biography. 3. Assassins—Israel—Biography. 4. Israel. Mosad le-modi'in ve-tafkidim meyuhadim—Biography. 5. Salameh, Ali Hassan, -1979—Assassination. I. Kfir, Moti, author. II. Title.
  UB271.I82R34713 2014
  327.1256940092--dc23
  [B]   2014019782

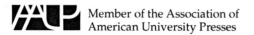

Contents

Illustrations follow page 108

Authors' Note

The story of the Mossad clandestine combatant Sylvia Rafael is based on extensive research, in the course of which countless interviews were conducted and documents gathered regarding her life and work. Due to security restrictions, some of the protagonists' names have been changed, as well as details pertaining to some of the Mossad's operations. In some cases the authors allowed themselves to exercise their literary imagination in order to conceal details that could not be made public.

Foreword

Among members of the intelligence community there is a saying: Intelligence is the second oldest profession in the world; the only difference between that and the oldest is that the intelligence profession has lesser morals.

The dramatic story of Sylvia Rafael, a Jewish Zionist and clandestine combatant of the Special Operations Unit of the Mossad, casts doubt on this adage. On the one hand, it illustrates intelligence operatives' belief that any subterfuge, no matter how questionable, is legitimate in order to achieve their aims. On the other hand, it shows how those operatives must maintain strict self-control and absolute loyalty—both to Israel's struggle with an Arab-Palestinian enemy (who will stop at nothing) and to a careful preservation of moral values—as well as a constant effort to avoid harming innocent bystanders, almost at any price.

The authors of this book chose to tell the story of Sylvia Rafael and the intransigent struggle against members of the PLO's Black September division in order to detail the long, careful process of sorting and selecting candidates for recruitment and the difficult tests and comprehensive, prolonged training that these combatants must undergo before they can be entrusted with operational missions.

The Lillehammer incident and the unintentional elimination of Ahmad Bushiki, an innocent Norwegian youth of Moroccan extraction, is in many ways the antithesis of a carefully considered, cautious operational policy. Unfortunately, sometimes the urgency of the need to take action overrides both restraint and the option of waiting until a better opportunity presents itself—and the decision is made to proceed with an operation in less than ideal circumstances. Sadly, that is what happened at Lillehammer; many such unfortunate incidents may be found not only in the annals of the Israeli secret service, but in those of every intelligence organization.

Sylvia Rafael was highly motivated and had absolute faith in her superiors. The Lillehammer blunder deeply disappointed her. The victim had been mistakenly identified, and the desire to act generated an unsuccessful plan of operation that resulted in the team's being arrested and imprisoned.

It is not surprising that after the fiasco Sylvia wrote, "Something in me broke after Lillehammer . . . it eroded my desire to continue serving with the people I respected so highly. My heroes had appeared to be men of absolute integrity, but suddenly I saw them in a different light. What a pity . . ."

Undoubtedly, the Mossad, the Israeli intelligence community, and the clandestine combatants of the Special Operations Unit learned a valuable lesson from Lillehammer. Nevertheless, those who plan and carry out such missions are never wholly immune from miscalculations and misfortune.

In fact, the failure at Lillehammer did nothing to weaken the resolve of the Mossad combatants, and their adherence to their mission finally paid off. Their uncompromising effort to track down and eliminate Ali Salameh, the arch-terrorist and commander of Black September, was ultimately successful. Sylvia Rafael, that courageous, highly motivated combatant, did derive some solace from this.

In conclusion, one must not forget that the greater part of the Mossad's activities—and that of the intelligence community in general—does not consist in tracking down and eliminating its enemies. Despite the great importance of such operations, they are exceptional and rare occurrences. The secret service's main function (and the yardstick of its effectiveness) is the more humdrum task of collecting information pertaining to issues vital for national security.

Major General Shlomo Gazit, IDF (Ret.)
Former IDF Director of Military Intelligence

Acknowledgments

The authors wish to thank the following people:

Dan Arbel
Tanchum Ben Ari
Ilan Ben David and the censorship team
Nurit Golan
Dina Gemer
Aryeh Zohar, Chairman of the Ministerial Book Censorship
Committee
Nehemiah Meiri
Yaakov Meidad
Eliezer Palmor
Danny Payanis
David Rafael
Annæus Schjødt

And all those who prefer to remain anonymous

1

A Murder Plot

The nine heavily armed men sat around the table. They were dark skinned, dark haired, and stony faced. Copies of a color photo were scattered in front of them. Each of them picked up a copy and studied it carefully. It showed a tall, elegantly dressed woman emerging from a fashionable boutique in downtown Oslo, the capital of Norway. On her arm was a shopping bag bearing the boutique's logo: Stimm and Stohrs.

The photo had obviously been taken with a magnifying lens from a long way away, but despite the distance, the woman's face could be clearly seen. She was attractive and seemed relaxed, untroubled, definitely not suspecting that anyone was following or secretly photographing her.

The atmosphere in the room was thick and intense. Cigarette smoke filled the air, and despite the tightly closed windows, noises from the street and the muezzin's call from the nearby mosque could be heard clearly. It was an early summer evening in 1977, in Western Beirut, Lebanon. People driving home from work were stalled in long lines of slow-moving traffic, and the street lamps were just lighting up.

At the head of the table sat Ali Hassan Salameh, a handsome, curly-haired man of thirty-seven. The others understood that the photographs in front of them were the reason this meeting had been called. They waited for their commander to explain.

"This is Sylvia Rafael," began Salameh.

Although none of them had ever met her, they were familiar with her name. As a matter of fact, they often spoke of her with respect and awe, aware that she had been instrumental in eliminating many of their friends.

"This woman must die," said their leader decisively.

None of those present batted an eyelid. Most of them were expert assassins, and getting rid of Sylvia would be all in a day's work.

Ali Hassan Salameh was a prominent operations officer in Black September, one of the world's cruelest and most dangerous terrorist

1

organizations. He had led terrorist attacks resulting in the deaths of many Israelis and Jews. He was also the architect of the murderous attack on the Israeli athletes at the Munich Olympics and had personally commanded that operation, which had made international headlines.[1] During the 1970s, when his organization was at the pinnacle of its activities, Ali was carried along on a wave of adulation that other terrorist leaders could only dream of. He was a born leader: creative, resourceful, brave, and determined. His men fulfilled his every command to the letter. He was considered a symbol of the Palestinian struggle, and Yasser Arafat, the leader of Fatah, in whose name Black September operated, announced on every possible occasion that Ali exceeded all his expectations. Arafat called him "my son."

Now, almost seven years after its inception, Black September's activities were being severely curtailed by internal squabbles and personal vendettas. Ali Salameh was struggling to maintain his position, determined to restore unity to the ranks and recapture Black September's days of glory. He missed his former celebrity status and the esteem that followed in its wake.

Ali Salameh was not only a leader in his own right. He also benefited from the reputation of his father, whose name had inspired respect among Palestinians beginning in the 1930s. Ali's father, Hassan Salameh, who used to circulate among his men wearing a bandolier of bullets across his chest and two revolvers in his belt, was numbered among the most prominent Arab leaders in Mandatory Palestine. He was under the protection of the Mufti of Jerusalem, Haj Amin al-Husseini, who supported Hitler and the extermination of the Jews. With the encouragement and support of the Mufti, Hassan Salameh had led Palestine's Arabs in a mortal struggle with the Jews prior to the War of Independence and during the early stages of that war. He was an experienced, intelligent, and crafty leader who chiefly led attacks against Jewish targets in central Palestine. He had set up headquarters in a fortified building in the heart of Ramle, from which he commanded bases of operations in Jaffa, Taybeh, and Tulkarm.

For the Jews of pre-state Palestine, Hassan Salameh's name was synonymous with destruction and annihilation. They realized that as long as he was at large, they would have no end of trouble with their Arab neighbors. His elimination was considered essential and urgent, and was given first priority; he was constantly trailed by Jewish forces determined to achieve this end. When it became known that Salameh could generally be found at the headquarters in Ramle, Jewish soldiers attacked the building, but did not succeed in penetrating its walls and killing their prey. In a further attempt, reinforcements from the Givati Brigade[2] attacked the Palestinian stronghold, killing thirty-nine of Salameh's men. He himself was not present at the time, but was eventually killed at the battle of Ras al-Ayn in 1948. His son and only heir, Ali Salameh, was nine years old at the time. When the boy came of age, he swore to avenge his father's death and drive the Jews out of the country. He would accomplish this by means of terrorist activity.

The Beirut conference room in which the senior officers of Black September were meeting with their leader was secured by armed bodyguards. A lookout posted by the windows kept a watchful eye on any suspicious movement. Ali knew that the Israelis were on his trail, and he feared that they might attack at any moment.

Ali was tough and merciless, intelligent and shrewd. He was responsible for numerous plane hijackings and death traps directed against innocent Israeli citizens. He dispatched terrorists to carry out spectacular attacks inside Israel, and he wiped out political opponents without hesitation. He was certain that the Mossad, Israel's intelligence organization, would do anything in its power to stop him, but he continually managed to escape the undercover agents sent to locate him, covering his tracks, assuming endless disguises, and moving from one hiding place to another just when the Israelis thought they had finally cornered him.

Ali had a deep hatred of the Mossad for killing prominent Black September operatives in Europe, many of whom had been his closest personal friends. On only two occasions had Black September managed to retaliate by eliminating Mossad officers. The echoes of these operations were faint, even nonexistent, in comparison with the wide press coverage given to every murderous Mossad attack.

Black September needed to rehabilitate its tarnished image immediately, and Ali Salameh realized that the best way to do this was to strike the Israelis where it would hurt most. Eliminating Sylvia Rafael seemed the ideal means of doing so.

Sylvia was one of the most seasoned Mossad operatives. She was a member of a select team of experienced clandestine combatants whose mission was to locate Ali Salameh. In turn, the leaders of Black September attempted repeatedly to locate and kill Sylvia, but to no avail. They craved her death, as over the years she had been a constant threat hanging over their heads. Here at last was the opportunity they had been waiting for, and they were determined to succeed.

Ali Salameh knew that Sylvia Rafael's death would not only arouse shock and horror in the Mossad, but would also be a source of consolation for the surviving members of Black September, who had lost their commanders and colleagues one by one through a series of Mossad attacks.

"It shouldn't be too complicated," he said. "Our men have been following her for a few weeks and have discovered that she goes around Oslo unarmed and unguarded. She doesn't suspect that anyone is threatening her life."

He announced that he would soon put together a team to eliminate Sylvia. "Only the best men will be chosen," he promised. "There will be no slip-ups."

Ali reported his plan to Yasser Arafat. The PLO leader liked the idea and gave it his approval. Since Ali's Black September funds were depleted, Arafat agreed to personally finance the operation, supplying plane tickets, hotels, and living expenses.

The plan of execution was soon ready. Libyan diplomats, who served Ali and his organization faithfully and had embassies in every European capital, smuggled revolvers into Oslo by means of their diplomatic pouch, stashing them away until needed.

Ali Salameh set the time of the operation for early summer. He assumed that as the weather became warmer, Sylvia would spend more time out of doors, making it easier to eliminate her.

The four assassins were chosen carefully. Only men who had previously participated in complex terrorist operations were selected. When they arrived in Oslo from various European cities, their fake passports were stamped by the Norwegian border police without arousing suspicion.

The team members booked into separate hotels and circled Oslo for two days in order to check out the lay of the land and find possible escape routes. Their orders were simple and precise: after Sylvia's elimination they were to scatter and depart for different European destinations, some by car and others by plane.

After they had completed their reconnaissance of the city, the team made sure to remain inconspicuous. They avoided using the telephone, hid out in their rooms, made do with sandwiches, and retired early.

As the date of the attack drew near, they collected the guns from their hiding place in the Libyan Embassy. It was decided that they would attack Sylvia from a public park opposite her home. When she came out of the door, they would open fire and leave her lying dead on the pavement.

They were confident that their mission would be successful.

2

An Unexpected Visitor

Clouds of dust blowing up from the desert hid the sun and the large sheep enclosures of the South African town of Graaff-Reinet. Through the thick fog, a loaded truck slowly made its way along the torrid highway. In the drivers' cabin sat two men. One gripped the steering wheel, and the other dozed, his head on his chest.

When the truck neared the northernmost houses of the town, the driver stopped by the side of the road. "Wake up," he said, shaking his passenger. "We've arrived." He pointed at the small houses and the white steeples of the Dutch Reform church that protruded above the dust. "That's Graaff-Reinet," he added.

The skinny, wild-haired passenger dressed in ragged clothes climbed down from the truck and waved his thanks. He was a heavy-limbed man in his mid-thirties, whose stomach was rumbling with hunger. For the past three days, since his ship had anchored in Port Elizabeth harbor in early August 1946, he had eaten only scraps of food that he had managed to collect from garbage cans, so that he could hold onto the small sum of money that was hidden in his shoes. He was unshaven and hadn't washed since leaving the ship, but he seemed totally unaware of his appearance. He derived strength from the goal that impelled him forward: to reach Graaff-Reinet. Achieving this objective had given him hope, even in the face of certain death.

The man had stayed alive only by a miracle. Before World War II, he had been a high school history teacher. After the war began, Ukrainian thugs had broken into his home and seized him, his wife, and their two children, and then marched them, along with hundreds of other Jews, to a deep valley among thick trees. There the Jews were shot down mercilessly, in a place that was later known as Babi Yar. Very few, among them the young teacher, fell into the hole before they were riddled by bullets; among the corpses, they pretended to be dead. They were the only ones to survive the slaughter.

After nightfall, when the cries of the dying were silenced, the man crawled out from among the corpses and stole back to his house. He pulled up the floor tiles in one of the rooms, under which his wife had hidden her jewelry, and stowed the valuables in his pockets, together with a letter bearing an address in Graaff-Reinet, South Africa. Well hidden from view, he walked all night on wooded paths. During the day he hid in the forest, eating berries, drinking water from rivers and streams, and mourning the death of his wife and children. After dark he continued on his way until sunrise. After a few nights he arrived at the home of Christian friends, who hid him in their cellar. In exchange for some of the valuables in his possession, they provided him with food and, most important of all, didn't reveal his existence to a soul. Twice the Germans conducted a careful search of houses in the area, but they failed to find the Jew who had escaped from death.

When the war ended, the man emerged from his hiding place and returned to his native city, a large part of which had been destroyed by bombing. He searched the ruins in the hope of finding relatives that had survived the inferno. Sleeping in cellars, he survived on fruit that he picked from abandoned orchards. A few weeks of unsuccessful searching and conversations with survivors convinced him that none of his relatives had survived. It was pointless for him to remain in Kiev.

He crossed Europe by hitchhiking and occasional train rides, knocked on the doors of relief organizations, and scanned hundreds of lists of survivors in an attempt to locate relatives and friends. All his efforts were useless. He had only one lead left, one faint hope—the envelope with the address in South Africa. He believed that he would find kind people there who would help him toward rehabilitation.

Mustering his last remaining strength and resources, the man from Kiev used an antique piece of gold jewelry, a family heirloom, to bribe a Russian clerk, who helped him obtain a passport and permission to board a Soviet freight ship that was leaving for South Africa. He was prepared to do any kind of work without payment in order to arrive at his destination, and he didn't complain when they loaded him with chores from morning till night, scraping off barnacles and painting the ship's metal hulk.

When the ship anchored in Port Elizabeth harbor, the man disembarked, carrying a worn-out bag containing a few clothes. In his pocket was the yellowing envelope that had become his most prized possession. On the back was written the sender's address; he set out in that direction.

Graaff-Reinet, a town of 10,000 inhabitants, which had been named after the first governor of the area, was located on the banks of the Sunday River. Its residents made their living by raising sheep for the local wool industry, exporting oranges, and producing wine from locally grown grapes. The survivor arrived there on a day plagued by a heavy east wind. The wooden shutters of the houses were tightly shut, and only those who had no choice could be found outside on the wide streets.

A policeman, wiping sweat from his forehead, directed the new arrival to the address he sought. With faltering steps and slow movements, he made his way toward an elegant residence. He hoped to find good people there who would help restore him to life.

The members of the Rafael family—a husband and wife and their five children—were gathered around the afternoon tea table. Two black servants provided them with dainty sandwiches, cakes, and dishes of jam.

A peaceful atmosphere reigned in this prosperous family's home. Ferdinand Rafael had emigrated with his family from the Ukraine to South Africa when he was a child. His parents had hoped to improve their economic situation in their adopted country. They worked in trade, bought a house, and employed black servants. Ferdinand grew up to be a talented businessman. He became wealthy from land sales, acquired a few flocks of sheep, and eventually took over ownership of the local cinema. He was also president of the club to which the wealthier residents belonged. They met there to dine sumptuously and listen to lectures on a variety of topics delivered by specially invited speakers. On festive occasions, they held formal dance parties.

Forty-two-year-old Ferdinand Rafael was a traditional Jew, who regularly attended the town's small synagogue on the Sabbath and maintained a Jewish way of life. His wife, Miriam, the daughter of a respected Boer family, was raised as a Christian.[1] She had never officially converted to Judaism, but had learned to keep a kosher home for her husband and family. She even fasted on Yom Kippur as a sign of identification with the Jewish people.

The doorbell rang, and they wondered who would be calling at such an hour, as they weren't expecting anyone.

The female servant opened the door and recoiled in shock.

"Come quickly!" she cried.

The family rushed to the door and saw a man lying unconscious on the doorstep.

"Who is that?" asked the eldest daughter, Sylvia.

"I haven't the faintest idea," answered her father.

In the dead of night in mid-February 1948, Hassan Salameh left his small stone house in the village of Qula in the Lydda district and walked toward his Packard, which was parked in the village center. Qula was a village of 1,000 inhabitants covering an area of 250 acres and overlooking Israel's Lydda Airport.

The Packard convertible was Hassan's pride and joy. Only the wealthiest Arab families possessed automobiles, whereas he, the son of a poor quarry laborer, had done the impossible by managing to acquire this most impressive status symbol, and an American one at that. Hassan looked after his car as though it were a thoroughbred stallion. He appointed one of his men to be in charge of washing and waxing it on a daily basis. He didn't bother locking the doors or posting guards around it; nobody would be foolhardy enough to steal it.

Until money had started coming his way, Hassan had known years of extreme poverty. He had often gone to bed hungry when there was no money in the house for food. All that changed when he began gathering men around him who were willing to sacrifice their lives in order to drive the Jews and the British from his country. When Hassan's pockets began filling with money, it was rumored that the funds had been stolen from the British banks raided by his men. There was also reason to believe that the Mufti of Jerusalem had financed the struggle of Palestine's Arabs during World War II with funds originating from Nazi Germany.[2]

On that particular chilly February night, Hassan was accompanied by his young son, Ali. He placed a heavy English rifle on the backseat, and they set off.

Behind the cactus hedge surrounding Qula village, a group of Hassan's most seasoned men were waiting on horseback, with rifles slung across their shoulders. They were joined by a few dozen men from the surrounding villages, Mazra'a, Rantis, and Hadid. Hassan's black car tore along the dirt road at the head of the riders, stirring up clouds of dust in its wake.

Ali was jostled to and fro in the seat next to his father, but he didn't complain. His eyelids were drooping with sleepiness, and his body craved the warm blanket that had been pulled off him when it was time to leave the house with his father.

Ali always obeyed his father, whether he wanted to or not. In fact, there wasn't a single person who didn't obey Hassan Salameh, the supreme commander of the Arab army of central Palestine. This burly, bespectacled, uneducated man knew how to stir up enthusiasm in the Arabs of the Lydda and Ramle districts and muster them for battle. He provided them with a personal example of bravery and military skill, and when the War of Independence broke out in June 1948, he already had to his credit a long string of operations that were meant to shake the confidence and determination of Jewish settlers and British conquerors alike.

Hassan Salameh was a rising star in the firmament of Palestinian leadership. He was renowned for his cleverness and ingenuity. These qualities usually enabled him to catch the Jews unawares by launching attacks at unanticipated times and locations. His sharp senses alerted him to any traps set for him. He took pride in the fact that more and more men were joining his ranks daily.

Salameh, a devout Muslim who proudly bore the title of "Sheikh," aspired to be the military leader of Arab Palestine after the Jews were finally driven from the land. His only source of dissatisfaction was Ali, his eldest son and heir. Ali was born and raised in the village of Qula, situated on the road from Rosh Ha'ayin to Lydda and overlooking the Plain of Sharon. On a clear day you could even see as far as Tel Aviv.

The slim, good-looking child enjoyed playing with his friends, but was less enthusiastic about working in the fields helping his family cultivate the soil, plant crops, and gather the harvest. The village was blessed with rich, fertile soil and abundant water. Most of the inhabitants were sons of farmers, and they expected their own sons to carry on that tradition. Ali, however, dreamed of being a film star when he grew up.

Hassan Salameh was a well-trained soldier. He had undergone extensive training as a guerrilla fighter by Nazi army experts, with the purpose of grooming him to lead the Arab uprising against the British mandatory forces in Palestine.[3] He had earned the reputation of being a talented leader, a fearless soldier, and an excellent shot. Unfortunately, his son was the direct opposite—a dreamy boy who enjoyed playing ball and riding his donkey among the ruins of the crusader castle upon which the village had been built. Hassan Salameh was ashamed of his son. He was jealous of those of his men who trained their sons to use weapons and brought them along to participate in attacks on Jewish settlements. Ali was the only child in the village who took no interest in bringing death and destruction upon the Jews. He grew bored when his father told him about the Arabs' rightful ownership of the land and their struggle to drive out the Jewish usurpers. He yawned when his father boasted about his military exploits. Ali's mother, Naima, was no less mortified than her husband by their son's lack of interest in becoming a fighter. She and her husband had long talks with the boy, explaining that he was bringing shame upon his family. He was Hassan's sole heir, and when the time arrived, the eyes of every Palestinian fighter would be upon him, expecting him to carry on his father's legacy. He must not disappoint them.

Ali hung his head obediently and didn't utter a word.

On Ali's eighth birthday, his father announced that from then on the boy would accompany him on some of his military exploits, hoping that this would inspire him to be a fighter someday. Before they set out, his mother supplied him with pita bread filled with olives and salty goat cheese. "Don't worry," said Ali, reading her thoughts. "I won't embarrass Father."

Hassan Salameh, with Ali in tow, arrived at his headquarters, a four-story building in Ramle that had formerly been a training college for British officers. The 150-room building functioned as an army headquarters in every sense of the word. On a daily basis, hundreds of Arab volunteers trained in the courtyard in the use of light weapons, hand grenades, and hand-to-hand fighting. In the basement was a huge arsenal of weapons, and parked outside the building were three armored cars that had been obtained from British soldiers in exchange for large sums of money. A short time earlier, a large Jewish force had attacked the building with the express aim of wiping out Salameh, but he was fortunate enough to have been elsewhere at the time of the attack. (He had in fact been spending time with his mistress in Damascus.)

Ali was far from enthusiastic, but in order not to hurt his father, he avoided expressing how he felt: namely, that planned army attacks simply didn't interest him.

Hassan Salameh presented Ali proudly to his men, took him out to observe shooting practice, and even handed him a rifle. Ali held the weapon unwillingly. The firearm was heavy and unwieldy, and Hassan held back the reprimand that was on his lips when Ali handed it back to him. The men standing around them regarded the boy with frank disappointment. They were convinced that a good beating on the part of his father would convince Ali to toe the line and take a greater interest in warfare. But Hassan, as cruel and pitiless as he was, never laid a finger on the boy.

The following day, Hassan and Ali were awakened at dawn by the sound of rifle fire and bursting grenades. It quickly became apparent that the Jews had opened an attack on a nearby Arab position. This was to be Ali's baptism of fire. Shaking with fear, he suppressed a tearful plea to return home.

A short time later, when his father's men joined in pursuit of the Jewish attackers, Ali went back to sleep. When Hassan returned, he shook his son awake and stood him on his feet. "Enough sleeping," he reprimanded him. "The war isn't over yet. We still have much work to do."

And so, at midnight on that February night in 1948, Hassan Salameh set out with his son at the head of a fighting unit in the direction of the town of Yazur, a few hours away on the road to Jerusalem. At sunup, the Arabs set up a roadblock of stones and took up firing positions among the eucalyptus trees on both sides of the road. Hassan pulled his son down next to him on the ground and pointed toward a Jewish convoy that was approaching their ambush positions. "Now you'll see us make short work of them," he said. Ali closed his eyes, praying that his father wouldn't force him to see the dead and wounded lying in pools of blood.

The armored trucks slowly proceeded up the narrow asphalt road. A few young Jews alighted from the vehicles and tried to clear away the barrier of stones that Ali's men had placed across their path. On top of the roadblock the Arabs had laid a dead dog with a booby trap inside it. As the Jews began clearing away the stones, the makeshift bomb inside the dog exploded, wounding some of them. Then Salameh gave the order to attack. Hundreds of Arab fighters began running in the direction of the road, shouting *"Itbah al-ye-hud!"* (Slaughter the Jews!) and shooting at the armored vehicles. The young Jews outside the vehicles were shot and killed instantly. Many of those emerging from the vehicles in order to collect the dead were also killed or wounded.

The remaining Jews opened fire through slits in the sides of the armored trucks, but it was a losing battle. Hassan Salameh's men would reach the vehicles at any moment, slaughter the remaining survivors, and appropriate their money and weapons. The trapped Jewish drivers maneuvered their vehicles onto the narrow road, turned around, and retreated. Pools of blood remained on the road. When nobody was watching, Ali stepped aside and vomited.

The Arab attackers congregated in one of the nearby orchards. Their mood was ecstatic. Some of them approached Ali and congratulated him on his bravery. Ali thanked them bashfully. He wanted to be as far away from there as possible, but didn't dare admit it.

Salameh gave the order to carry on with the operation. Blocking the road to Jerusalem was essential, he said. "The Jews are attempting to bring supplies to the besieged city, " he announced. "We can't let that happen."[4]

Ali remained at the roadblock with Hassan and his men for two days. He slept on the ground and ate pita bread, olives, and the fruit that he managed to gather from the trees. He was present at additional ambushes, heard the bullets whizzing over his head, and witnessed both Arab and Jewish casualties.

On the third day, Salameh left the operation in charge of his second-in-command and returned with his son to the village of Qula. He was confident that Ali had learned an important lesson and that his son finally realized that he was duty-bound to follow in his father's footsteps. There were some encouraging signs: the boy hadn't complained even once and hadn't run away from the battlefield. Even though Ali hadn't expressed enthusiasm, Hassan considered this an important first step from Ali's childhood to becoming worthy of taking over from his father. He told his son, "I'm glad you were with me," and Ali replied, "So am I, Father."

A mile from the village, their way was blocked by a line of refugees. Hassan and his son recognized them as inhabitants of Qula. The refugees carried their few possessions on their backs and in hand carts, having thrust the keys to their houses deep inside their pockets. Hassan's wife and her parents were among them. They recounted in sorrow how a unit of Jewish soldiers had invaded the village, overcome the weak resistance put up by the village men, and occupied the area. All the inhabitants had quickly gathered up their belongings and fled. Hassan gritted his teeth, drove his family to the home of friends in Ramle, and announced that he was returning to the front.

"I'm going to liberate Qula," he said, ignoring his wife's tearful imprecations. "Look after yourself," she implored him.

"Don't worry," he replied confidently. "*Alla ma'ana.* God is with us."

The Rafael servants carried the unconscious unknown visitor into the house, and Ferdinand called a doctor.

"He's suffering from exhaustion," announced the doctor, after performing a thorough examination. "Let him rest, and when he regains consciousness, try to feed him a little, mainly liquids."

He packed up his medical bag. "How did this man arrive here?" he asked.

Miriam said that the servant had found him lying on the doorstep.

"You'd better be careful," said the doctor with a grim expression. "Who knows? Maybe he's a thief, or a murderer."

This alarmed Ferdinand. He put his hand in the man's pocket and drew out a Soviet passport in the name of Alex Rafael, a native of Kiev.

"That's strange," he murmured. "We have the same family name, but I have no idea who he is."

He noticed that in his left hand the man was clutching something that looked like an envelope. Ferdinand managed to extricate it from the man's grasp and read what was written on it. It was addressed to Alex Rafael in Kiev, the Ukraine, and bore the return address of Ferdinand Rafael, Graaff-Reinet, South Africa. Only then did Ferdinand recall that he had sent money to a cousin on the occasion of his bar mitzvah. Was it he who was now lying unconscious in his house?

Since the beginning of the war, Ferdinand had heard nothing from his relatives in Europe. He had tried to contact them by mail after the war, but his efforts had been fruitless. He still hadn't completely lost hope that at least some of them had survived.

At lunchtime the following day, Alex opened his eyes. Miriam fed him hot chicken soup, and he sipped it gratefully. Slowly and painfully, in halting English, he sadly informed the Rafaels that the whole family had perished in the war, and that his own survival had been a miracle. Sylvia wept bitterly at hearing this tragic news.

Until the moment they met Alex, the horrible events of the war had seemed distant and vague to the five Rafael children, Sylvia,

Joyce, Harriet, Jonathan, and David. The newspapers that arrived in Graaff-Reinet had carried war reports, and Ferdinand had told the children about those relatives who had remained in Europe, but these were people they had never met and whose existence they were hardly aware of. They only realized the magnitude of the disaster that had befallen their kin when this stranger arrived, with only a faint glimmer of life still left in him.

None of the Rafael children had received a traditional Jewish education, and none of them regretted this. They were receiving a general education at the local school, and they participated in traditional holiday celebrations only out of respect for their father.

Under the devoted care of the entire household, the unexpected visitor gradually recuperated, and Ferdinand invited him to stay with them as long as he liked. After a few days, Alex could sit up in bed and converse with his hosts. He told Sylvia, who was around eight, that his daughter, Judith, had been just her age when she was taken to Babi Yar and shot by Ukrainian thugs and S.S. officers. Sylvia was thirsty for more information, and Alex told her about the family in Kiev, their daily lives before the war, and the extermination of hundreds of thousands of Ukrainian Jews.

"Why didn't they defend themselves?" Sylvia inquired.

"Because they didn't have guns," answered Alex softly.

Her father had told her that he had had three uncles and twelve cousins.

"Why did they kill them?" she asked. "What did they do wrong?"

"They didn't do anything wrong," explained Alex. "Their only crime was being Jewish."

"I'm Jewish!" she replied nervously. "Will they kill me, too?"

"The Jews have nothing to worry about in South Africa," he reassured her.

Sylvia wanted to know more about Judaism, and every day Alex sat beside her and, in his broken English, told her stories from the Old Testament, about the wandering tribes and the chronicles of the kings of Judea and Israel, and about the heroic stand at Masada and the destruction of the Second Temple.[5]

That week at school, Sylvia wrote a composition that was highly praised by her teacher:

> Our entire family in Europe was killed before we even had a chance to meet them. My father told me that they were very

nice people. They had houses and gardens and children and they were happy and sad just like everybody else. Suddenly everything was destroyed, without anyone suspecting that it would happen. They were taken from their houses and killed, just because they were Jews. The Ukrainians and the Germans had rifles and cannons, but my family didn't even have a revolver to protect them. The Jewish people had already suffered enough. There were always bad people who wanted to destroy the Jews, and only rarely did they defend themselves. The Jews believe in God; they pray to Him every day and fulfill His commandments. I asked my father why God didn't protect his Jews, why didn't He save our family, and Father only said: If the Jews don't defend themselves, nobody else will do it for them.

Sylvia's interest in Judaism steadily increased. At her request, her father ordered English books and albums from Palestine. During her summer vacation, she traveled as far as Port Elizabeth to join a youth group organized by the local Jewish community, and participated in a play about the heroic stand of Joseph Trumpeldor at Tel Hai.[6] Her father and mother, sisters and brothers, as well as Alex, came to see the performance. Sylvia's activities in the community center were highly praised by all.

After the play, just as they were preparing to return home, Alex collapsed. He was admitted to St. George Hospital in Port Elizabeth, where the best doctors were put at his disposal. Sylvia begged to stay with him until he recovered. Friends of Ferdinand's, who lived near the hospital, invited her to stay with them.

Being an outstanding student, Sylvia was given permission to miss school in order to take care of Alex. Every day she sat by his bedside and talked with him. The disasters of war had taken a severe toll on his health. Now his body had succumbed to cancer, and there was nothing left to be done. The Rafael family rushed to the hospital to be present during his last painful hours. Alex's last words were: "Take care of yourselves . . . do everything in your power to prevent any more Jewish deaths."

The Rafael family accompanied him to his final resting place in the Jewish cemetery.

The day after Alex's funeral, the South African newspapers announced the United Nations decision to create a Jewish state in Palestine.[7] Ferdinand Rafael's grand residence in Graaff-Reinet was the only building to fly an Israeli flag. His eldest daughter, Sylvia, was the first to raise the flag on a pole in front of the house. Passersby stared at it curiously, only a few of them knowing which country it represented.

The next day there was another newspaper item from Israel. Ferdinand Rafael sadly read it aloud to his family. An Egged bus had been ambushed by Arabs near Petah Tikva, and six passengers had been killed.[8] Half an hour later, another bus was attacked, resulting in two additional casualties.

"They're killing Jews yet again," sighed Sylvia's father.

The U.N. decision regarding the partition of Palestine and the establishment of a Jewish state deeply upset Hassan Salameh. He felt that all his efforts had been in vain and that the armed attempt to rid Palestine of its Jewish settlers had failed; but there was still hope that the State of Israel would not become a reality. The invasion of the Arab armies in 1948 was directed at preventing the U.N. decision from being realized; the aim of the invasion was to hand over control of Palestine to the Arabs.[9] Hassan Salameh waited eagerly for the armies of the Arab League to arrive. He hoped that his own forces would play a major part in defeating the Jews. After all, who else had embittered their lives for so many years? Who was more worthy than he of enjoying the fruits of victory? Salameh, however, quickly came to understand that this was a false hope: the commanders of the Arab armies weren't asking for his assistance; they were confident that they would easily overcome any Jewish or British resistance. They had not yet decided how to divide the spoils of victory among themselves, never mind giving Hassan Salameh a share. With a heavy heart, Salameh realized that he had been deposed as leader of the armed struggle over Palestine. This was no longer his war, but the war of all the Arab nations.

Nevertheless, despite his temporary loss of status, he would not surrender or bow before the commanders of the Syrian and Iraqi armed forces, thus relinquishing his right to receive any benefit from the impending struggle. Hassan Salameh believed in what he was doing and was sure that he was no less capable than any professional military officer. He reassured himself that in the end there would be no choice for the victors but to give him a portion of the rewards of victory. Allah would see to it that he received his just deserts.

On May 15, 1948, immediately after the U.N. declaration regarding the foundation of the State of Israel, the Iraqi army invaded the country. Two weeks later, an Iraqi patrol unit conquered the Arab village of Ras al-Ayn, located southwest of Kafr Kassem. Ras al-Ayn commanded an area east of the Antipatris Fortress, the last remnant of the city built by King Herod on the ancient caravan route linking Jaffa with Amman, Jordan.[10] The historic stone building rising above the buried Herodian city was not the only salient feature of the town. Ras al-Ayn was strategically important due to its location at the source of the Yarkon River, which supplied the city of Jerusalem with its drinking water.

As the Iraqis reinforced their position, digging trenches and constructing fortifications near the springs flowing into the river, the Etzel prepared to attack. Those were days of confusion and panic for the Jews; against the Iraqi invasion and that of the pan-Arab "Army of Salvation" stood a few Jewish underground forces: the Haganah, the Etzel, and the Lehi.[11] At that stage, the Israel Defense Forces existed only on paper.

The fighters of the Etzel were less prepared than the professional Iraqi soldiers. Their weaponry was meager, and their experience with attacking well-fortified positions was limited. Nevertheless, they did have an obvious advantage: they were defending their homeland, and they firmly believed in their ability to win.

The attack exacted a heavy price of dead and wounded on both sides, but ultimately the Etzel was victorious and took up positions along the line of defense constructed by the Iraqis.

Hassan Salameh heard about the occupation of Ras al-Ayn while planning a series of attacks on Jewish settlements in the center of the country. He was well acquainted with the place. Four years earlier, after visiting the Mufti of Jerusalem in Germany, Salameh was chosen to take part in an extensive terrorist offensive in Palestine. The Mufti had planned the operation in conjunction with the Nazis. Salameh, another Arab fighter, and three Nazi officers underwent an intensive training program, after which they were taken to a small airport near Berlin, where a Henkel plane was waiting to fly them to Palestine. The plane circled Jericho, and the five fighters parachuted, carrying backpacks containing gold, weapons, forged documents, and a deadly poison that was meant to contaminate Jerusalem's water supply. The British tracked them down, capturing the second Arab and two of the Germans. Hassan Salameh and the remaining German managed to escape.

According to the Mufti's instructions, Salameh was supposed to spill the poison into the source of the Yarkon River. He was familiar with the place, as it was close by his native village of Qula, but intensive Jewish activity in the area heightened the risk that he would be caught in the act of poisoning the water source, so he canceled the operation. Later, however, he had the opportunity to return to the source of the river and block off the Jews' water supply. He was confident that when he recaptured the place from the Jews, the Iraqis would reciprocate by restoring him to his former position.

Salameh quickly assembled a few hundred of his men and they set off in the direction of Ras al-Ayn.

The Jews who had occupied the Iraqi positions were ready for a counterattack. At sunup, when Salameh's men opened fire and invaded the village in armored cars, the Israelis immediately prepared for battle. Each side fired on the other with rifles and machine guns and operated mortars and antitank artillery, but the Jews' fighting spirit was stronger and their aim was better. As Hassan Salameh was attacking the fortified hilltop, the Jews began firing mortar shells in his direction. Shrapnel punctured his internal organs; seriously wounded, he was rushed to the hospital in Ramle.

Salameh was admitted to the hospital on May 31, 1948, and the doctors tried in vain to stabilize his rapidly deteriorating state. When it became clear that Hassan would not recover, his men, who were posted outside his room around the clock, rushed off to bring his wife and son to his bedside. Naima, at the end of her pregnancy, and her son, Ali, held Hassan's hands, wept bitterly, and prayed to Allah to save their loved one.

"Naima," whispered the wounded man, "when my soul goes to Heaven, remember that you have a grave duty: to train Ali to take my place and make sure that he continues the struggle for Palestine."

"I promise," she replied softly.

To Ali he said, "My son, do not ever forget who your father was. Remember that fate meant you to follow in my footsteps, to fight to the death against the enemies of the Arab people. Thanks to you, the name 'Salameh' will continue to be inscribed on the banner of the struggle."

Hassan Salameh died on June 2, 1948. His men marched to his funeral carrying huge posters bearing his likeness. The women wore black and wept when the coffin passed the outskirts of Ramle on its way to the local cemetery.

When she was sixteen years old, Sylvia organized a celebration for the members of the Jewish youth movements in Port Elizabeth in honor of the State of Israel's sixth anniversary. She read out an English translation of "The Silver Platter" by Nathan Alterman, a choir sang "Bab al-Wad" and "The Friendship Song" by Haim Gouri, and colored slides of various Israeli landscapes were projected on a large screen.[12] The celebration was attended by heads of the local Jewish community as well as non-Jewish dignitaries. The next day, the local press published articles about the occasion, accompanied by photographs.

Sylvia was a pretty girl, tall and attractive, a talented student, lively, creative, quick-witted, and a born leader. In class and with her friends, she often spoke about her plans to go to Israel and help the Jews build their country.

But when she confronted her parents and asked their permission to go, they both insisted that she remain at home.

"You're still young," her mother said. "Finish university first; give yourself more time. Then you can decide what you want to do with your life."

Sylvia realized that she had no choice but to obey her parents. After she graduated from high school, she enrolled in a liberal arts program at the university, returning home four years later with an academic degree. She worked for a year as a music teacher at a school in Port Elizabeth, but her desire to go to Israel hadn't diminished, and she continued making plans to go there for an indefinite period.

Around this time Sylvia became attracted to a young man whom she met at the home of friends in Port Elizabeth. Avery Simon was six years older than Sylvia, the son of a wealthy Jewish family, and a fledgling lawyer in a successful legal firm. He fell in love with Sylvia the first time he met her. He was delighted by her appearance, her cleverness, and her gentle manner, and his overtures led to a passionate romance. A few weeks later, on his birthday, Avery invited her to dinner with his parents. His father was a powerful building contractor, and his mother was active in various charity organizations. They received Sylvia warmly and maintained a light, friendly atmosphere around the dinner table. After dinner, the father presented his son with a set of keys for his birthday. They were the keys to a beautiful house that had been custom-built for him.

The next day, Avery took Sylvia to see the new house. She was impressed by its size and the views from the windows. "This will be our house," Avery said, his eyes shining. "We will raise our wonderful family here."

Sylvia's parents liked Avery from the moment they met him, and they both agreed that they couldn't hope for a better son-in-law.

Sylvia and Avery seemed to be the perfect couple. They both were attractive, intelligent, and cosmopolitan. They often discussed their future together. Sylvia spoke of her desire to immigrate to Israel, but Avery tried to convince himself that she would eventually forget about it. When he subsequently asked her to marry him, Sylvia reminded him that she had other plans and told him she was not ready for marriage. What mattered to her, she said, was to realize her dreams and fulfill her potential. When she suggested that Avery accompany her to Israel, he sadly replied that it would be impossible. "I'm just starting my career," he said, "with a good chance of eventually making senior partner. What would I do in Israel? I don't know the language, so how could I practice law there?"

Sylvia told Avery that she respected his decision, but he must understand that her place was in Israel. "Every Jew must go there in order to help build the state and defend it," she claimed. "That is our country, not South Africa."

Avery's parents took his side and tried to get Sylvia to change her mind. As a compromise, Avery suggested that she go to Israel for a few months and work there as a volunteer. "I'll wait for you," he promised. She looked at him tenderly. "Israel is my dream," she said. "I don't know how long I'll stay there. If you join me, it will prove that you really love me."

Sylvia's father spent long hours having heart-to-heart talks with her, hoping to convince her to change her mind. "Israel will get along without you," he said. "Here you have a loving family and a young man who worships you and wants to marry you. What have you got there? Nothing."

Surprisingly, it was her non-Jewish mother who supported her decision.

"Leave her alone," Miriam admonished her husband. "She can

do as she pleases with her life and should realize her potential as she sees fit. We haven't got the right to intervene."

Sylvia's decision to go was tinged with sadness. She loved Avery, enjoyed his company, and knew that she would have a wonderful life with him; but her dream of Israel was too strong. When she announced to him that she had decided to leave, a shadow crossed his face. He could not understand why she was so stubborn. Sylvia also failed to convince her father that Israel was their real homeland.

It was in Sylvia's nature to have no qualms about behaving differently from what was expected of her. She had no intention of marrying Avery, although that seemed the obvious thing for her to do; she insisted on going to Israel, despite her father's strong objections. Psychological tests performed on Sylvia some time later yielded the following results: "Sylvia has a deep-seated need to give her life meaning. This can clearly be seen in her having left her fiancé in order to immigrate to Israel. Moving to an unknown young country fired her imagination far more than having a comfortable existence in a quiet South African suburb."

At twenty-two, more determined than ever, Sylvia packed her bags and was driven to the airport by her parents. Before she boarded the plane, her father hugged her affectionately and gave her the gift of an expensive camera.

"We'll all be here waiting for your return," he said.

She hugged him tightly, but knew in her heart that she wouldn't be seeing him for a very long time.

If it hadn't been for his mother, sister, aunts, uncles, and cousins, not to mention his dead father's many friends, Ali Hassan Salameh would have had a much more pleasurable life, doing whatever he wanted, wasting money on restaurants and nightclubs. But those around him never ceased to remind Ali of what he would have most loved to eradicate from his mind: the 1948 war, the dead and the wounded, and all the blood that had been spilt.

He remembered very little of what had happened following his father's death. Here and there he had vague memories of escaping from Ramle in a relative's car. They had driven on narrow, bumpy roads through villages on the West Bank of the Jordan, often getting off the road to avoid meeting up with Jordanian army units on their way to the Israeli front. His mother had hidden under her clothes considerable sums of money left by her husband, part of which he had collected from robbing British institutions and blackmailing prominent Arabs who had not cooperated with him. His widow was aware that Hassan had also received large sums from the Mufti of Jerusalem with which to purchase arms, distribute monetary incentives among his men, and bribe British officers to spare him from being tried as a terrorist. She had no way of knowing how much remained out of the sum of her husband's fortune, but there was enough left hidden in the metal box buried in their yard to finance her family's needs indefinitely.

After four days of seemingly endless meandering through the Hashemite Kingdom of Jordan,[13] the family arrived in Beirut and moved temporarily into one of the refugee camps where the Christian authorities were housing the Palestinians who arrived there. Fearing a growing Muslim presence in the country, the Christians refused to grant the refugees Lebanese citizenship or the right to purchase houses and land.

The Salameh family was forced to spend some time in the refugee camp, and only after Lebanese friends came to their rescue did Naima Salameh manage to rent a house in the al-Hamra Quarter, which was inhabited by wealthy Muslims. She covered the walls of the new house with photographs of her husband in army uniform, on the rifle range, on horseback, and standing next to a mortar ready for firing. She named her daughter, who was born a short time after Hassan's death, Jihad, meaning "Holy War." She had not abandoned the idea that when the time came, Ali would take his father's place as the great hero who would liberate Palestine from the Jews. Any means were justified to reach this end. At almost every family gathering, Naima reminisced about her native village and recounted her husband's heroic exploits. "Ali is Hassan's heir," she repeated endlessly. Ali listened, but remained silent.

On June 2, 1958, on the tenth anniversary of Hassan Salameh's death, a memorial ceremony was held in front of a huge crowd in Beirut's central square. Present at the ceremony was Yasser Arafat, then twenty-nine years old, who with some of his friends dreamed of establishing an organization that would restore Palestine to Arab hands. Six years later, as a result of the first Arab summit meeting, the Palestine Liberation Organization (PLO) was founded. A year later Arafat, a former engineering student at Cairo University, took command of Fatah, a suborganization within the PLO that advocated the use of force.

Meanwhile, on the tenth anniversary of Hassan Salameh's death, Hassan's widow, son, and daughter stood on the stage that had been set up in the square, in front of an audience of Hassan's men, who were holding up enlarged photographs of their dead leader. On the stage, Yasser Arafat embraced Ali and kissed him in front of the crowd. "The entire Arab nation anticipates that one day you will pick up your hallowed father's rifle and will lead the battle against the Jews." The audience cheered its support.

Ali Salameh was then eighteen years old, a student who divided his time between Bir Zeit University and the nightspots of Beirut and Berlin. He was supposedly a student at the Faculty of Social Sciences, but was seen in class very rarely. Studying was far less important to him than the endless temptations the world had to offer, including nightclubs, loose women, and fast cars. Ali had endless money and enjoyed spending it. He could afford to hang out in expensive restaurants and clubs and wear only the most fashionable clothes. He drove from one delight to another in his custom-made blood-red sports car.

Ali was a captivating young man whose exotic green eyes were the cause of many a broken heart. His classmates could barely overcome their jealousy when he abandoned his school books at the height of studying for final exams in order to enjoy the charms of a beautiful dancer whom he had met at a nightclub. Girls sent him perfumed love letters; women hotly pursued him.

For many years Ali's mother followed her son's escapades with disappointment mixed with anger. Friends informed her about how he passed his time and demanded that she save the family's honor by putting a stop to it. She frequently held discussions with her son, begging him to take his studies seriously and stop getting involved with women and visiting nightclubs. Her nagging infuriated Ali, but she was still his mother, so he accepted it with resignation. He hoped that in time she would find other things to occupy her mind, but he underestimated her determination. Naima refused to give up on her plans for him. She knew that as long as Ali's head was filled with dancing girls, there was no chance that he would do anything serious with his life, let alone take up the heavy burden of the Palestinian cause that his father had bequeathed to him with his last dying breath. It was essential that he calm down, become a respected member of society, and start taking himself seriously. She decided that for this to happen, he must marry.

Naima carefully checked out the available possibilities. She made a list of single girls, daughters of successful businessmen, army officers, and politicians. Eventually she singled out Zeinab, a relative of Abdel Kader al-Husseini, a man who had commanded the Palestinian troops in battles against the Jews during the War of Independence until he was killed during the Battle of Qastal on the road to Jerusalem.[14] Zeinab, who had inherited large sums of money and property from her father, was also related to one of the most prominent personalities in the Arab world, the Mufti of Jerusalem, Haj Amin al-Husseini, who had exerted great influence over both Hassan Salameh and her father. Another family member, Faisal al-Husseini, would later hold the Jerusalem portfolio of the Palestinian Authority.

Worn down by his mother's incessant nagging, Ali traveled to Jerusalem to meet Zeinab. He was warmly welcomed into her family's home and exchanged pleasantries with the girl and her relatives, all the while attempting to hide his indifference. His intended bride had made no impression on him whatsoever, but his mother and other family members wouldn't leave him in peace. They repeated again and again that no greater honor was possible for them and for him than the union of two such well-known and highly respected Palestinian families. His mother shed tears of emotion, telling him that this marriage would surely gladden his father's soul in Paradise.

Ali eventually succumbed to the pressure, and at a grandiose ceremony attended by hundreds of guests from the elite of Palestinian society, he was married to the girl his mother had chosen for him. The tables groaned under the weight of the delicacies that were served, and Ali was given an especially large portion of stuffed pigeons, whose flesh was traditionally believed to enhance male sexual prowess. After the ceremony, Ali slipped away to a nightclub to dance the night away with other women.

The volunteers' office of the Kibbutz Artzi kibbutz movement was located in one of the office buildings on Leonardo da Vinci Street in Tel Aviv.[15] Twenty-two-year-old Sylvia arrived there early one morning in the summer of 1959 directly from the airport. A few excited young people of both sexes were already waiting outside the office's closed door for the kibbutz representatives who would interview them and determine which kibbutz they would be sent to. Waiting on the benches outside the office were an assortment of youngsters, both Jews and Gentiles: volunteers in their twenties or thirties carrying backpacks, singles seeking adventure, students on vacation, girls hoping to find a husband in Israel. Most of them told Sylvia that they intended to stay in Israel for a few weeks. They asked her how long she would be staying.

"I'll stay as long as I can be of some use," she replied.

By nine o'clock Sylvia was sitting opposite the young kibbutz member who dealt with new volunteers. The girl studied her briefly, wrote down her name, and asked about her state of health.

"Fine, as far as I know."

"Do you have a profession?"

"I'm a music teacher."

The interviewer didn't seem enthusiastic.

"Our kibbutzim don't need music teachers," she said indifferently. "Can you do anything else?"

"I'll do whatever is required of me. I'm not afraid of hard work."

A short time later, after having been given a letter of referral, Sylvia was on her way to Gan Shmuel, a ten-minute ride from the town of Hadera. She had never heard of this kibbutz and had no idea what she would find there. In fact, she knew very little about kibbutz life. She had read about the communal lifestyle, the monastic conditions, the hard work, but all that didn't worry her. The main thing was for her to make a contribution, to be useful, whatever difficulties were involved.

She had been given a ticket for a bus leaving from the Tel Aviv Central Bus Station. The bus to the kibbutz passed by tenements, private homes, orange groves, and fields, and Sylvia was fascinated by the changing scenery rolling by her window. She also studied her fellow passengers with interest: kibbutz members dressed in khaki, elderly men wearing suits, soldiers in uniform, both male and female. It was the first time in her life that she had encountered Israeli soldiers and also the first time she had heard so many people speaking Hebrew.

She arrived at Gan Shmuel in the afternoon. She passed kibbutz members returning from work, and they gave her a friendly smile. Teenagers wearing the Hashomer Hatzair uniform—blue shirts with white string ties—ran past her, shouting loudly.[16] She was amazed by the well-tended lawns and deeply inhaled the scent of flowers growing along the paths. After a short conversation with one of the kibbutz members on her rights and obligations as a volunteer, she was taken to the volunteers' quarters, a row of wooden huts where the residents lived two to a room. After Sylvia was assigned a bed and given sheets, a blanket, work clothes, and toiletries, she joined the other volunteers at supper in the kibbutz dining room. Back in her room, she became acquainted with her roommate, a tall, crop-haired Swedish girl, climbed into bed, and slept soundly until she was woken up early the next morning for her first day at work, in the kibbutz canning factory.

The morning was cool and pleasant, but the sun came up quickly, hinting at the hot, stifling day ahead. The factory's machinery gave off intense heat, and Sylvia began sweating profusely. Having grown up in South Africa, she was accustomed to hot summers, but the heat and humidity in the kibbutz exceeded anything she had ever experienced. Surviving her first day at work took considerable effort; she hadn't expected it to be so hard.

After finishing work late that afternoon, she returned to her quarters on the outskirts of the kibbutz. She showered in the communal women's facility, put on clean clothes, and went outside to chat with the other young people from around the globe who had come to help out in the kibbutz. She was the only one from South Africa.

The following days were even harder. Together with kibbutz members and other volunteers, she was co-opted to work extra hours during what was supposed to be her free time, helping out in the factory, which was at its peak season. She worked willingly, even though overcome by tiredness.

Sylvia, unlike the other volunteers, knew a little Hebrew, so she could conduct simple conversations with the kibbutz members, but that wasn't good enough for her. She spent all her spare time studying Hebrew in the kibbutz *ulpan*,[17] where she greatly improved her command of the language. She borrowed Hebrew books from the kibbutz library, reading late into the night.

According to kibbutz tradition, each volunteer was assigned a family so that he or she would feel at home and acclimatize more easily to life in the unfamiliar social framework. David and Dorit, a young couple who had both been born on the kibbutz, were Sylvia's adopted "parents." Dorit was a kindergarten teacher, and her husband worked in agriculture, growing vegetables.

When Sylvia arrived at their nicely furnished room for the first time, they received her so warmly that she fell in love with them instantly. Dorit and David asked about her first days at work. "They were hard," she answered in a mixture of Hebrew and English, "but I wasn't expecting them to be easy." They took her to the dining room, where members and volunteers had their meals together. The walls were decorated with paintings by kibbutz members and slogans in praise of physical labor. Sylvia loved the bustle of the dining room, the vegetables served to the tables fresh from the fields, the bread that was baked daily in the kibbutz bakery. It reminded her of the bread her mother baked back home in South Africa.

David instructed her in the principles of kibbutz life—how work was assigned, how the children lived together in communal houses, how the kibbutz was run by an elected secretariat and a general meeting. He sketched out the history of the kibbutz from its beginnings in 1910 and told her about the reclamation of the land, the early days of poverty, the hostile Arab population, and the never-ending struggle to achieve the best possible yield from the soil.[18] She was especially impressed by the story of Uri Ilan, a native son of Gan Shmuel, who was captured by the Syrians while on a special mission in enemy territory. He committed suicide in prison, at the height of an interrogation involving torture. When his body was returned to Israel, they found a note upon which he had written with burnt-out matches: "I gave nothing away."

"I would have done the same," Sylvia told her adopted parents.

The first few weeks in the kibbutz aroused Sylvia's enthusiasm. She worked nonstop, and on Friday evenings in the dining room she was drawn into the circle of dancers moving to the strains of the accordion. But her enthusiasm rapidly waned. She felt that she could make a greater contribution if she was given more challenging work and consulted with Dorit and David about what she should do. They empathized with her. "From the moment I met you," confessed Dorit, "I could see that you were not the type to be satisfied with menial labor. I understood that you were seeking far greater challenges. Canning preserves, as important as it is for the kibbutz economy, is apparently not for you."

Dorit made an attempt to find other employment for Sylvia on the kibbutz, but she was unsuccessful. It was up to the young volunteer herself to decide what she should do. She thought that working in education would suit her better than boring factory work, but all the teaching posts in the kibbutz were already filled.

After four more months of boring routine, Sylvia packed up her few belongings, said goodbye to David and Dorit, left the kibbutz, and moved into a flat in Tel Aviv together with another girl. She gradually collected around her a small group of young Israeli men and women, who appreciated her brilliant conversation, her sense of humor, and her ability, when necessary, to assume the role of psychologist or priest in the confessional.

Meanwhile, she sought a teaching position and was eventually hired as an English teacher at a high school in Holon, near Tel Aviv. Some of her pupils found it hard to cope with the strange language, so she stayed after school giving them special tutelage. Sylvia invested all her energies and talents in teaching, preparing lessons filled with humor and original ideas. The principal praised her highly, and her skills were valued by both teachers and parents. She got on very well with her students, and all in all she was quite contented; but she aimed higher. She felt that teaching tapped only a small part of her abilities and that she could utilize them to better advantage elsewhere.

While continuing her work as a teacher, Sylvia searched intensively for a new challenge, preferably some kind of pioneering project. She was particularly attracted to the largely undeveloped and uninhabited expanses of southern Israel. She traveled down to the Dead Sea Works and offered her services there, but was told that she could only be employed as a secretary, and she wasn't interested in that.[19] She traveled all the way down to Eilat, but didn't find what she was looking for there, either. "I love this country," she wrote to her parents, "but I still haven't found my true place here."

She was no longer in touch with Avery, but one day he sent her a telegram:

Waiting anxiously for your return. Love you with all my heart.

She sent back a short answer:

Dear Avery, I'm staying here a while longer. It's not easy, but I still haven't given up.

One chilly spring evening, Sylvia was in her room marking students' exams. Classical music was playing on the radio, but it was suddenly interrupted by a dramatic announcement. The Knesset had been informed by Prime Minister David Ben-Gurion that the Nazi war criminal Adolf Eichmann had been captured in Argentina and brought to Israel to stand trial. News items followed in rapid succession, stating that Argentine reporters attributed the kidnapping to the Mossad. This was the first time Sylvia became aware of the existence of Israel's Secret Service.

Adolf Eichmann, the chief perpetrator of Hitler's plot to exterminate the Jews, had escaped to Argentina at the end of World War II, assumed the false identity of an Argentinean named Ricardo Clement, and purchased a small house in a derelict neighborhood of Buenos Aires. Mossad agents picked up his trail and kidnapped him on May 11, 1960, as he alighted from a bus on his way home from work. He was then drugged and transported by plane to Israel. Less than two weeks later, Ben-Gurion declared, "The bitter enemy of the Jewish people, Adolf Eichmann, has been captured by the Israeli Security Forces and will be brought to justice in Israel on charges of genocide."

Eichmann's kidnapping and the trial that followed made headlines around the world, firing Sylvia's imagination. Those were exciting days for her, although she cried bitterly when she listened to the broadcast testimonies of extermination camp survivors.

Eichmann's capture heralded one of the most remarkable chapters in the Mossad's history. The organization's name was on everyone's lips, evoking respect, even reverence. The capture of the most wanted Nazi filled members of the Israeli intelligence community with pride and gave them the feeling that they were capable of completing any mission successfully, no matter how difficult.

Sylvia continued working as a teacher in Holon for another two years. Although teaching occupied a major part of her life, she felt unfulfilled. Constantly searching for something more challenging, she consulted with friends and went to job interviews, but turned down offers that seemed beneath her abilities. She continued working as a teacher, wondering if this was all she was capable of contributing to the country. Her work no longer interested her, and the months were flying by. She thought that if no opportunities presented themselves soon, she might just as well return to South Africa, get married, and raise a family.

But Sylvia's life was about to take a surprising turn.

As if fate were sending her yet another reminder, Sylvia read about the Israel Secret Service's response to the Egyptian rocket initiative. Egypt's president, Gamal Abdul Nasser, had proudly announced a plan to construct ground-to-ground rockets that would be capable of reaching any Israeli target. He recruited German and Austrian ballistics experts to carry out this plan, arousing much anxiety among Israelis. Memories of the Holocaust were still fresh and painful, and now again a Jewish population was in danger of extermination, through the joint efforts of German and Austrian scientists (some of whom were known to be ex-Nazis) and Egypt, Israel's most powerful enemy.

Israel's intelligence services were on high alert, working feverishly around the clock to devise ways to thwart the Egyptian scheme. Unit 188, the crack unit of the Intelligence Corps that was responsible for special operations outside the borders of Israel, was at the very heart of these preparations. Its commander, Yoske Yariv, an inspired, determined, and experienced officer, was given the difficult task of hindering the progress of the Egyptian rocket initiative and, in conjunction with the Mossad, leading an offensive against the German scientists involved in it.

The headquarters of Unit 188 were located in an old building in the Sarona quarter of Tel Aviv, which had formerly belonged to residents of the German Templar colony. The Templars were members of a Christian religious sect upholding the belief that settling in the land of Israel would accelerate the Second Coming of the Messiah. Many of them had collaborated with the Nazis during World War II, causing the British authorities to deport the entire community to Australia.

Symbolically enough, this building in the quiet neighborhood of Sarona, with its red-tiled roofs and pleasant, narrow streets, became the headquarters of the intelligence unit that was to wage the battle against ex-Nazis who had found refuge in Arab countries, German scientists who were developing the Egyptian rocket industry, and other enemies of Israel in Egypt.

The office responsible for sending the German scientists to Egypt was located in a building on a busy street in Frankfurt, Germany. A parcel bomb addressed to the chief rocket scientists working in Egypt was secretly smuggled into this office. The seemingly innocent parcel was duly dispatched from Germany to the arms factory in Hilwan, Egypt, where the rocket laboratory was located. When it was opened by the scientists, it exploded in their faces, wounding several of them. This daring operation, a cooperative effort between Israeli intelligence operatives stationed in Europe and Egypt, attracted universal attention. In its wake, various world leaders intervened and eventually put a stop to the Egyptian missile project.

Unit 188 operated quietly and discreetly, far from the public eye. Those who joined its ranks were required to sign a confidentiality agreement, pledging to reveal their true activities to no one. Sylvia had never heard of this unit, but Unit 188 had heard about her. Sylvia's roommate, Hannah, had a friend named Zvika, who was an instructor at the unit's School for Special Operations. During one of his visits to the flat, Zvika was introduced to Sylvia and had a long conversation with her. He was impressed by her intelligence, her native English, and her burning desire to serve the State of Israel.

"I think she could be right for us," he told his colleague, the commander of the School for Special Operations.

Unit 188 was among the first intelligence units in Israel to grant equal status to men and women. The first attempt to enlist women into field intelligence work was made during the 1948 War of Independence, when it met with considerable success. In fact, women had been serving in the Israel Intelligence Service long before Unit 188 was founded. For instance, Shulamit Cohen-Kishik, a native of Argentina living in Jerusalem who at age sixteen had married a Lebanese Jewish businessman and moved to Beirut, was a vital source of information regarding the Lebanese army, which was then at war with Israel. Later, after the establishment of Unit 188, a young woman named Dafna, who had grown up in Bat-Yam, near Jaffa, joined the unit. Her father had served in World War II as a British officer in Egypt. She married Shlomo Gal, a Mossad operative. A few years later, Dafna, although heavily pregnant, joined her husband on a successful information-gathering mission in an Arab country.

The clandestine combatants of Unit 188 showed absolute, unequivocal loyalty to their work and to those who sent them. A striking example was Wolfgang Lotz, son of a German father and a Jewish mother, who assumed the identity of a former Nazi, founded a riding school in Cairo, became friendly with top Egyptian and German officials, and managed to obtain a complete list of the rocket scientists working in Hilwan. Another outstanding example was Eli Cohen, who arrived in Damascus disguised as a businessman and managed to infiltrate Syrian president Hafez al-Assad's inner circle, forming close ties with ministers and top army officers. The

Egyptian-born Cohen was recruited to Unit 188 after a prolonged training period in Israel. He maintained an extensive social network in the Syrian capital until he was caught by Russian surveillance experts in the act of transmitting encoded messages to Israel.

Potential women candidates for Unit 188 were generally recruited from among new immigrants and foreign students who had come to study in Israeli universities. Women were recruited not only in Israel, but also abroad. One of these female recruits, who became a resident of a country hostile to Israel, served for many years in a large public institution in that country.

Many of these female recruits became operatives who lived in constant mortal danger. Their activities demanded powerful motivation, absolute loyalty, and operational skills that were equal to those of the opposite sex. However, they did enjoy a certain advantage in their work, as women generally aroused much less suspicion than men.

3

Night in an Arab Village

It was evening in late October 1962. The summer heat had passed, and there was a light chill of early autumn in the air. Sylvia was in bed reading *The Jewish Wars* by Josephus Flavius.[1] After a tiring day at school, she had decided to read a chapter or two before falling asleep. Suddenly the phone rang. Someone she didn't know apologized for the late hour, introducing himself as "Gadi," a representative of a government agency looking for employees. He asked if she was prepared to meet with him. "I have an interesting offer for you," he said.

Sylvia didn't conceal her surprise.

"Who told you that I was looking for work?" she asked.

"Friends of yours," was the man's cryptic answer. "I thought you might be suitable for this position, and I would like to tell you about it."

"What kind of a position is it?" she asked.

"I can't discuss it over the phone. Are you free tomorrow morning?"

"I teach in the morning."

They arranged to meet in the afternoon after Sylvia finished work, at Café Hadley on Judah Halevi Street in Tel Aviv.

Gadi, whose real name was Moti Kfir, the commander of Unit 188's School for Special Operations, was waiting for Sylvia at the rear of the café at the appointed time, at a table for two a bit isolated from the other tables. Sylvia entered the café, took a quick glance around, and immediately approached him, guessing that he was the man who had invited her to meet with him.

He shook her hand, and she confidently returned his firm handshake.

"Pleased to meet you. I'm Gadi. What will you have to drink?"

Sylvia asked for coffee.

Gadi wanted to make it clear that their conversation must remain confidential, but was worried that Sylvia might be alarmed by the mystery surrounding the job he was about to offer her. So he softened this by saying, "Whatever is said here must remain between us."

Sylvia looked at him questioningly.

"If it's supposed to remain between us, why are we meeting in a café?" she inquired in Hebrew.

Gadi didn't think it appropriate to reveal to her that no candidate for a secret assignment in Israel or elsewhere was ever invited to the central headquarters, whose location was known to very few people.

"A café is an excellent meeting place because of the noise," he explained unconvincingly. "In this racket nobody can hear what we're saying."

"You wanted to offer me a job," she reminded him.

"I would like to ask you a few questions first, if you don't mind."

"Go ahead."

He asked her about her family background, what had impelled her to immigrate to Israel, her activities in the present and her plans for the future, her roommate in the rented flat in Tel Aviv, what she did in her spare time. She answered quickly and easily, frankly, and with humor.

"How satisfied are you with your life? Give it a mark from one to ten," requested Gadi.

"I would say about eight. I work as a teacher. It's interesting, but I'm sure that I have the ability to accomplish much more."

"What would you like to do?"

"Something more interesting, more challenging."

"For example?"

"For example, enlisting in the army," she replied, eyes shining.

"What's stopping you?"

"I'm too old, and apart from that my mother is Christian, so according to Jewish law I'm not really Jewish. So even though I feel Jewish, I don't think they'll recruit me into the army."

"I can't help you get recruited into the army," said Gadi, "but I can try and find you a job in security."

"Whom exactly do you represent?" Sylvia inquired. Her direct gaze studied the man across the table carefully.

"I represent a government body that works in affiliation with the Department of Security."

"Could you explain exactly what kind of a job you're offering me?"

"Not at this stage. First you will have to undergo tests and examinations, so that we can be sure that you are suitable. Only then can we discuss what you would actually do."

"At least give me some idea of what you're offering," she implored him. Not many people could refuse Sylvia anything she asked for, and she knew it.

"Well . . . ," he hesitated for a moment. "It's a hugely challenging job, involving quite a lot of travel abroad."

Sylvia considered what had been said up till then. She was of course interested in finding a new, exciting job, but she still hadn't the foggiest idea what he was suggesting. It all seemed too mysterious, too wrapped in secrecy. She couldn't even guess what it was all about.

During their conversation, Gadi noticed that both the men and the women in the café hadn't taken their eyes off Sylvia. They continued to follow her with their eyes as the two concluded their conversation and she preceded Gadi toward the door. Generally, when candidates attracted too much attention, it was better to think again before accepting them into Unit 188. In fact, candidates were taught to be as inconspicuous as possible; but Sylvia had made a very good impression on Gadi, and he was quite sure that she would be capable of handling any situation and of exploiting the attention she attracted to good advantage.

At their next meeting a few days later at another café, he asked her, "If I told you that I could arrange for you to be recruited into the Intelligence Corps, what would you say?"

"I'd be delighted."

"The truth is that I have a job like that for you, but . . ."

"I know. You already told me that I have to pass some tests first."

"Correct."

"What kind of tests?" she asked.

"First of all, psychological examinations. After that there will be a security investigation."

"How long will it take?"

"A few months."

"Can you give me more details? It's hard for me to decide without knowing anything about what you're offering me."

"I can only tell you," said Gadi quietly, "that what's being offered is an interesting, exciting, unusual job."

"Is it dangerous?"

"Sometimes."

She smiled and sat back comfortably.

"In that case, it will suit me just fine," she said.

"One more thing. My real name isn't Gadi, but you will continue to call me that. If you get the job, we'll call you Elana, until we decide otherwise."

After a few more meetings with Sylvia, Gadi told his colleague Shimon about her. Shimon was responsible for recruiting clandestine combatants to Unit 188 and testing them for suitability. He had been one of the founders and instructors of the legendary Mista'arvim unit of the Palmach (a special unit of the army) before the establishment of the State of Israel, and was a veteran, a skilled field officer, expert in the language, culture, and customs of the Arabs. The Mista'arvim was in fact the foundation upon which Unit 188 was established, and those who served in it were well acquainted with the Arab world.[2]

"What impression did she make on you?" asked Shimon.

"She seems to be an outgoing, intelligent young woman, both brilliant and resourceful," said Gadi. "My impression is that she would be able to restrain her extroverted personality if she needed to."

Shimon listened to Gadi with interest.

"Tell me more about her," he said.

Gadi told Shimon about Sylvia's family in South Africa, her arrival in Israel as a volunteer, and the fact that she was currently working as a teacher.

"Do you think she would be capable of being stationed in an enemy country?" Shimon inquired.

"Yes, I think she would."

"She sounds interesting. I'd like to meet her."

On condition that she successfully pass the tests awaiting her, Sylvia was earmarked to serve in Unit 188, which had formerly operated under the auspices of the Intelligence Branch of the Israel Defense Forces (IDF). The director of the Mossad, Isser Harel, had repeatedly tried to get the unit transferred to his organization, but the commander in chief of the IDF, Moshe Dayan, was against it. In October 1963, the commander of the Intelligence Branch, Meir Amit, was also appointed temporary director of the Mossad, and the controversy was settled: the unit was transferred to its natural home, the Mossad, where it was merged with Hamifratz, the former Foreign Special Operations Unit under the command of Yitzhak Shamir, who later served as prime minister of Israel. Colonel Yossef Yariv was later appointed head of the newly formed unit. Meir Amit, who nicknamed Yariv "the pathfinder," wrote to him when he joined the Mossad: "Your unit's accomplishments bring honor and glory to the entire nation and make an immeasurable contribution to our security . . . I am glad fate brought us together as work colleagues. The situations that you cope with are perhaps the most delicate and complex of them all, not only because you deal with matters of life and death, but mainly because, although you are hidden and invisible, the eyes of the world are upon you."

With the establishment of the new Special Operations Unit, all of Unit 188's personnel became an integral part of the Mossad system. Theoretically, the transition to the new framework shouldn't have made any profound changes in their activities. But, although the goals and mission of Unit 188 didn't change, the organization acquired greater prestige and an enhanced sense of pride and worth, which encouraged its members to improve their operational skills even further.

For security reasons, all of Sylvia's sessions with the psychologist took place in his private home.

"Tell me about your childhood fears," the psychologist asked Sylvia. His voice was gentle and his eyes friendly. He wanted to uncover her weak spots in order to evaluate her personality accurately.

"I wanted to be the best student in the class. I was frightened of not succeeding."

"And did you succeed?"

"Yes."

"What else?"

"I had a recurrent dream. I saw people with masks breaking into our house and shooting us all to death. That sort of thing happened quite often in South Africa. Some of our neighbors had been killed when they resisted the burglars. I would wake up in fear and trembling from those dreams. I would have the feeling that it could happen in our house at any time, and then it actually happened. I was eight years old. I woke up in the middle of the night. It was quiet. Our dogs didn't start barking, but I heard a strange noise in the guest room. I got up and walked toward the noise, and then I saw two figures trying to break in through the window. I remember that there was a moment when I froze to the spot and was petrified with fear, but I quickly realized that I had to do something to stop them. I ran to my parents' bedroom and woke my father. He picked up the hunting rifle that was lying near his bed. We tiptoed in the direction of the living room. We saw that the window had been broken and that two men were rolling up the carpet. My father aimed the rifle at them and shot. The bullets hit the two burglars. One of them was killed instantly, and the other was wounded, bleeding and screaming in pain. My father phoned the police, and I went out to see what had happened to our dogs. I discovered both of them dead, killed by the burglars. I returned to the living room. I looked at the dead burglar and the one who lay wounded on the floor near his friend's body and said to him, 'You both got what you deserved.' He looked back at me with frightened eyes."

"Did you feel scared then?"

"No. I felt angry."

Later in his evaluation the psychologist wrote:

> Sylvia's memory of the break-in to her home when she was a child is a good illustration of her courage and resourcefulness. Having courage is in fact a sign of the ability to solve problems under pressure. Sylvia hears noises in the house, but does not translate this into panic, but to a need to take effective action. Even after her father shoots the burglars, causing death and injury, she recalls that the mission was successful, rather than the shock and horror of witnessing killing and blood for the first time in her life. "The problem was solved," she seems to be saying, apparently exhibiting detachment. We see an emotional reaction only when she discovers that their dogs have been killed. Sylvia trusts her father. It is to him that she runs, him she wakes up, expecting him to deal calmly with the burglars. Her father doesn't protect her, but rather includes her as a team member, allowing her to witness the shooting. He relies on her not to shout or get in the way. They work as an organized team. The conclusion from this is that Sylvia relies on authority and authority can rely on her. Responsibility and problem solving are central elements in her life. Resourcefulness inspires her not to shrink from unknown situations, unex-

pected change, risks, or breaking new ground, but rather to welcome them into her life.

"Did you have any other childhood fears?" asked the psychologist.

"I don't remember any."

"What frightened you as you grew up?"

"I was afraid that I would remain an old spinster. I didn't have a boyfriend until I was sixteen."

"Did you ever wake up from dreams that didn't involve break-ins to your house?"

"Very rarely."

The psychologist asked: "When you think about the possibility that you will pass all the tests successfully and be accepted for the job, is it clear to you that you might have to face considerable dangers, even mortal ones?"

"I understand that."

"Does it frighten you?"

"A bit."

"Are you afraid to die?"

"No. I am afraid of failure."

"Let's say that you are sent on a mission. Something goes wrong, and you might possibly be killed. Would you give up, return to your case officer, and explain to him that the mission was impossible?"

"If I had the possibility of carrying out the mission successfully, I would continue with it."

"Even if this would endanger your life?"

"I probably wouldn't think about my own life when I was pulling the trigger."

Like every candidate for the Special Operations Unit, Sylvia had to undergo a prolonged security investigation and be examined by various psychologists. Their reports invariably expressed immense respect for her. They emphasized her identification with the Jewish people, her courage, her honesty, and her proactive personality. One of the reports quoted a statement she had made during one of the sessions: "The word 'impossible' doesn't exist in my lexicon." The psychologists came to the conclusion that Sylvia was perfectly suited to becoming a clandestine combatant. She loved working independently, had the presence of an actor on a stage, was brilliant at conversation, and attracted male attention without even trying.

Her personal file containing these psychological evaluations was transferred for consideration to Unit 188's central headquarters.

At the meeting during which Sylvia was assessed, with the participation of the unit commander, the commander of the School for Special Operations, the director of the Recruiting Department, and the head of the Operation Department, all agreed that she should be accepted for training.

Their final evaluation stated:

> The Special Operations Unit is a uniquely suitable place for her. She has a marked inclination toward independence, steady resourcefulness, a talent for bonding with others, and quickness of movement, but only on condition that these are structured. Sylvia functions well within a framework, on condition that she is allowed a degree of freedom. She is proud to have found a framework that she can rely on, something that she can truly belong to with pride. She has difficulty with too much closeness, but she does need a certain amount of it. The Mossad, its instructors, and case officers represent for her the right balance between closeness and distance.

Sometime later, at a café, Sylvia met with Shimon, the man responsible for recruiting clandestine combatants. He shook her hand warmly. "You've been accepted," he told her. "Now you'll enter the training phase. If you pass it successfully, we'll make a combatant out of you."

Sylvia couldn't believe that she was really on the way to becoming a member of the Special Operations Unit. Weak in the knees, overwrought, and near tears, she sat opposite Shimon, dumbstruck with excitement. This was a great day, maybe the greatest of her life so far. She felt that a new chapter was beginning, that a fascinating, unknown world was about to open up before her.

Sylvia emerged from the café. The city bustled noisily around her, passersby crowded the sidewalks, cars honked, but she floated above it all on a cloud of happiness. She could have been satisfied by the feeling of elation that filled her heart and the waves of joy that washed over her, but she had a strong desire to celebrate, to

mark the occasion properly, to set up a landmark that would sym-
bolize the great turn her life was about to take, a symbolic gift that
she could give herself at such an auspicious moment.

After quitting her job at the school and phoning her parents to
inform them that she was about to be appointed to an important
government post, she considered a few options. She could of course
invite her girlfriends to dinner or to go to a play or a concert, but
neither of those options seemed suitable to the occasion. Finally, she
had an idea that appealed to her most of all. She went to the Tel Aviv
Central Bus Station. Three hours and two buses later, she stood at
the foot of Masada, the fortress in which a thousand Jewish rebels
led by Elazar ben Yair were besieged by the Roman legions camped
below them. When the Romans finally managed to storm the enclo-
sure, they found the bodies of the dead rebels, who had chosen to
kill themselves rather than be taken captive by the Romans.

Sylvia joined a group of English-speaking tourists and ascended
the winding Snake Path with them. It was a hard climb, but her
physical fitness and willpower helped her reach the top. At the end
of her climb, she saw a huge inscription that had been written on
one of the walls by an anonymous hand: "Masada will never fall
again."

She looked out over the Dead Sea and the Judean Desert beneath her and saw in her mind's eye the tents of the Roman legions
surrounding Masada. Everything she had read and learned about
the siege appeared before her eyes, palpable and magnificent. Her
glance swept over the ruins, and she imagined the cries of hungry
children emanating from them. She was amazed by the determination of the besieged warriors, who did not surrender even after all
was lost. Sylvia knew that Masada was a symbol of the heroism of
the Jewish people, undeniable proof that whatever hardships the
nation suffered, it would never surrender to its enemies. There, at
the summit of the mountain that had witnessed the death of proud,
unbending Jews, she told herself that the organization she was joining now had been founded in order to perpetuate the heritage of
those brave fighters, and she vowed to be personally responsible for
making sure that history didn't repeat itself.

The three-room apartment was situated on the second floor of an
old building in the busy center of Dizengoff Street in Tel Aviv. It belonged to an elderly, childless couple who had lived there for many

years. The husband was a veteran intelligence operative who had been on many secret missions abroad. His wife managed a book-store.

Tolka Rosen, who was responsible for locating apartments and renting them for the training needs of the Special Operations Unit, had approached the residents of the Dizengoff apartment. She asked the old couple if they would agree to rent one of their rooms on a temporary basis. They answered in the affirmative, even though not a word was mentioned about who would use the room and for what purpose. They were not the only ones who put their apartments, or parts of them, at the disposal of candidates for the secret service. All the clandestine combatants went through their first training period in rooms or apartments that were rented from veteran intelligence operatives or their associates.

Accompanied by a few personal effects and a small transistor radio, Sylvia arrived with Gadi at her training location. The apartment's residents were waiting for them. Gadi introduced Sylvia to them as "Elana." Even at such an early stage, she needed to become accustomed to a false identity.

The hosts didn't ask any unnecessary questions. They liked Elana from the start, but immediately after giving her a key to the apartment, they hurried off to another room and closed the door. They had been briefed beforehand not to make any real contact with her.

Abraham Gemer had been chosen by Gadi to be Sylvia's instructor. Gemer had joined the unit after serving in a paratrooper commando unit, in which he had participated in daring retaliation activities, ambushes, and patrols deep in enemy territory. After completing his service as an officer, he was recruited to the Mossad and, with Gadi's help, had made his way to Unit 188, rising through the ranks. Before being assigned as Sylvia's instructor, he had already trained other recruits, who became an integral part of the combatant team.

Abraham Gemer was born in Ness Ziona. His father was murdered by an Arab gang when Abraham was a year old. [3] His widowed mother, left with little Abraham and an older child, decided to apply for membership in a kibbutz. After several rejections, she was accepted by Kvutzat Schiller, which became home to her and her two children.

Abraham was a good-looking, well-built man, quiet and introverted, modest, and a long-distance trekking enthusiast. A strong friendship had developed between Abraham and Gadi from the time they were growing up in neighboring kibbutzim. In their youth they had played basketball together, and later they both served in combat units.

Sylvia's room faced a quiet backyard. Someone had placed a vase containing a bouquet of fresh garden flowers on the small writing table in her room.

She wasn't supposed to stay there to sleep. The room was meant for training only. She surveyed it with a quick glance and returned to the flat that she shared with Hannah.

Early the next morning, she hurried back to the training apartment. A short time afterward, she heard the doorbell ring. Sylvia opened the door. Gadi was standing there, accompanied by a tall, dark-haired man of impressive appearance.

She knew that this man was due to arrive. He had been appointed as her instructor, and she was very curious: until that moment she had never met him face to face.

"My name is Oded," Abraham Gemer introduced himself. Instructors from Unit 188 always concealed their true identities, and the trainees understood that this was necessary.

Oded stood in front of Sylvia for a long moment. He studied her, and she studied him back, like two strangers that fate had brought together to achieve a common goal. Sylvia was an expert at breaking the ice between people. Her sense of humor was a useful tool for accomplishing this.

She smiled at Gadi and asked with a playful wink, "What is this supposed to be?"

"I don't understand," said Gadi.

"I thought that I'd already passed all the preliminary tests," she added with a mischievous smile. "Now you want to see if I'm capable of withstanding the charms of a film star?"

All three of them burst out laughing, but Sylvia didn't really relate to Abraham as an attractive man. Later on, Gadi told her about a friend of his, an instructor who had conducted a passionate love affair with a trainee. "He didn't report it to those responsible for him," he told her, "but the girl did. She understood the importance of describing everything that was happening to her, especially her relationship with the instructor. A short while later he was fired from the unit."

"Why didn't they kick her out, too?"

"Because she told the truth, and he didn't."

Gadi told her that as a result of that incident, he had ordered his instructors to keep their distance from their female trainees.

The first day of training would be devoted to getting acquainted and providing Sylvia with an overview of the training. The next morning Sylvia got up early, and on her way to the training apartment she bought fresh rolls and other food items in the neighborhood grocery. Abraham brought oranges. She invited him to join her for breakfast.

At the end of the meal, she peeled two oranges, one for each of them.

He watched her with a smile.

"Let's assume that you are working under the disguise of a Swedish journalist," he said. "The people you met on one of your newspaper assignments invite you to their home for dinner. They don't know that you are connected with Israel. At the end of the meal, the hostess serves each one of her guests an orange for dessert. What would you do with it?"

She didn't understand the question.

"I would peel it and eat it, of course."

"They would immediately realize that you were Israeli," he said with a laugh.

"How?" she asked in surprise.

"Because only Israelis peel oranges like you do," he replied.

She was embarrassed.

"I didn't think of that," she mumbled.

"That just goes to show that an intelligence operative worth his salt must learn everything, even the table manners of the country where he operates."

She sighed.

"I understand," she said. "What you meant to say was that I have a tremendous amount to learn in order to properly carry out the job assigned to me."

"That's exactly what I meant, Elana."

They worked every day for long hours, until nightfall. The lessons were going well, and Abraham complimented her on being a fast learner. She made sure to repeat every detail, to perform every exercise with the greatest precision, and to cope with a huge amount of new information. Every few days, she reported to Gadi about her progress.

In the course of the training, Sylvia and Abraham had very little time for private conversations. Here and there between lessons, during a coffee break or a meal, she tried to find out something about his life, his hobbies, his family. He answered briefly, if at all. His reluctance to talk about himself was due not only to his introverted personality, but also to the strict secrecy regulations of Unit 188.

Every morning Abraham would arrive at the training apartment on Dizengoff Street and teach Sylvia the skills necessary for being a clandestine combatant: reading city maps and ordinance maps, deciphering aerial photographs, memorizing operational commands, weighing situations, defending oneself, making contact, encoding messages. They went over methods of trailing potential victims, ways to detect if one is being followed, and how to evade suspicious-looking people and escape from dangerous locations. Sylvia learned the basics of managing world travel (visas, passports, car rentals, hotels). Abraham brought along an expert to instruct her in Morse code and took her out to a training ground where an explosives expert illustrated ways to booby-trap innocent-looking objects. She learned that envelopes didn't always contain letters and that what seemed to be a bar of soap could really be a deadly explosive. She was taught that bathroom scales are an ideal place to hide a transmitter and that nail polish can serve as invisible ink. Sylvia was an eager learner and absorbed information quickly. In his weekly reports to the school commander, Abraham praised her broad general knowledge, her successful execution of the exercises, and her strong motivation. She complimented him on his training methods. He impressed her as being a true professional.

Sylvia and her instructor spent the entire winter and half the summer closed up together in the apartment. When Abraham left after a day of training, Sylvia would return to her living quarters. The sharp transition from her secret life to her ordinary one was not easy. She of course told Hannah nothing about what she was doing, and when her roommate asked her about it, she claimed that she was taking part in a course for archive clerks in the Department of Security. The isolation and secrecy weighed heavily upon Sylvia. Naturally she would have preferred to share what she was going through with someone else, but she knew that this was strictly forbidden. For the first time, she experienced one of the major hardships of the task she had taken upon herself. Nevertheless, she did not regret it for a moment. She fought loneliness by every means at her disposal: reading books, mainly accounts of Holocaust survivors; corresponding with her parents and her brother David; and painting landscapes in watercolors and oils.

In one of her letters to her parents, Sylvia wrote, "I quit my job at the school in Holon, and I'm learning a new profession in a commercial firm with branches all over the world. The work is hard and interesting, and the people I'm working with are just the kind of colleagues I always dreamt of. They are brilliant professionals, intelligent, fair, and honest, and they respect me a lot. It is hard not to admire them, with their devotion to the job, their modesty, and their attention to every detail. They are outstanding people, ideal role models."

One morning Abraham brought a film projector to the training apartment and set it up. Sylvia had no idea what would happen next.

He closed the shutters, drew the curtains, turned out the lights, and started the film. It was about a young French girl who fell in love with her teacher. The girl invited him to her birthday in the village. Her friends, her parents, her other relatives, and her beloved teacher all sat around a table under a spreading tree. The girl's mother served food.

Suddenly Abraham stopped the film. The room was in total darkness.

"Try to remember what the father was wearing," requested her instructor.

The film's images flashed through her mind.

"A white shirt, a hat, dark trousers . . ."

"What did they eat?"

"A meat stew in a casserole, a large salad, country bread."

"And what did they drink?"

"Red wine."

"Were there labels on the wine bottles?"

"No."

"Excellent."

The film continued, but was stopped by Abraham at set intervals. Sylvia was asked to identify additional details: to describe the room in which some of the scenes took place, to recall how many cows were grazing in the pasture where the girl and her lover went for a walk, to repeat exactly what the actors had said to one another in different circumstances.

She remembered everything.

On the table in the center of the training room were scattered some family photos, two pens, a notebook, an envelope, a telephone, reading glasses, and a wallet.

"Study the table for a moment," Abraham instructed Sylvia. "Now, close your eyes." He spread a piece of material over the objects on the table.

"Tell me which objects were located on the upper left-hand corner of the table," he requested.

Sylvia succeeded in doing this, too. From childhood she had been capable of remembering small, seemingly trivial details. At school she was able to recite by heart long passages from books that she had read only once.

Most of Sylvia's training exercises took place indoors, where she learned to cope with staged situations. But she was always grateful when they took place outside the apartment, allowing her to breathe fresh air and not be confined in a limited space. At a small base located in a dry riverbed in the Plain of Sharon, far away from the flat, she learned about the qualities of different kinds of explosives and how to avoid the common accidents that could occur when dealing with dangerous materials. One of the instructors at the base was an intelligence operative who some years before had prepared a booby-trapped book that was meant to cause the death of the director of Egyptian intelligence in the Gaza Strip, General Mustafa Hafez, who was also the commander of the *fedayeen*, terrorist units that attacked Israel.[4] The instructor told Sylvia that Hafez was an extremely cautious man, so it was impossible to send him a letter bomb, because he would carefully examine every package he received. Israeli intelligence experts came up with a truly brilliant idea: they decided to use a double agent, Mohammed al-Talalka, who was working both for the Israelis and for General Hafez. Al-Talalka wasn't aware that the Israelis knew about his Egyptian connection. One day the Israeli intelligence agents told al-Talalka that the commander of the Gaza police, Lutfi al-Akkawi, was an Israeli agent and needed a miniature radio hidden in an ordinary-looking book. The double agent was asked to bring the book to Akkawi, and he readily agreed to do so. Of course the first thing he did was to take the booby-trapped book to Mustafa Hafez and inform him that the commander of the Gaza police was a traitor. Al-Talalka handed the book to Hafez and told him that there was a miniature transmitter hidden inside it that was meant for the police commander. Hafez thanked the double agent for the information, and opened the book without hesitation. The explosion killed him instantly.

Sylvia's instructor told her about just this one case, but she was sure that he had been involved in many other, equally exciting ones.

The exercises that Sylvia had to perform were extensive and varied. For example, she was asked to travel from one place to another in the city, checking constantly to see if she was being followed. When she suspected that someone was after her, she was instructed to enter a shop and exit by the back door. If someone took the same detour, she could be sure that she was being followed. Another way to tell whether she was being followed was to get onto a bus and get off at a stop in the middle of nowhere. If someone else got off at the same stop, then there was a good chance that that person was following her. In some cases, there really was someone from the Special Operations Unit following her to see how she would manage. She was taught how to behave when she felt that her pursuers were closing in on her and she had nowhere to hide.

Sylvia especially loved maneuvers where she was asked to blend into her surroundings—for instance, by chatting with a neighbor in a café about neutral subjects such as health or house pets. She had an amazing ability to establish contact with strangers. Her joy of life, her friendliness, and her boundless energy made people around her immediately feel as though they had known her for years. She discovered a quality in herself that she had previously been unaware of: the ability to get people to open up and tell her their most intimate secrets by giving them a sense of security and support. She was told by her instructors that the ability to form personal ties without arousing suspicion was one of the most valuable qualities of a secret service operative.

Every clandestine combatant needs a cover story that becomes an essential, integral part of his being. At times the operative reveals his true identity and at times he assumes a fictitious one. A good cover story is an essential ingredient of any successful operation. It is also a vital first line of defense in cases where the combatant is unmasked, arrested, and interrogated. Special operatives have forged passports at their disposal that are tailor made for them. During his mission in Egypt, for example, Wolfgang Lotz used his original German passport. When he was arrested, his interrogators examined his identity and discovered that there was nothing amiss and that the name written on it was his real name. Luckily for him, having had a Christian father, he was not circumcised. At first they thought Lotz was a German working for the Israeli secret service. It never occurred to them that he was really an Israeli Jew.

Wolfgang Lotz is a prime example of the difference between a clandestine combatant and a secret agent. Lotz was a combatant, a member of Unit 188. An agent is a spy acting against his country, generally for money. When he is caught, he is always accused of one crime: namely, treason.

In an effort to test Sylvia's ability to make contact with public figures, she was obliged to construct a convincing cover story. The only condition was that the story be unconnected with South Africa. She worked on an appropriate cover story for several days; finally, she announced that she had chosen the identity of a reporter from the *London Daily Mirror,* hoping that this would pave her way toward meeting a well-known Israeli personality. Abraham equipped her with a foreign passport and tested the veracity of her cover story by asking questions that she might be asked by her interviewee.

"Where do you live in London?"

"In Swiss Cottage, on 25 Greencroft Street."

She had found the address in a British paper, in an ad for an apartment for sale, so she was glad she could answer appropriately.

"What was the last article you wrote for the *Daily Mirror?*"

"An interview with the author John le Carré."

She had that answer ready too.

"What if the person you are interviewing was to ask you the name of the editor of your paper. What would you tell him?" he asked, testing her.

"I hadn't thought of that," she mumbled.

"And what if they asked you the phone number of the editorial board?"

She felt as though the ground was giving way beneath her.

Abraham shook his head.

"Not good enough, Sylvia. Not good enough."

Having been revealed as a sloppy amateur incapable of putting together a perfect cover story deeply worried Sylvia. The training and the studies were harder than she thought they would be, and although she did everything that was demanded of her with absolute devotion, she was afraid that in the end she would not manage to become a clandestine combatant. She was well aware that only those who passed all the practical tests successfully would finally be chosen for that coveted role. She shuddered to think what would become of her if she failed.

Abraham sent her to interview Beba Idelson, the secretary of the women's organization Pioneer Women (today called Na'amat). Sylvia phoned Idelson's office, introducing herself as a representative of the *Daily Mirror,* and set a time for the interview. When she arrived at the appointed time, she was both friendly and convincing; nobody even asked to see her press card.

After the mistakes Sylvia had made in the general rehearsal with Abraham, she had prepared much more thoroughly for the interview with Idelson. She had gathered additional information about the newspaper that had ostensibly sent her and had read a lot of material about poverty as it affected adults and children as well as about Pioneer Women's projects in these areas. She memorized Idelson's biography as a former member of the Knesset and an experienced organizer with many successful ventures behind her. Idelson answered all Sylvia's questions with alacrity and complimented her on being so familiar with the background material.

After the interview, Sylvia returned to the apartment to meet Abraham.

"How did it go?" he asked.

"Excellently," she answered. Her mood was exultant. She felt that she had passed another test with flying colors.

The night of January 1, 1965, was cold and rainy, a perfect setting for undercover activities. It was the kind of night when security guards were less on the alert than usual. On this night a terrorist attack was to take place that was meant to echo around the world.

Hidden by the wet weather and the darkness, three men, members of Fatah, crossed the Jordan where it flowed through the Beisan Valley. Their dark clothes were soaked, and they shivered from the cold. On their backs they carried large explosive charges wrapped in waterproof covers.

The three crawled into Israeli territory, freezing to the spot when a routine IDF patrol passed close by them. After the danger had passed, they got up and quickly made their way toward the pump-

ing station of the National Water Carrier at the northwest corner of
Lake Kinneret, the Sea of Galilee. The purpose of the station, which
had been inaugurated only a year previously with an investment
of hundreds of millions of dollars, was to pump large amounts of
water that flowed into the Sea of Galilee from the Banias River in
Syria and the Hatzbani River in Lebanon to arid, thirsty areas in
southern Israel.

The plan to blow up the pumping station has been initiated
by Yasser Arafat. It was Fatah's first exploit, and Arafat was waiting anxiously in Jordan to hear about its outcome. He was hoping
that the operation would gain prestige for his organization in Arab
countries, place Fatah on the public agenda in the rest of the world,
and win support for his continuing efforts to free Palestine from its
Jewish usurpers.

The rain pelted the three terrorists as they made their way
through the fields, slipping and sliding in the mud. They were supposed to get to the nerve center of the water system, climb over the
fence, position the explosives in the main hall of the pumping station, and set the timing device three hours forward. They were then
to retreat to the point where they had forded the river and return to
base.

The operation began without a hitch, but the three didn't manage to reach the pumping station. A detachment of the Israeli Border
Patrol had seen their muddy footprints, and the operatives quickly
found themselves surrounded. There were commanded to surrender; instead, they tried to escape. Two died instantly from the resulting gunfire, but the third managed to escape.

One of those killed was twenty-three-year-old Abed, a relative
of Ali Salameh. Yasser Arafat visited the family's Amman home in
order to pay his respects and praise their son's courage. There he
met Ali, who was at the house with his mother and sister. Arafat
said proudly that even though the terrorist operation in which Abed
had participated had actually failed, it had managed to bring to the
attention of the entire world that there was an organization called
Fatah and that they would continue to terrorize the lives of the Jews
until the Jews were eventually forced to vacate the land in favor of
the Palestinians. Fatah's slogan was: "What was taken by force will
be restored by force."

Arafat hugged Ali.

"We need you now more than ever," he said. "Join us."

This time Ali found it hard to refuse. Abed was not only a relative, but had been a close friend since they had studied together at Bir Zeit University, near Ramallah. The mourning family said to him imploringly, "Abed would have wanted you to continue in his footsteps."

In fact, Ali had no plans for the future. He didn't have a vocation that he particularly wanted to pursue. He just wanted to be left alone to do what he liked best: to enjoy life. But the pressure of his immediate family, Arafat, and the bereaved family to continue his father's legacy increased, not leaving him much choice. He hoped that giving in to their pressure and joining Fatah wouldn't stop him from continuing to taste the pleasures life had to offer. In the long run, he thought, the personal sacrifice he was being asked to make wasn't really that great.

Ali's mother approached him.

"This is the moment for making decisions," she said passionately. "Don't forget that you are Hassan Salameh's son. Thousands are waiting for you to continue his mission. Don't disappoint them."

Ali stood very tall.

"I will join you," he said to Yasser Arafat.

Arafat looked at him, his face shining.

"I've been waiting such a long time to hear you say that," he replied, embracing Ali warmly.

Once a week the instructors at Israel's School for Special Operations got together to discuss how the training process was going and how their trainees were progressing. The school's office was located in an ordinary apartment on the third floor of an old walk-up building at the corner of Allenby and Mazeh Streets in downtown Tel Aviv. The three-room apartment had high ceilings; its windows, which faced the street, were sealed by tall wooden shutters, making it impossible for anyone in the nearby buildings to see what was going on inside.

Two of the rooms were rented by Unit 188. They contained some old furniture and metal filing cabinets. Two paintings of landscapes by Reuven Rubin were hung on the walls.[5] The Spartan decor suited the general atmosphere of the Special Operations Unit, whose high command and the combatants were always expected to manage with the bare minimum—simple offices, small budgets, and modest salaries.

The two rooms were rented to the Special Operations Unit by the

Wertzmans, a retired middle-aged couple whose sons had occupied prominent positions in the security forces. The couple lived in the third room of the apartment and always greeted the office workers with a huge smile and a cup of tea. They spent most of their time at home, pretending that they had no idea what was going on in the rooms they rented out. The only thing the husband could say to the renters in public was, "Don't worry—I'm looking after your offices for you."

At their meetings the school's instructors discussed innovations in the art of warfare and how they could be adapted to their special needs. They also considered how to update exercises and teaching programs, as well as how best to supervise the candidates' training and evaluate their performance. In everything related to self-confidence, determination, and motivation, Sylvia was given the highest marks at these meetings.

The ideal Unit 188 clandestine combatant is one whose personality represents the ultimate balance between qualities that seem to be total opposites: bravery and discretion, adventurousness and self-control, daring and self-criticism, independence and obedience, imagination and practicality, simplicity and the ability to carry out elaborate stratagems, decisiveness and aggressiveness, leadership and the ability to accept the leadership of others. The School for Special Operations was responsible for assuring that its recruits possessed these qualities.

Sylvia's training continued step by step, gradually becoming more complex. As time passed, she was expected to perform ever more difficult and challenging tasks, until the moment finally came when she and her trainers would find out how she would react when faced with real operational conditions in a totally Arab setting. The examiners know that every candidate has weak points. For this reason all the trainees must undergo an ordeal to ascertain how they would behave during an actual operation in enemy territory. The psychologist who interviewed Sylvia was convinced that she was brave and daring, but neither the psychologist nor Sylvia's instructors had any idea how she would react at the moment of truth. They prepared a particularly challenging test for her.

In preparation for the test, the Department of Maps was requested to print a single copy of a falsified ordinance map. The important modification was to move the Jordanian border west into Israeli territory. All Israeli settlements were erased from the map, while a large Arab village, which was actually in Israel, suddenly found itself in Jordan.

The map was spread out before Sylvia.

"Your mission is to get to this village," she was told. "You must collect information about the exact location of the central water well, ways of access, and the buildings around it."

She studied the map carefully.

"Is it in Jordan?" she asked.

"Yes, it is."

"It won't be easy," she said.

"Do you prefer not to do this?"

"Definitely not," she said decidedly. "I can't wait to get going— you've finally given me a serious assignment."

Sylvia spent long hours studying the map down to its last detail, mentally photographing the roads leading to the village and committing to memory the path that would lead her there. She repeatedly went over her cover story: she was a tourist from South Africa who had been visiting Antipatris, the ancient fortress of Herod not far from the border, and lost her way. On the day before the assignment, Abraham took her to the remains of the fortress, so that she would become acquainted with the area and be able to stick to her cover story convincingly.

"What will you do if they ask to see your passport?" asked Abraham.

"I'll tell them I left it at the hotel."

She knew that if she were arrested by the Jordanians, they were liable to ignore her cover story and accuse her of spying, shoot her, and bury her body in a field, and nobody would ever be the wiser about what had happened to her. Their reaction would depend on the amount of self-confidence she displayed and her ability to convince them that she wasn't an Israeli spy.

A few days later, on a foggy autumn night, a Special Operations Unit vehicle let Sylvia off at the remains of a Muslim burial ground. She recalled its location on the map.

"The border is just ahead," her colleagues told her. "Good luck!"

Sylvia had to get to the outskirts of the village on her own, stop near the well, and return with an exact description of the place. She had not been given a weapon.

"You mustn't make contact with anyone," her guide told her. "Do everything in your power to avoid it."

The moon was hidden behind heavy clouds as Sylvia began making her way toward the village. Darkness enveloped her, a cold wind blew through her hair, and she was overcome with a feeling of dread. She was sure that she was in Jordanian territory and that she was liable to fall into the hands of Jordanian soldiers or angry villagers.

As she neared the village, she smelled acrid smoke emanating from the houses, which were heated by dried cow dung, and she heard dogs barking angrily. It was almost midnight. The first houses she saw looked like threatening black hulks. She broke off a branch from one of the trees and waved it at two dogs that approached her, baring their teeth and growling angrily.

Sylvia found the well and memorized its exact location. Someone came out of one of the houses and disappeared into an adjacent one. A car arrived and stopped in front of a one-story stone house. She hid at the back of a nearby building, and when the coast was clear, started walking back in the direction from which she had come. She walked rapidly along the dirt track, not yet out of danger. Someone might still spot her.

The way back was easier since she was now familiar with the path. Another hour passed, and she could already see the outline of the monument. She breathed a sigh of relief when she saw the car waiting for her.

"Did you get what we wanted?" he asked. He didn't reveal to Sylvia that she had actually been on the Israeli side of the border the whole time.

"Yes." She promised to present him with a full report in a few hours, including all the information she had gathered.

"Excellent," said the man, who was not accustomed to handing out compliments. "I have only one question: were you frightened?"

"A bit."

When Ali Hassan Salameh parked his sports car in front of the headquarters of the Fatah organization in Amman on a wet, rainy day in October 1965, he was surprised by the feverish activity that was taking place inside the building. Armed men bounded up and down the stairs, darted in and out of the rooms, and conversed among themselves excitedly. Loud shouting issued from Yasser Arafat's office. Everyone emerging from there looked exhausted and helpless. Ali tried to find out what was happening. "A great disaster," answered a man carrying a loaded Kalachnikov rifle. "A huge disaster."

Ali waited patiently outside the door of Arafat's office. It was his first day in Fatah, and he and Arafat were supposed to discuss Ali's future in the organization, but the leader only became free to talk with him a couple of hours later.

When Ali finally entered the room, he found the Fatah leader in a gloomy frame of mind. His handshake was limp and his eyes looked pained.

"Pardon me," he said to Ali. "I'm having a very hard day."

Ali Salameh looked at him with interest, wondering what was causing Arafat to be so upset.

"Since I founded the Fatah," said Arafat, "nothing like this has never happened."

In a sad voice he told Ali that after the failed attempt to sabotage the Israel Water Carrier, Fatah had carried out several shooting attacks on citizens within the borders of Israel. "But it hardly made any impression, not on the Arabs and not on the Israelis. We knew that we had to carry out a bigger operation, one that would make waves. We decided to ambush a bus on the Tiberias-Beisan road, open fire on it with machine guns, and return immediately to Jordan. We were certain that the operation would be a success. We were wrong. At the exact location where the ambush was to take place, Israeli soldiers were waiting for our people. All the members of the team were killed instantly. We thought it was a coincidence and tried to ignore it. A few months later, we planned another big operation in the strictest secrecy. We collected our best men and ordered them to infiltrate into Kibbutz Ashdot Yaakov and kill as many people as possible. When the preparations were completed, we prayed for their success. I was confident that this time nothing would stop our operatives from carrying out their mission. But when the detachment crossed the Jordan with a large stock of weapons, ammunition, and bombs, an Israeli ambush was waiting for them. Almost all our men were killed in the first burst of fire, and those who remained alive were captured and taken in for questioning. This second failure really worried me, since I came to the conclusion that the IDF's ambushes were not coincidental . . ."

"Do you mean to say that there is a traitor in our midst who is passing on all the details of our operations to Israel?" Ali completed the leader's thought.

"I'm not sure." Arafat's voice broke. "Only members of my operational staff knew about the planned operations. I know each and every one of them very well. They are very reliable. There's not a chance that any of them could be working for the Israelis."

"You'd better not waste any time finding out if your intuitions are correct," suggested Ali.

Arafat's servant brought cups of bitter coffee. The two men drank them down in one gulp, followed by glasses of cold water.

"You have given me food for thought," Arafat said. "Are you acquainted with Salah Khalaf Abu Iyad?"

"I've heard of him," answered Ali. Abu Iyad was an old friend of Arafat's. A native of Lydda, Abu Iyad was one of the founding members of Fatah and head of the intelligence branch of the organization.

Arafat sent for him.

A bulky man with a large stomach, a black moustache, and piercing eyes entered the room. Arafat introduced him to Ali.

"Your father's name goes before you," said Abu Iyad to Ali. "He was a born leader. I hope you will follow in his footsteps."

They wasted no more time on polite conversation. Arafat asked Abu Iyad to set up a security department that would specialize in locating agents working for Israel. "That is now our most acute problem," he said. When Arafat suggested that Ali be appointed head of this department, Abu Iyad gave his wholehearted approval.

The idea actually appealed to Ali. This wasn't a routine assignment. It would require honed senses, quick thinking, and a sharp eye. Although Ali was totally inexperienced, he was intelligent and resourceful, ambitious, and wily, exactly what the new post demanded.

"Thank you," he said to Arafat and Abu Iyad. "I will do the best I can, and may Allah grant me success."

In anything connected with nightlife, Beirut surpassed Amman in every way. Compared to the lively capital of Lebanon, which was replete with clubs, restaurants, and women who were there for the asking, the Jordanian capital was no more than a sleepy town, whose inhabitants generally went to bed early. Businesses closed at nightfall, and the lights went out in the streets and houses of Amman before the partying had even begun in Beirut.

Ali Salameh's new position demanded that he move to Amman

with his wife and small son and give up a good part of the pleasures offered by Beirut. He didn't like the Jordanian capital: it didn't
contain a single restaurant that was to his taste, and no garage in
Amman knew how to service his Mustang. There weren't really any
nightclubs, and the Jordanian girls were too conservative for his
taste. When his wife told him that she preferred life in Amman, he
turned on her angrily. He realized that she felt that way because he
would have fewer opportunities to be unfaithful to her.

At the same time, despite all its drawbacks, Amman did have
one striking advantage: it provided Ali with an interesting occupation and the possibility of rapid promotion. His new position as the
man responsible for locating agents working for Israel who had in-
filtrated the Fatah organization was one that he thoroughly enjoyed.
For the first time in his life, he was faced with a real challenge. People expected him to succeed, and Arafat and Abu Iyad depended on
him. This was a new, exciting experience for him.

The fact that he had to exercise extreme caution and maintain
absolute secrecy also appealed to him. For security reasons, the intelligence headquarters of Fatah moved from place to place. When
Ali first arrived, the headquarters were located in a well-guarded
building in a refugee camp near Amman. Fewer than ten employees
worked there, and they mainly gathered information about possible
Israeli targets. Until Ali arrived, none of them had ever dealt with
uncovering secret Israeli agents. Ali was assigned a private office
and set to work. He knew that the task assigned to him was complex
and difficult to accomplish, but he was confident of success. From
the beginning, he trusted no one and preferred working alone. He
began by spending several days preparing an accurate list of all the
people who were generally included in meetings that dealt with secret operations. Next, he checked the procedures for how operational plans were conveyed from Fatah headquarters to the men in the
field. The first recommendation he made to Arafat and Abu Iyad,
the head of intelligence, was to keep any information about the location of an attack absolutely secret from those meant to carry it out
until the last moment. His suggestion was immediately accepted,
but it soon proved to be ineffectual. The IDF continued to neutralize almost every Fatah attack and to decimate the teams before they
managed to carry out their operations. Fear reigned in Fatah's training bases. The general feeling was that whoever was sent out on a
mission would probably not come back alive.

Arafat's mood worsened with every additional Israeli sabotage of Fatah's operations. He and Abu Iyad feared that these recurring failures would severely harm the organization's standing, and they urged Ali to continue his investigations. At an emergency meeting attended by the three of them only, Ali Salameh told them simply, "They seem to have planted an agent in the operational branch."

Arafat went pale. "It can't be!" he cried. "All the members of the operational staff are my confidents. None of them is capable of betraying us."

"I hope you're right," replied Ali and then asked for permission to investigate the members of the staff. Arafat reluctantly gave his approval.

"On one condition," he emphasized. "Make sure they don't find out that we're tailing them."

4

Arrest and Investigation

Georgina Rizk was a pretty, round-faced girl with auburn hair. Her father, a dark-skinned Christian Lebanese tycoon, always appeared in public dressed elegantly; her light-skinned, fair-haired mother was a native of Hungary. The mansion in which the family lived— three floors filled with elegant furniture and manned by an army of servants—was located in Beirut's Ashrafiya Quarter, which was populated by other affluent Christians. The house was located a short distance from the golden sands of a beach that bordered the blue Mediterranean.

Georgina and her sister, Felicia, studied at a private school, one of the best and most expensive in Lebanon. They were driven there and back in a chauffeur-driven limousine. Their clothes were imported from Paris, and when their hair needed cutting, it was done at home by a fashionable hairdresser who arrived especially for that purpose.

Georgina was brought up like a princess. Her parents adored her and indulged her every whim. Her teachers complimented her, boys from wealthy families courted her passionately, and a private maid was at her disposal night and day, making up her bed, serving her food, and standing ready to do the bidding of her young mistress.

Ali Salameh was twenty-seven years old when he took his first steps as a member of Fatah. Georgina was fourteen at the time. Like most people in Beirut, Ali had heard of the Rizk family, and quite often when he was in town he would pass by the protective wall of their mansion. There was no chance of his ever gaining admittance, since her father never invited terrorist activists to his home. He did contribute large sums to the Palestinian charity organizations active in Lebanese refugee camps, but he was careful to keep his distance from organizations such as Fatah. Thus, the chance of Ali Salameh's ever running into Georgina Rizk was slim; but when they finally met several years later, the encounter would change their lives forever.

When she was sixteen, Georgina's father granted an interview to the Beirut paper *Al Hayat*. A news photographer took pictures of the house and also of Georgina. It was the first time that her picture had appeared in the newspaper, and it attracted much attention. A few days later, the organizers of beauty pageants phoned her and suggested that she contend for the title of Miss Lebanon.

Georgina was excited by the prospect of winning the title that so many young Lebanese women coveted. She asked her father for permission to participate in the contest. He responded furiously, "It would be shameful for you to appear in front of an audience that would undress you with their eyes." He thought that his daughter's participation in a beauty contest was beneath the dignity of a respected family such as his. It could, he continued, harm his reputation, maybe even affect his business. But Georgina's mother was of a different opinion, and she set out to defend her daughter with a vengeance. She didn't see anything wrong with such an event, and she made every effort to convince her husband that not a few girls from good Arab families had participated in beauty contests in the past. She recruited relatives and friends to pressure her husband into changing his mind.

The raging arguments eventually ended with mother and daughter emerging triumphant.

The pageant was held in a packed auditorium in central Beirut. Out of the twenty-one contenders, the judges unanimously chose Georgina, as she was the most beautiful of them all. The former Miss Lebanon placed a golden crown on Georgina's head. After the ceremony, television cameramen and newspaper photographers flocked around her enthusiastically.

Within a week, Georgina's picture was appearing on the cover of every magazine in Lebanon. Several shops on Hamra Street, in Beirut's most exclusive shopping area, placed her picture in their display windows. Journalists and television producers asked her for exclusive interviews. When he could no longer stand its constant ringing, her father had their phone disconnected.

At first Georgina enjoyed her new popularity, but she quickly began to feel that she was receiving far too much exposure. She hadn't expected to become so open to public scrutiny, and she was upset by the letters she received from disgusted Muslim citizens, who condemned her for having participated in the pageant. She stayed at home for a whole week, hoping that the press would find a new topic that would distract their attention from her. But then, exactly when she thought the wave of publicity had passed, she received an official letter inviting her to participate in the Miss World contest in the United States.

Apprehensive of angering her father even further, Georgina turned down the offer.

A soft spring breeze ruffled the calm waters of the Yarkon River, and the smell of seaweed filled the air. As the sun slipped below the horizon, its rays lit up the kayaks floating on the river and the face of the young woman who was walking on the riverbank. She was tall, with green eyes and dark hair. In one hand she held a fishing rod and in the other a large cloth bag. She was headed northward, toward the river.

A while later, she sat down on the bank of the river not far from some fishermen who were staring at the water, waiting for the balls floating at the end of their lines to twitch as a sign that another fish had swallowed the bait. They glanced at her indifferently as she placed a worm on her hook and cast the line into the water. This was the first and last time in her life that Sylvia attempted to go fishing, but she had no choice in the matter. She was masquerading as an angler in order to get closer to the concrete channel that partially protruded from the water, half covered by the branches of a willow tree on the riverbank. While the other fishermen directed their attention to their lines, she furtively glanced at the channel and weighed the best way of getting to it.

From among the trees on the riverbank, Abraham and another instructor from the School for Special Operations closely followed Sylvia's movements. They hadn't taken their eyes off her from the moment she approached the river and took up her position among the fishermen on the bank.

The sun set, and it started getting dark. One after another, the fishermen packed up their equipment, collected their daily catch, and went away. The young woman remained. The river was enveloped in darkness.

Her two observers strained their eyes. They saw the departing fishermen passing by. They couldn't see Sylvia any longer and knew that at that moment she was beginning an assignment that was part of her advanced training at the School for Special Operations. The test facing her would measure her ability to overcome both physical and mental difficulties.

Under the cover of darkness, Sylvia changed into a lightweight sports outfit. She packed the fishing rod and the clothes she had discarded into the bag and left the bag in the thicket.

She slid from the riverbank into the water and approached the channel she had studied so carefully while she was supposedly fishing. When she arrived at the channel, she headed for its opening. During an earlier visit, she had noticed a layer of metal covering it. The metal was rusty. Sylvia removed it effortlessly and crouched down inside.

She had been given this assignment a few days earlier, and she knew it wouldn't be easy. First of all there was the cover story, which was supposed to give her a good reason for being there, disguised as an amateur angler fishing in the Yarkon. It had worked. Even the regulars hadn't paid much attention to her. The concrete channel presented a greater problem. Its purpose was to convey into the Yarkon water that was used to cool down the giant turbines of the Reading Power Station. The water, which was pumped from the sea, was drained from the power station by means of a concrete channel flowing into the Yarkon, which returned the water to the sea. Sylvia's instructors had warned her that the water was liable to be hot, so she had equipped herself with boots carried in her fishing bag. In fact the water was a lot hotter than she had counted on. Its heat penetrated her boots and burned her feet painfully. She had two choices: either to retreat or to advance. She chose the second option.

Sylvia had taken into consideration that the way through the channel would be long and difficult. The air inside was humid and dense, and the heavy darkness hindered her progress. She found it hard to breathe or to see where she was going, and she supported herself on the sides of the channel so as not to slip, hoping that this nightmare wouldn't have to go on much longer. She stopped a few times to rest, gritting her teeth and suppressing a cry of pain, but she was determined not to give up, not to fail.

In her hands she held a parcel that she was supposed to place near one of the turbines. Absolutely no one must notice her. The power station, being a potential target for terrorist activity, was well guarded. If she was spotted by anyone, she knew that the security guards would be alerted and she would be arrested. That would mean she had failed, which was of course the last thing she wanted.

After what seemed forever, Sylvia finally heard the sound of the power station's turbines. The farther she advanced, the stronger was the flow of hot water surrounding her. Slowly she crawled toward the opening, trying to avoid any sudden movements that might attract attention. She peered out and saw two workers standing not far from her. Luckily, they didn't notice her.

The turbine room was large and well lit. In its center were located the two huge motors that supplied electricity. Sylvia crawled behind one of them, far away from the workers' line of vision. With her sleeve she obliterated her boot prints, which had left a wet trail across the floor. In one quick motion, she leaned the parcel against one of the motors and glanced quickly at the workers. They still hadn't noticed her. But someone else had been following her all the time. From a hiding place in the room, the man had watched her every movement, from the moment she jumped out of the channel until she laid the charge. It was one of her instructors supervising her performance.

Sylvia crawled back to the dark channel and was swallowed up by it. The way back was quicker and easier. The more she advanced, the cooler the water became, and she breathed a sigh of relief when she finally stood in the warm river water.

Cars passed by on the road nearby. A full moon floated in the sky, and not a soul was walking on the paths parallel to the river. Sylvia climbed up the riverbank, her clothes soaking. She took her dry clothes out of the bag and put them on, changed her boots for sports shoes, and began making her way toward the lights of the city shining just a short distance away.

The two instructors jumped out of the bushes and blocked her way.

"How did it go?" asked Abraham.

She was hungry and thirsty.

"First buy me something to eat," she said.

The instructor who had followed Sylvia's movements in the power station joined them.

"You did an excellent job," he said, and told her that he had been following her the whole time.

They took her to a falafel stand and bought her a portion of spicy chickpea balls and salad in pita bread. Sylvia wolfed it down.

"It wasn't that complicated," she said, her mouth full.

"When you get home, sit down and write your report," said Abraham. "We'll start later tomorrow, so you can get some rest."

Ali Hassan Salameh didn't need to infiltrate power stations or other well-guarded locations in order to prove that he was worthy of being part of the Fatah machine. His father's glory as a legendary leader was his ticket into the organization, and it formed an integral part of his image from the moment he first sat down at his desk in the intelligence department. The senior members of Fatah adopted him immediately as a beloved family member, the guards at the entrance to the building saluted him deferentially when he arrived and when he departed, and he felt as though nothing could hinder his way to the top.

This warm embrace gave him confidence, but Ali knew that it wasn't enough. He must first of all prove himself worthy by succeeding in the assignment that had been given him. It was his first test, and it was almost impossibly difficult and complex. The information he had collected about the operational staff revealed that, apart from Abu Iyad and Ali himself, six other Fatah veterans were permanent members, all of whom had been part of the organization from its inception. They were all close associates and personal friends of Arafat and Abu Iyad, and most of them were family men who were highly motivated and with an impeccable history. There was no apparent reason to suspect any of them; nevertheless, it was clear to Ali that the operational staff could have been the only source of the leak that caused so many operations to be disrupted by the Israelis.

Ali examined the personnel file of every one of the staff members, which contained information relating to each man's activities from the time he joined Fatah to the present day. Some of them had accompanied Arafat from the very first day he had established the organization. Each had planned and carried out activities that were meant to harm the Israelis. A sophisticated, stubborn effort would be necessary in order to disclose which of them was working with Israel, and Ali felt in need of help. He couldn't turn to Arafat and Abu Iyad for assistance. They put unquestioning faith in their men and couldn't accept that any of them were capable of betraying the organization.

Ali had an idea, which on the surface seemed difficult to carry out; but the longer he considered it, the more convinced he was that it was the best plan possible. He asked Arafat for special permission to go to East Germany in order to meet with the director of the Stasi, Erich Mielke, and request his help in uncovering the "mole" in Fatah's operational staff. The Stasi was a well-organized espionage organization that acted in cooperation with, and under the supervision of, the Soviet Union. It served as the uncontested ruler of communist East Germany and extended its activities to all parts of the world, including the Middle East. Its leaders had given much assistance to Arafat, meeting with him more than once and supplying him with information and arms. Ali was hopeful that they would be able to help him.

Arafat gave his permission for the journey unwillingly. He didn't think it would be effective, but he didn't want to stand in Ali's way or cause him frustration so early in his days as a member of the organization.

Ali's journey was wrapped in complete secrecy: only Arafat and Abu Iyad knew about it. Ali flew to Poland on his own passport, confident that the Israelis were still unaware of his existence and wouldn't attempt to harm him. He traveled to East Berlin by train from Warsaw and booked a room at the Moscow Hotel. Grayness and dilapidation reigned in the faded city, and the hotel blended into the general atmosphere. It was a multistory building that mainly housed party activists and their guests. The food was sparse, and entertainment was nonexistent. On every floor of the hotel sat a woman superintendent who had keys to all the rooms and kept a careful record of all comings and goings. Ali knew that every room was equipped with an eavesdropping device, so he was careful to make only one telephone call, to Mielke's office.

The meeting between the two of them took place in Stasi headquarters on Lichtenberg Street. Erich Mielke greeted Ali warmly. He was a balding fifty-five-year-old man of average height, who worked out every day at the gym, ate a healthy diet, and shunned tobacco and alcohol. Ali introduced himself in German, a language he had learned during his studies in Berlin, and told Mielke the purpose of his visit. Mielke listened in silence and then said, "Give me the list of suspects. I promise you that we will do our best."

Mielke, an amateur hunter, invited his visitor to accompany him on a hunting trip to a nearby forest. He fitted Ali out with a camouflage uniform, and the two of them slowly surveyed the forest for prey. The Stasi director killed a young deer. Ali missed every time. "You're not a professional hunter yet," Mielke commented to his young companion. "It takes a lot of experience to hunt animals and humans. You'll learn!"

Mielke gave the order, and the German secret agents in Beirut and Amman immediately began collecting information about the six members of Fatah's operational staff. They especially looked into these men's connections with foreign elements outside Jordan. After a few weeks they picked up the trail of a young Lebanese woman who had been the girlfriend of one of the suspects. An undercover investigation revealed that the man, who was married with children, was paying the young woman's rent and showering her with expensive presents. They conveyed this information to Ali, who checked the man's financial records and discovered that he had a large bank balance, despite the fact that the salary he received from Fatah would barely suffice to support his family. It was clear that the suspect was receiving funds from additional sources.

The surveillance of the man intensified. Two of Ali's trusted colleagues followed the suspect on his next trip to Beirut and surprised him in his girlfriend's apartment. He denied ever having passed on information to the Israelis, but couldn't explain the source of the funds he was using to maintain his girlfriend in such opulence.

Arafat was deeply shocked when he received the results of the investigation. This man was considered to be one of the pillars of Fatah's operational division, but from the moment it was discovered that he had betrayed the organization, his days were numbered. A hit team was sent after him, and he was shot to death one night on his way home.

Arafat claimed that the Israelis were responsible for the assassination.

"Who are you?" asked one of the investigators in Hebrew. He was about forty, tall and sturdy, with a dark complexion and black hair. Sylvia looked into his eyes and saw that they were totally lacking in compassion.

His friend was smoking a cigarette and blowing the smoke in her face. He was younger and shorter than the other one, with a fat belly hanging over his belt.

"I don't speak Hebrew," she said.

They reverted to English.

"Who are you?" she was asked again.

"A tourist."

"Your name?"

She gave them the false name that was an integral part of her cover story.

"Where are your documents?" the first interrogator asked.

"I lost them."

"Did you report the loss to the police?"

"I didn't manage to. It only happened yesterday."

"Where do you live?"

"In a hotel."

"Which one?"

"The Sea View in Tel Aviv."

"What's the address?"

"Number 28 Ben-Yehuda Street."

The second interrogator leaned toward her.

"Do you think we're stupid?" he asked coldly, his voice hoarse from smoking.

Behind his back was a large mirror. She saw her image reflected in it: wild hair, pallid face, frightened eyes.

"You were arrested in an army camp that is off limits for civilians. What were you doing there?"

"I was on a nature hike and I got lost."

"People don't just go walking in army camps. Who sent you?"

"I told you—I got lost."

"Why were you hiking in that particular area?"

"I was told that it was beautiful there."

Only a few hours had passed since Sylvia had walked, under cover of darkness, through the gate of the fence surrounding the camp. This was yet another important test that she needed to pass. According to the instructions she had received, she was to infiltrate Camp Allenby in Jerusalem and return with detailed information about access roads, buildings, and sentry posts. Abraham had rehearsed her cover story with her beforehand.

Getting into the camp wasn't easy, but it wasn't impossible. She arrived there late in the evening, at a time when most of the soldiers were already asleep. It was raining, and the sentry at the gate preferred to stay shut up in his hut. She stole inside without being detected and wandered around among the buildings, collecting data. Not far away, she saw a guard of soldiers patrolling the fence. They didn't notice her.

The camp was enveloped in silence. Apart from the patter of raindrops, there was no sound, no people or vehicles. Sylvia committed to memory the position of the command headquarters and the sentry posts and was preparing to leave when suddenly a bright light blinded her. Within seconds, she found herself surrounded by four armed soldiers.

"What are you doing here?" demanded one of them.

"I'm a tourist. I've lost my way," she answered in English.

"Don't you dare make a move!" he shouted. The soldiers blindfolded her, put her and her belongings into an army vehicle, and transported her to the detention center at the Russian Compound in Jerusalem. Sylvia hadn't expected this to happen, but she assumed that very shortly her instructors would understand that she hadn't completed her mission and would come looking for her. She hoped they would hurry.

Now the tall interrogator leaned in toward her.

"Look, ma'am," he said quietly. He rubbed his hands together; they were the hands of a boxer. "You have two choices, and only two. One is to tell us the truth, and the other is to keep quiet. For your own sake, I hope you have enough brains to choose the first option. If you answer our questions, we'll bring you food and let you go to sleep. If you choose the second option, you'll curse the day you were born. Keep in mind that nobody has ever been questioned by us who didn't eventually tell us the truth."

She knew that this wasn't an empty threat, that they had the means to break her. She knew this since she had been instructed regarding interrogation methods. She was well aware that those who had sent her to infiltrate the camp expected her not to say a single word, even under torture.

"I've got nothing to say," she stated. The shorter interrogator approached her and thrust his fist in her face. She waited for the blow, but it didn't come.

"Lie down on the ground."

She lay down on the cold stone floor, and he tied up her hands.

"Call us when you decide to talk," he growled.

The two exited the room and left her lying on the floor. They took up positions in the next room opposite the one-way mirror facing the interrogation room, where Sylvia was lying on the floor. On the blind side of the mirror, she was unaware that her instructors and the commander of the School for Special Operations were also seated on the other side and were watching her every movement.

The interrogation room was dimly lit by one electric bulb. She couldn't tell if it was night or day. Her watch had been taken from her when she was arrested.

The ropes were starting to bite into her flesh, and it was uncomfortable lying on the hard floor in such an awkward position. All she had to do in order to ease the discomfort was to call her interrogators and tell them the truth; but Sylvia bit her lip and remained silent. Whatever happens, she thought, I won't break down. It was unthinkable to disappoint those who had sent her.

Sylvia assumed that a few hours had passed since they tied her up and left her. Her whole body ached, and blood was dripping from her wrists. She tried to sink into sleep to dull the pain, but she didn't succeed in closing her eyes. She was well aware that many people under interrogation had been broken after being tortured in this way, and that she would be expected to confess everything in the next few hours. She was determined not to let that happen.

She shouted toward the door, and the tall interrogator entered the room.

"I need to go to the bathroom," she said.

"Okay," he said. His voice was soft and pleasant for a change.

He undid the ropes and accompanied her to the toilets.

When she had finished, he said, "I understand that we can now continue with the interrogation."

"There's no point," she answered coolly, with self-control. "I've already told you that I have nothing to say."

He led her silently down a long corridor and took her down a few steps until they stood at the entrance to a small cell.

"Every few hours someone will come to see if you've changed your mind," he said. "Enjoy yourself."

He quickly opened the door, pushed her into the cell, and turned the key. The door was windowless, and the cell was filled with the strong smell of disinfectant. It contained an iron bed, a small sink, and a lavatory in the corner. She was exhausted, but she couldn't sleep. She was kept awake by a naked electric bulb hanging from the ceiling.

After what seemed like an eternity, a slit in the bottom of the door opened and a plate of food was shoved through it. Sylvia was hungry and thirsty, and she reached for the food. It was tasteless and meager. Tears of frustration rolled down her cheeks, but she forced herself to maintain self-control. This was only the beginning; surely even harder ordeals lay ahead.

Later—she still couldn't tell if it was day or night—she was taken from her cell and led once again to the interrogation room. She noticed that something had changed in the room. The chair where she had sat before was no longer there, so she was obliged to stand.

"Have you had enough time to think?" asked the tall interrogator. "What have you decided?"

"I haven't changed my mind."

He smiled.

"You're a strong girl," he said, "but we're stronger than you are. You'll eventually tell us what we want to know."

They questioned her for a long time. She didn't answer. Afterward he left the room and the second interrogator entered. Sylvia's legs hurt from the prolonged standing. She knew that they weren't letting her sit down as part of the wearing-down process.

She looked at the new man in silence. For some reason she felt no fear.

They continued questioning her all through the day, until her legs could no longer support her. She fell in a faint to the floor, waking up a few hours later in her cell. The electric light blinded her. Then she noticed something unexpected: at the foot of her bed sat a woman in a prisoner's uniform. She was older than Sylvia, plump, and extremely talkative. "They arrested me so that I would tell them where my husband is," she said. "They suspect him of passing on information to the Arabs, but he left me a few months ago, and I haven't since seen him since." She asked Sylvia why she had been arrested.

"I was wandering around in a restricted area."

"What were you doing there?"

"I was there by mistake."

"So why are they holding you?"

"Because I'm not telling them anything."

"Tell them what they want," said her new cellmate. "Why are you being so stubborn?"

Suddenly, as one feels after a great physical effort, a shiver passed through Sylvia. She felt that the strength was leaving her body, and a feeling of nausea crept up into her throat. She was enveloped by a feeling of dread. Was she about to break down?

She curled up in a corner of the cell. Again they brought her food, but she pushed it away. Her cellmate didn't stop talking, and her voice was oppressive and annoying. For a moment Sylvia wanted to shout at the woman to shut up, but she forced herself to pull herself together. Her senses grew alert again, and her strength returned. No, nothing would break her, not now and not during the next interrogation session.

The cell door opened. The two interrogators stood in the doorway. Sylvia's cellmate was ordered to leave. She got up from the bed and left the cell without a word.

"How are you feeling?" asked the tall interrogator.

"I'm surviving."

"Come with us," he said.

They returned to the interrogation room. Her legs still hurt. The interrogator opened the door, and Sylvia's eyes opened wide in amazement. Abraham, her instructor, was in the room. He hugged her warmly.

"Congratulations," he said. "I'm proud of you."

When he had sent her to infiltrate the army camp and to report on the location of the offices and the barracks, Abraham made it clear to Sylvia that she was forbidden to divulge the truth if she were caught. She had fulfilled his instructions to the letter.

"Did the interrogators know who I was?" she asked.

"Of course."

"I didn't suspect them for a moment," she said in English, smiling. "They really put me through hell."

He told her that the woman who entered her cell was a case officer of the Israel Security Agency who was supposed to persuade her to admit her guilt.

"You withstood that test, too," he said.

"Were you really here the whole time?"

"We followed the interrogation from the next room by means of the one-way mirror and an eavesdropping device."

"Did I make any mistakes?"

"Not a single one."

"You must all think I'm a pathological liar."

"We think it is easy for you to tell lies to others while being totally honest with us. How are you feeling?"

"Exhausted."

"Well, Sylvia, I told you that it wouldn't be easy, and these are only the entrance exams."

He dropped her off near the hotel where she was staying in Jerusalem in order to perform other assignments in the city, which included surveillance, observations, making contact. The Special Operations Unit had chosen Jerusalem as a training base, since as far as Sylvia was concerned, it was a foreign city. She wasn't familiar with a single street.

"You must be famished," he told her.

"I'm dying to sleep."

"Good night. We'll continue tomorrow."

Ali's success in unmasking the Israeli agent in the Fatah general staff was generally kept a secret. Arafat and Abu Iyad were too embarrassed to admit that Israeli intelligence had managed to infiltrate their organization, but their closest associates knew the truth and appreciated the excellent job that Ali had done. This made him feel more strongly than ever that for the first time in his life, he had done something important and valuable, making him even more enthusiastic about his new profession.

He would arrive at his office every morning as early as possible to deal with any tasks that were imposed on him. He generally spent his time planning how to ensure maximum security at meetings of the Fatah high command. The organization couldn't allow itself any more traitors.

In early June 1967, on the eve of the Six-Day War, the joy of victory had already spread among millions of Arabs before the first shot was fired. They felt totally prepared for the war and were impatient for it to begin. Their huge stockpiles of ammunition and large armies made victory a certainty. On the other side, the Israelis were showing signs of weakness and indecisiveness.

When the Israelis finally pulled themselves together and went to war, the Arab armies found themselves a lot less prepared than they thought they were. In the early hours of June 5, the Israel Air Force attacked the air force bases of Egypt, Syria, Jordan, and Iraq and put all their fighter planes and cargo transport planes out of action. In six days, the united Arab front totally collapsed. Gaza and the West Bank found themselves under Israeli occupation.

In the Arab countries, early hopes of victory were replaced by a sense of defeat and burning frustration. Against this backdrop, the heads of Fatah met for an emergency meeting, in which they decided to increase terrorist attacks on Israel in order to restore a modicum of Arab pride. They didn't take into account that there were now new players in the field who would make even greater effort in that direction than they would—for example, George Habash.

Habash (code named "The Doctor"), forty-two years old, a

Christian, and a native of the Israeli city of Lydda, had escaped with his family to Lebanon at the outbreak of the 1948 war. He was a graduate of the Faculty of Medicine of the American University in Beirut and had worked for a few years in the refugee camps' clinics. He advocated driving the Jews out of Israel and returning the refugees of 1948 to their homes. After the Six-Day War, he founded an extreme Marxist organization called the Popular Front for the Liberation of Palestine (PFLP).

Unlike Arafat, Habash was convinced that terrorist activity within the borders of Israel and the surrounding territories was ineffective and didn't have the power to elicit a universal response. He came up with a far-reaching plan that called for showcase attacks outside Israeli territory, in order to make headlines and sway public opinion in favor of the Palestinian struggle. In 1968, after months of careful and secret preparations, three terrorists of the Front boarded an El Al flight from Rome to Lydda disguised as tourists, and in the middle of the flight announced to the shocked passengers that the plane was being hijacked. Threatening the pilots with weapons, the terrorists forced them to fly to Algeria. After exhaustive negotiations, the hijackers released the passengers and crew in exchange for the release of terrorists who were imprisoned in Israel. The hijacking encouraged the PFLP to carry out a series of additional hijackings, not only of Israeli planes, and to attack Jewish institutions in Europe. Reports of these terrorist attacks echoed around the world, especially in Arab countries, where the Popular Front's reputation rose to heights that caused the top echelons of Fatah many sleepless nights. The writing was on the wall, and Arafat couldn't avoid reading it. He realized that Habash was right: the time for major terrorist attacks had indeed arrived. It was unthinkable to lag behind George Habash, whose small organization was succeeding far better than Fatah, with its thousands of fighters. It was imperative for Arafat to succeed, and he soon formulated a plan that would move him and his group in the right direction.

Ali was urgently summoned to Arafat's office.

"Pack a suitcase," Arafat commanded. "You're flying to Cairo tomorrow."

He explained that the purpose of the journey was for Ali to train a promising group of young Fatah members at an Egyptian Secret Service base. The nine members of the group, some of whom spoke foreign languages and were university graduates and others of whom were professional killers, were to be trained in Cairo to assume false identities, perform sophisticated terrorist acts, assassinate political rivals, establish safe houses, and escape effectively from the law. Upon their return to Amman after a few months' training, the nine would form the basis of a special unit that would initiate and carry out spectacular terrorist attacks outside the borders of Israel. This unit, called Force 17, would eventually develop into one of Arafat's greatest sources of pride.

Sylvia didn't have much spare time during her training period, but at least her weekends were free. She spent them taking trips to all parts of the country, swimming in the sea and photographing scenery and people. However, she was careful never to photograph anyone or anything connected with her training.

Sylvia told her instructors about her hobby, and the information was duly noted in the reports passed on to the unit commanders. They were glad to hear about it, since photography was to play an important role in the cover story that was being developed for Sylvia. It was decided to turn her into a professional photographer.

While she was still in training, she was instructed to sign up for an advanced photography course with Paul Goldman, one of Israel's foremost news photographers. She introduced herself to him as a new immigrant who was an amateur photographer and explained that she had decided to improve her abilities in the field.

"Why did you choose to come to me?" asked Goldman.

"Because I admire your photographs." The Mossad had supplied her with numerous examples.

"It won't be cheap," he emphasized.

"I don't care about the price."

Goldman, who was a native of Budapest and smoked a pipe that he held between clenched teeth, lived in a small apartment in Kfar Saba with his wife, Dina, and their daughter, Medina. He was a brilliant news photographer who had established his reputation in Israel and around the world. One of his most famous photographs, showing David Ben-Gurion standing on his head at the seaside, was purchased by dozens of newspapers in many countries. He was often asked to supply these newspapers with other original photos.

Although he was a brilliant photographer, Goldman had some negative qualities. He despised most of the people surrounding him; he was bad-tempered and quick to insult anyone who annoyed him. If he weren't in need of the money, he would have probably refused to share any of his professional expertise with Sylvia or with anyone else.

The tall, skinny photographer, whose hunched back made him appear to be burdened by the weight of the world, regarded Sylvia coldly and asked to hear about her previous experience as a photographer. He snorted derisively when she showed him some of her work.

"You know nothing," he grumbled.

He unwillingly devoted their first lesson to acquainting her with the various functions of the camera. He taught her things that she hadn't known existed.

"Tomorrow I'm going to photograph Ben-Gurion again," he said. "Accompany me and follow my work methods, but take into consideration that I won't have time to explain anything to you. I rely on your being intelligent enough to figure out for yourself what I'm doing."

The next day they drove to Ben-Gurion's house on Jewish National Fund Avenue (now Ben-Gurion Avenue) in Tel Aviv. The prime minister's wife, Paula, eyed Sylvia suspiciously until Goldman introduced her as his assistant. "She's too pretty to be a photographer," Paula commented wryly. Ben-Gurion himself took an interest in Sylvia's life story and was impressed by the fact that she had arrived in Israel as a volunteer. He suggested that she photograph him as well, but one angry look from Paula made him withdraw the offer.

Goldman and Sylvia returned to his studio in Kfar Saba, where he included her in the developing and printing process. The strong smell of the chemicals gave her a headache, but she didn't complain. When the prints were ready Goldman turned on the lights, and she marveled at their quality. "I'll never reach such a high standard," she said. He answered unsmilingly, "You'll never be as good as I am, but with considerable effort, you might come close."

Sylvia learned from Goldman with enthusiasm and felt herself improving with every lesson. He taught her how to photograph landscapes and people close up and at a distance, how to focus on her subjects and pay attention to every detail. Sylvia eagerly drank in every comment he made, every instruction he gave. She knew that learning photography was essential to her future as a clandestine combatant in the Special Operations Unit. She visualized herself being sent on spying missions where she would be required to photograph secret enemy installations or pick up the trail of arch-terrorists.

For three months she met regularly with the celebrated photographer. She observed how he decided which shots were the best ones to be sent off to newspapers at home and abroad, read the complimentary letters he received from the editors of major European and American papers, and recognized how vastly improved her own photos became as a result of his tutelage. One day, when she showed Goldman the photos she had taken of a boy in a public park, he complimented her for the first time: "Not bad."

Sylvia's unit commanders also studied the photos and were pleased with what they saw.

At the end of her training, Sylvia met with Abraham, her instructor, and Gadi, the commander of the School for Special Operations, in the special apartment used for her training. She had brought with her a thick notebook in which she had written her impressions of the training program.

"In the course of my training," she read from her notes, "all my instructors exhibited professionalism and a deep knowledge of the study material. I would like to thank you for the opportunity you have given me to work with wonderful instructors, who are both talented and highly motivated. Despite the fact that they often gave me a hard time and pushed me to the limits of my abilities, they reinforced my sense of having a mission. I am deeply grateful to each and every one of you for the knowledge you have imparted to me and the unforgettable experience of being trained by you."

"The exercises that made up the program," she continued, "left me plenty of room for initiative and tested my ability to improvise. Some of them demanded a large amount of both physical and mental strength, and at times I found myself close to the breaking point. I hope this was not too obvious. The main problem I had to cope with throughout the training period was loneliness. As you know, I have been cut off from my family and haven't formed any close social ties. I often longed to be able to feel free and easy with other people, but I understood that keeping them at a distance was the price I had to pay if I wanted to be a combatant. I repeated to myself that I was being offered the possibility to realize my ultimate goal, and that outweighed any personal considerations. I was glad to have succeeded in overcoming my private feelings."

"Thank you," said Moti Kfir—Gadi—with emotion. He revealed his real name to her for the first time.

Sylvia went over to the cupboard in her room, which concealed the safe in which she locked up her learning materials. She opened the safe and took out two portraits she had painted, one for Abraham and the other for Moti.

"A memento from me," she said.

They studied the paintings with amazement and mumbled their thanks.

That evening they took her to a festive farewell dinner at the Zion Restaurant in Tel Aviv's Yemenite Vineyard quarter.

"We have a present for you, too," said Abraham after they had been seated at their table.

He handed Sylvia a wrapped parcel containing a set of watercolors and a copy of Rudyard Kipling's famous poem "If":

If you can keep your head when all about you
Are losing theirs and blaming it on you,
If you can trust yourself when all men doubt you,
But make allowance for their doubting too;
If you can wait and not be tired by waiting,
Or being lied about, don't deal in lies,
Or being hated, don't give way to hating,
And yet don't look too good, nor talk too wise:

If you can dream—and not make dreams your master;
If you can think—and not make thoughts your aim;
If you can meet with Triumph and Disaster
And treat those two impostors just the same;
If you can bear to hear the truth you've spoken
Twisted by knaves to make a trap for fools,
Or watch the things you gave your life to, broken,
And stoop and build 'em up with worn-out tools:

If you can make one heap of all your winnings
And risk it on one turn of pitch-and-toss,
And lose, and start again at your beginnings
And never breathe a word about your loss;

If you can force your heart and nerve and sinew
To serve your turn long after they are gone,
And so hold on when there is nothing in you
Except the Will which says to them: "Hold on!"

If you can talk with crowds and keep your virtue,
Or walk with Kings—nor lose the common touch,
If neither foes nor loving friends can hurt you,
If all men count with you, but none too much;
If you can fill the unforgiving minute
With sixty seconds' worth of distance run,
Yours is the Earth and everything that's in it,
And—which is more—you'll be a Man, my son!

A few days later, Abraham issued the following memo:

Top Secret

To: The Commander of the School for Special Operations

Dear Sir,

With the completion of Sylvia Rafael's basic training period, I would like to make a number of comments:

1. The candidate was discovered to possess outstanding character traits. She is very thorough, extremely intelligent, and has the capacity to learn and absorb large amounts of information. The candidate has an excellent ability to make contacts, has a well-developed sense of humor, doesn't shirk from difficulties, is capable of distinguishing between the essential and the marginal, and exhibits high motivation and absolute identification with the Jewish people.
2. The candidate carried out every task assigned to her to the letter, even if it was sometimes difficult for her to do so.
3. I never heard her complain about any hardship. When she was required to learn material for the next lesson, she would sometimes study into the night in order to be prepared for the next day.
4. All her instructors sing her praises. She received excellent

grades throughout the training period. She exhibited initiative and ingenuity in infiltrating highly guarded areas and successfully completed investigative missions.

5. In my estimation, she has a unique ability to adjust to difficult situations, act independently, and carry out what is required of her in the best possible way.

Sincerely yours,
Abraham Gemer

Sylvia's days in the School for Special Operations were over. Now it was time for the Operation Department to oversee Sylvia's next important step in the direction of actual service in the field.

Ami, the director of the Operation Department, was in his forties, tall, bespectacled, and German-Jewish in origin and behavior: exacting, meticulous, generally unsmiling. Moti brought Ami to Sylvia's apartment and introduced him to her.

"You are about to assume a different identity," Ami told Sylvia without any preliminaries. "This is a process that will take a few months. One of us will help you through the first stages. Afterward, a personal case officer will be assigned to you, from whom you will receive your assignments."

"I understand."

"You will usually have to work alone, at times in enemy territory. It won't be easy: there generally won't be anyone around to give you orders, so at times you will have to be both commander and combatant. You will have to utilize all your abilities and apply everything you have learned so as to act independently."

She nodded.

"Your instructors tell me that you've successfully completed every assignment without shrinking from difficulties. Now the time has arrived for the true test, the biggest challenge of your life. Are you ready to accept it?"

"Yes, I am," she said excitedly.

After lingering for a short while longer, Ami wished Sylvia the best of luck and parted from her with a firm handshake.

Sylvia realized that it wouldn't be easy. One of the obstacles that every combatant had to overcome was the almost constant conflict between his or her personal life and the demands of the job. The person must understand that a mission takes precedence over everything. In such circumstances it is difficult to plan a family. When preparing to set out on a mission, the combatant must put his or her personal life on hold and come up with an endless supply of convincing excuses. He or she must approach an operation free from any other commitments for an unlimited period. Romantic attachments, sports activities, and hobbies must always take second place. All attention must be focused on the mission. It must always take first priority; coping with this situation is only made possible by a will of iron and powerful motivation.

Like Beirut, Cairo was a city of many faces, the opposite of Ali's home city of Amman. Most of the grueling training at the military intelligence base outside the city took place during the day, so the nights were available for enjoyment. Ali was in an exhilarated mood. He felt absolutely liberated, freer than ever. His wife and his son, Hassan, weren't with him, and he rejoiced in being far removed from stifling family life.

Cairo offered pleasures that he had almost forgotten existed. He had received a generous budget from Fatah, and he spent it, without any qualms, on excellent meals in the restaurant of the elegant Shepherd's Hotel on the banks of the Nile. He danced the night away at the Haroun al-Rashid nightclub, flirting with young women, smoking Havana cigars, and tipping the waiters and the dancing girls lavishly. But there was a difference between his present situation and his former life as a playboy: now he drew a strict line between work and pleasure. He took the training maneuvers seriously and displayed enthusiasm and commitment to even the most basic exercises. He often expressed to his instructors the hope that the training would prepare him to avenge his father's death.

Ali invested considerable effort in the training. As always, he wanted to stand out and win praise and popularity. He improved his abilities as a sniper, became an expert navigator, and generally was a prize pupil. He passed both the practical and the theoretical tests successfully; his instructors, members of the Egyptian secret service, praised him unconditionally and gave him the warmest recommendations.

When he returned to Amman, he spent most of his time at Fatah headquarters and dining out with his friends, arriving home only to sleep. He didn't tell his wife anything about his stay in Egypt.

The special unit comprising the nine men who had trained in

Egypt with Ali began planning international terrorist activities. Ali was to be responsible for one of the first phases: setting up a Fatah cell in Rome and recruiting Palestinian students and local supporters to carry out terrorist attacks on European soil. Ali jumped at the chance to travel to Italy. He loved missions that involved traveling to destinations far away from boring old Amman. Arafat didn't put a time limit on his stay in Rome, and this improved Ali's mood even further.

The thought of spending time in Rome sent adrenalin coursing through his veins, and the reality turned out to be even better than he had imagined. Rome offered a thousand temptations and distractions, from the cafes on the Via Veneto, replete with beautiful women, to the nightclubs of the Italian capital, which offered excellent cocktails, dining and dancing, and frivolous girls who were ready for any adventure. It was easy for Ali to succumb to temptation. Setting up a Fatah cell was not a particularly taxing assignment, nor was there any problem with recruiting members from the local Palestinian community or from among the students supporting the Palestinian cause.

Ali would wake up late in the morning, generally with a hangover due to too much alcohol and the previous evening's other pleasures. He gulped down a few cups of strong coffee and devoted the rest of the day to finding a suitable location for the organization's nerve center. He finally rented a flat on the ground floor of an old building near the Trevi Fountain and camouflaged his group by dubbing it the "Arab-European Friendship Club." He spent long hours in local universities setting up cells of Arab and European students who supported the Palestinian cause, forming a nucleus of young men who, when the time came, could assist Fatah in organizing and carrying out complex terrorist acts. On one occasion he was even invited by the students' union of Rome University to lecture on the tragedy of the 1948 refugees. Israeli and Jewish students prevented him from opening his mouth, and fighting broke out in the large hall until the police were called in to break up the skirmish.

When Ali had completed his assignment in Rome, he received a message from Arafat requesting him to "perform a small service for my friend, Muammar Qaddafi, the Libyan premier." The message stated that within a few hours Ali would receive a parcel that had been sent by diplomatic pouch to the Libyan Embassy in Rome.

A few minutes later, a Libyan diplomat who was an enthusiastic

Fatah supporter phoned and arranged to meet him at the railway station parking lot. When Ali arrived at the designated spot, the diplomat handed him a parcel containing three guns with silencers and ammunition and the address and daily routine of an émigré from Tripoli who was Qaddafi's sworn enemy.

"You must kill this man," the diplomat said.

Ali had never heard of this person, but he understood that Qaddafi would be grateful to Arafat for being instrumental in eliminating a man he hated so deeply. With the help of two Jordanian students who had been recruited to the ranks of Fatah in Rome, Ali located the potential victim and even decided to personally take part in the operation.

On a dark, gloomy night, after prolonged surveillance outside the man's home, the subject was spotted emerging from his front door. The two students shot the man and fled. Ali stayed where he was. He approached the wounded man lying on the sidewalk, shot him at close range, and, after verifying that he was really dead, disappeared into the darkness. It was the first time Ali had ever killed anyone. It gave him feelings of pleasure, satisfaction, and elation.

Sylvia's commanders were pleased to learn that she had successfully completed her training period. The Operation Department needed clandestine combatants of her caliber.

However, there was still a long, hard way to go before Sylvia would be ready to set off on her first mission. She needed to obliterate any traces of her connection with Israel and with South Africa and assume a new identity. Nobody had informed her yet about the nature of that identity or where she would be sent in order to assume it. She only knew that she was soon to meet the person who had been chosen by the Operation Department to lead her, step by step, into her new existence.

His name was Yitzhak. He had been born in Germany, the son of a well-known physician who had served as a medical officer in the German army during World War I and had been awarded the Iron Cross. His family lived in a beautiful house, enjoying a comfortable income and the respect of relatives and friends. But Yitzhak warned his parents that disaster was coming. He observed with fear and trembling the rise of Nazism in Germany on the eve of World War II. Believing that the Jews' situation would gradually worsen, he begged his parents to immigrate to Palestine. They refused, convinced that the Nazis wouldn't harm them due to his father's excellent service record in the previous world war. But the Nazis were of a different opinion, and Yitzhak's parents were sent to a concentration camp, where they met their death. Yitzhak succeeded in immigrating to Palestine alone.

He lived with an adopted family in Haifa, studied at the Hebrew Reali School, and volunteered for service in the British Army, serving as a gunner in the War of Independence.[1] Shortly after his release from the IDF with the rank of lieutenant colonel, he joined the Mossad and was responsible, among other things, for organizing the secret immigration of North African Jews to Israel.[2] Now he was called to unit headquarters to discuss the next stage in transforming Sylvia Rafael into a combatant. It was a few days after his return from a mission in South America, and he was busy attempting to placate his irate wife, who had received postcards indicating that he was on a safari in Africa. Only upon his return did she discover that he had been in a different part of the world altogether.

Yitzhak was a short man, quiet, reserved, and totally unremarkable. He could easily blend in with any crowd without anybody noticing or remembering him later. But he was intelligent and clever, brimming with self-confidence, dependable, brave, and cautious. He spoke seven languages fluently, and it was well known in the Special Operations Unit that he could act any part, assume any disguise, and blend into any background, as unfamiliar as it may be.

Due to his remarkable talents, Yitzhak was recruited to join the team sent to eliminate the "Hangman from Riga," Herbert Zuckers, a pilot and engineer from Latvia who collaborated with the Nazis and brutally murdered thousands of Jews during World War II. Zuckers, a red-faced, gray-haired mountain of a man, lived near São Paolo, Brazil, where he had found refuge after the war. According to survivors' testimony, Zuckers had stolen large amounts of cash and valuables from his victims, but he had used up much of his spoils in order to escape to South America and obtain Brazilian citizenship. There he had remained, almost penniless, managing to earn a meager living by operating a boating harbor and an old seaplane in a vacation area. His wife, son, and daughter-in-law were also involved in this enterprise.

Yitzhak was sent to meet Zuckers in the guise of an Austrian businessman representing wealthy clients interested in investing in the South American tourist industry. "Be careful," Yoske Yariv, the commander of the Special Operations Unit, told Yitzhak while he was being briefed for the assignment. "According to our sources, Zuckers knows his life is in danger. He is suspicious of almost everyone, and probably won't buy your story easily."

"We'll see," smiled Yitzhak.

The Special Operations Unit provided Yitzhak with an Austrian passport in the name of Anton Kinsella and sent him to Austria to construct his cover story. He rented an office, prepared business cards, opened bank accounts in the name of the phony company he established, and collected any proof he could regarding his place of residence, including laundry receipts, bus and cinema tickets, and a receipt for reading glasses he had purchased, stuffing them into the pockets of the trousers he packed for his trip to Brazil. He was careful only to take clothes that he had bought in Austria and local toiletries. Even his toothbrush and electric shaver were Austrian-made.

Once in Brazil "Kinsella" introduced himself as a wealthy European investor, made contact with the Brazilian minister of tourism, and opened business accounts in various banks. He drove to São Paolo and invited a group of local businessmen to a meeting at his hotel. He told his visitors that he represented a group of investors who were interested in developing tourist areas in South America and that he had been sent to find Brazilian partners. He was taken on a tour of local tourist spots, including a visit to the lake where Zuckers had his boating harbor. "Kinsella" showed an interest in viewing the site from the air, and Zuckers gladly took him up in his seaplane, thus establishing an initial relationship between them.

Gradually, according to a detailed plan he had formulated, Yitzhak and the other team members began setting the trap that would ensnare the Hangman from Riga. Yitzhak, who spoke perfect German, presented himself as a former German officer who had been wounded at the Battle of Stalingrad. He was careful to interject frequent anti-Semitic jokes into his conversation. He also knew how to knock back remarkable amounts of alcohol without losing his head, thus ingratiating himself with Zuckers and becoming a welcome guest in his home. The murderer, who had been searching for ways to get out of his financial trouble for some time, didn't hide his glee when Yitzhak suggested that Zuckers be appointed to represent the South American investors in exchange for a high salary.

Yitzhak communicated his progress to his case officers by means of letters written in code, which he sent to the Mossad post office box in Europe.

When Yitzhak was sure that he had won Zuckers's confidence, he invited him on a business trip to Montevideo, the capital of Uruguay. After picking up the Latvian at the airport, he took him on a tour of properties that were on the market and could be prospective investments. They even negotiated with the owners to purchase some of them. At first Zuckers cooperated willingly; but when they arrived at the fourth location, he became suspicious: the place was in total darkness. His instincts warned him of danger, and he attempted to escape, but it was too late. Three special operations combatants attacked him. Zuckers, who was in excellent physical condition, didn't surrender easily. He fought like a lion, trying to shake off his assailants, who had him by the neck. He knew that his life depended on shaking off his attackers, but they overpowered him. Finally, three shots fired from a gun equipped with a silencer put an end to his life.

Yitzhak and his team hid Zuckers's body in a large wooden box that had been prepared beforehand and upon which they affixed a sticker stating in English that Zuckers had been condemned to death for butchering Jews. It was signed: "Those who will never forget." Afterward, the Mossad men escaped to the airport. Yitzhak even managed to return the rental car and receive the deposit he had paid. They left Uruguay and returned to Israel with a feeling of elation and satisfaction. They were sent home to rest up after a job well done.

Upon returning from Uruguay, Yitzhak was called by the commander of the Special Operations Unit, who gave him a new assignment: to establish a perfect cover story for Sylvia Rafael and to help her through her first steps toward becoming a clandestine combatant.

He was required to leave Israel yet again, this time for Canada.

Upon his return from Rome, Ali Salameh was received in Amman by Yasser Arafat with a warm hug and resounding kisses on both cheeks. The Fatah leader showered him with praise and remarked that he had completed his assignment flawlessly. The Fatah cell in Rome was functioning smoothly, and the exile whose death Qaddafi craved had indeed been eliminated without leaving any traces that could lead the Italian police to the perpetrators. Most important of all was the list that Ali had compiled of young Italian sympathizers who would be willing to carry out attacks when required. Arafat announced that Ali wouldn't be returning to Abu Iyad's intelligence department; he was to be promoted to a more elevated post.

While he was away in Rome, Jordan had changed so much as to be unrecognizable to Ali. It had begun with an IDF attack on Karame on March 21, 1968. The Israelis had been outnumbered and had lost 28 soldiers, with 3 more missing in action, together with a few tanks, trucks, and armored cars. In the raid, 188 Jordanian soldiers and terrorists had been killed. Arafat managed to escape unharmed on a motorcycle. The Israelis retreated the way they had come.

The Palestinians wrote this operation up as a "historical victory." In the period after the Six-Day War disaster, it was a ray of light shining in the darkness enveloping the Arab world. Fatah moved its bases to the heart of Jordan and brought in hundreds of volunteers to serve the organization. This increased Palestinian presence rapidly overshadowed the kingdom's predominantly Bedouin character. Fatah now had full control of the refugee camps, running them, punishing refugees who resisted their authority, collecting taxes, and totally ignoring officials of the Jordanian regime. In the towns and cities, large, boisterous Fatah detachments patrolled the streets, demonstrating total self-confidence in their power. They filled the cafés, behaved rudely toward the local populace, and taunted any army personnel that attempted to intervene. Fatah was literally running a state within a state by having established a dominant Palestinian presence in Jordan. This was an intolerable situation from the point of view of the Jordanian authorities, a powder keg that could blow up at any moment. It was clear to King Hussein that if he didn't take aggressive action, Fatah would soon storm his palace and put an end to his reign. The king frequently went on tours of army installations in an attempt to lessen the agitation that held sway there as a result of Fatah's provocations. The Bedouin regiments that remained loyal to the king demanded the destruction of Arafat's organization before it was too late, but the king hesitated in giving the command. He understood that the resulting bloodshed could lead to the total destruction of his kingdom.

Time was not on Hussein's side. His restraint encouraged Fatah to be even more audacious. They set up roadblocks and conducted wide searches, claiming that they were tracking down collaborators with Israel. Every night in his palace, the king could hear bursts of gunfire from the direction of the city center, and his anger and frustration mounted.

Bitterness spread throughout the ranks of the army. The general feeling was that instead of dispatching a strong military presence from the bases to the raging city streets, the king was weakening the army by not letting it take a role in restraining Fatah. In early September 1970, as the king was reviewing an armored detachment camped near Amman, he saw some woman's brassieres fluttering on one of the tank's antennas.

"What is this?" asked the king.

"Those are our new uniforms," he was insolently informed by the tank commander. "Ever since you turned us into women, that's what we wear."

The king became pale. He returned to his palace in a terrible mood, aware of the need to act without delay. While he was debating how to proceed, the Palestinians presented him with a particularly embarrassing situation. George Habash's Popular Front for the Liberation of Palestine (which, like Fatah, was affiliated with the Palestine Liberation Organization) hijacked four planes from various airline companies and landed them in Dauson, a desert airport near Zarka, Jordan. Three hundred ten hostages were transported to Amman and released from there. That was the last straw for the king. Even though it hadn't been Fatah that hijacked the planes, the king understood that they had been the instigators and that if he didn't react, then the perpetrators' self-confidence would continue to grow and such attacks would multiply. He convened an emergency meeting of the army high command and ordered them to declare war on the Palestinians.

That same night, large army detachments of Bedouin soldiers loyal to the king attacked the refugee camps and opened fire on every man who was armed or was suspected of belonging to a PLO terrorist organization. Hundreds were killed in the first hours of the attack; the wounded cried for help in the narrow alleys but were prevented by the Jordanians from receiving medical aid. Simultaneously, the army attacked Fatah training bases, killing and wounding everyone found in them, destroying stockpiles of weapons, and setting fire to offices and command headquarters. In towns and cities throughout the kingdom, Fatah operatives were dragged from their houses, stood up against the wall, and shot without trial. Dozens managed to escape, crossing the Jordan and begging Israeli soldiers to give them sanctuary.

Syria rushed to Yasser Arafat's aid and dispatched 300 tanks across the Jordan, thus threatening the king's regime. In a panic, Hussein appealed to the United States for help, and Israel was asked by her ally to send detachments of tanks to confront the Syrian armored forces. Long lines of Israeli tanks made their way through the Golan Heights toward the Syrian border. The Syrians retreated, and soon not a single Syrian tank could be found on the Jordanian border.

Like most of Beirut's residents, Lebanese beauty queen Georgina Rizk watched the televised reports from Amman. On the screen flashed scenes of fierce battles between Fatah activists and the Jordanian army. The reporter described dozens of dead in the refugee camps and the mass exit of the Fatah leadership from Amman. The reports interested her only slightly, as she didn't know anybody who belonged to Fatah and found it hard to follow what the fighting was all about.

At that same moment, Ali Hassan Salameh and his wife and son were bumping in their car over winding dirt roads in an attempt to avoid falling into the hands of Jordanian army patrols. Zeinab felt terrible throughout the trip, being pregnant with her second child.

Other vehicles belonging to Fatah leaders were following the same route. The escapees moved in small convoys, mainly at night, crossing the Syrian border and driving from there to Beirut. Ali Salameh rented a house in western Beirut, not far from the new residences of Yasser Arafat and Abu Iyad, who had arrived previously. A constant series of news bulletins from Amman described the Jordanian army's continuing persecution of the Palestinian terrorist organizations, resulting in hundreds of casualties. Many of those killed had been members of the Fatah high command.

"Our revenge will come," Arafat promised angrily.

He labeled the massacre "Black September," the name that would also be given to one of one of the most violent and sophisticated terrorist groups ever to act in the name of Fatah.

Ali Salameh would stand at the helm of the new organization.

Patricia Roxenburg was thirty years old and a junior secretary in the wills and legacies department of a large law firm located in Montreal, Canada. She loved opera and nature walks, and never suspected that while she was enjoying her quiet, orderly life, a double would emerge who would assume her name, her identity, and even an accent similar to hers, that of a native-born Canadian.

The original Patricia lived in a small apartment in the heart of the city together with two Siamese cats. One spring, she went with her Jewish boyfriend on a trip to Niagara Falls. While they were sitting in a café enjoying the spectacular view, her boyfriend asked her to lend him her passport.

"Why?" she asked, surprised.

"Friends of mine are looking for a Canadian passport," he answered.

Patricia asked for an explanation, but her friend didn't offer many details.

"I can only tell you that the State of Israel needs your passport for a very important purpose."

She knew that the man she loved was a loyal supporter of Israel.

"How long do they need it for?" she asked.

"Only for a year or two."

Building a cover story for a Mossad operative is a complicated process. Before it is put into play, Mossad experts examine the fabricated identity in order to verify that it suits the clandestine combatant who will assume it. First, the combatant's personal description must match the details found on the new passport. Second, he or she must have absolute command of the language spoken in the adopted country, as well as intimate knowledge of people's daily lives there.

After the complex missions in which he had taken part, Yitzhak didn't think that building a new identity for Sylvia would be particularly difficult. Most of the burden would fall upon her shoulders. She would need to invest time and patience in fitting into a new environment, and this would require a high degree of motivation, but such a task didn't generally involve any kind of danger. Yitzhak estimated that he could successfully build Sylvia's new identity in a matter of months.

The process began with the Mossad experts modifying Patricia's passport to be suitable for Sylvia. All the details written in the passport corresponded with those of the combatant, except for the fact that Patricia was three years older than Sylvia. The Mossad document experts needed to alter Sylvia's photograph to make her look Patricia's age. Sylvia objected to the change. "Why have you made me look so old?" she complained when she first saw the passport.

Yitzhak explained that this was an integral part of building Sylvia's new identity. He hinted to her that she would probably be sent somewhere far away, where there was no chance of anyone recognizing her and sabotaging her attempts to establish a cover story.

After prolonged discussion, the Special Operations Unit decided to send Sylvia to Vancouver, on the western coast of Canada. One of the reasons for this decision was that every Canadian province was independent, so there wasn't the slightest chance that someone from Montreal would discover that Patricia Roxenburg's passport was being used in faraway Vancouver.

From that point onward, Sylvia would introduce herself as a news photographer. That was her cover story, and it suited her in many respects. She had a sharp eye, an easy manner of approaching people, and good control of photographic techniques. From the unit's point of view, there was a slight risk involved, since no Mossad clandestine combatant had ever before been disguised as a newspaper reporter. The reason for this was that, on the one hand, reporters were liable to arouse suspicion among a hostile Arab population that keeps a watchful eye out for any stranger who attempts to get too close. On the other hand, a news photographer has easy access to any location and can collect vital information and get away without difficulty. In addition, Sylvia took excellent photographs and behaved naturally with a camera, making it relatively easy for her to pose as a news photographer.

Yitzhak referred Sylvia to camera shops in Vancouver where she could buy sophisticated photographic equipment. She paid for it out of her expenses. Like her salary, her budget was very modest, and all cash outlays had to be carefully reported at set intervals.

Sylvia found herself all alone in Vancouver, preparing for an extended acclimatization period. She rented a furnished apartment in a six-story building on one of the narrow streets leading to the harbor. From her window she could see elegant yachts and the large excursion boats that took passengers on three-day pleasure cruises to Alaska. The weather was generally wintry, but the temperature never fell below zero, and it rarely snowed. Vancouver was a beautiful city, calm, peaceful, and not too crowded, and it took pride in its restaurants—Thai, Chinese, Vietnamese, and Japanese. Its fish restaurants had gained an international reputation.

Sylvia established a typical Canadian daily routine, making sure to pay her taxes and avoiding running up a bill at the local supermarket. She was on good terms with her neighbors, telling them about her job as a news photographer. She photographed all the children in the building and distributed the prints to their parents for free. She made sure not to stand out, but at the same time left ample evidence that she actually lived there in case anybody checked up on her. Thus she became a frequent visitor in the homes of some of her neighbors and was a welcome guest at birthday parties and other family occasions. She always made sure to bring a modest gift. Only years later did she learn to her surprise that a short while previously another secret service operative had lived in that same building. He was Oleg Vladimirovich Pankovsky, a Russian colonel who had supplied military secrets to the West about the Red Army's secret missiles and had also traveled to meet with British and American intelligence officers in various locations around the globe. When his activities were uncovered by the KGB, he was tried, convicted of treason, and executed in the presence of family and friends.

Sylvia patiently continued with her routine lifestyle. Every other day, she went food shopping at the local supermarket, gradually making friends with the people who worked there. She spent considerable time familiarizing herself with the city. She committed to memory every main thoroughfare and landmark and the location of shopping centers and major stores. She learned how to imitate the local accent, bought a bicycle manufactured by the popular Canadian company Rocky Mountain, and spent weekends riding on the bicycle paths outside the city. A few times a week, she fed bread crumbs to the birds in Stanley Park, painted the local scenery in tempera and oils, and reported her progress to Yitzhak. On Sunday afternoons, she drank English tea at the Vancouver Hotel. In the winter, she photographed daring swimmers on Kitsilano Beach and managed to sell one of her photographs to the *Vancouver Sun,* a daily newspaper. The name "Patricia Roxenburg" appeared beneath the photo, absolute proof of her actually being a professional photographer. She was paid $150 for the picture, which she used to buy classical records, paints, and an easel.

During her entire stay in Vancouver, Sylvia was careful not to encounter Israelis or South Africans or to read Israeli newspapers. She obtained information about what was happening in Israel from the local press. At that period, Yitzhak was still instructing her from Israel.

* * *

The organizers of the Miss Universe beauty contest in Miami were shocked by Georgina Rizk's negative reply. In the history of the contest, no one had ever turned down the opportunity to participate, and Georgina's refusal was incomprehensible to them. The organizers, who were keen on the idea of including an Arab contestant, didn't give up easily. They sent representatives to convince her, but to no avail. Finally they took it upon themselves to personally travel to Beirut. They visited her home, sent influential personages to put pressure on her, and convinced local journalists to advocate for her participation in the contest. For two years, Georgina continued to refuse, claiming that the wide press coverage awaiting her at the Miss Universe competition just wasn't to her liking. Eventually, however, she gave in, on condition that her parents be allowed to accompany her.

As anticipated, the popular media in Miami received her enthusiastically. Photographers were waiting at the airport. Members of the Rizk family residing in Portland, Oregon, and Quebec, Canada, arrived especially to participate. Beirut television sent a special crew to Miami to cover the occasion.

The contest took place in Miami's huge auditorium in the spring of 1971. The contestants, including Miss Israel, Etty Orgad, mounted the stage, which was decorated like a glittering queen's palace. They wore long white dresses and marched along a catwalk that divided the hall in two. Television cameras broadcast the ceremony live to the homes of millions of viewers.

It was generally thought that the beauty queen of Brazil or the Netherlands would win the coveted title. Both were models, beautiful and famous, and nobody dreamed that the judges would award the crown to anybody else. As it turned out, they decided otherwise; they chose Georgina Rizk. It was a historic choice: Georgina was the first contestant from the Middle East ever to win the title of Miss Universe.

In a dream of happiness, Georgina Rizk approached the master of ceremonies, ready to accept the queen's scepter from his hand. Her lips quivered as she murmured, "Thank you!" She was again surrounded by a sea of newspaper reporters, microphones, and cameramen, who photographed her with her father and mother.

In the weeks that followed, Georgina did everything that Miss Universe was expected to do: she traveled all around the world, appearing at receptions in New York and London and at charity balls in Peru and Vietnam. She met heads of state and ministers in South

Africa and the Persian Gulf. Almost everywhere she went she was asked if she supported the Palestinian cause. She answered in the affirmative, but didn't go into detail. "Ask me about myself," she requested of reporters who tried to get her to discuss politics. "Ask me what you would ask any other Miss Universe."

She returned to Beirut six weeks later and was received with applause at the airport. On her way into the city, she saw along the highway welcoming banners bearing a photograph of the new queen wearing her crown. She arrived home to find it filled with dozens of bouquets of flowers.

At the age of nineteen, Georgina Rizk had become the most popular celebrity in the country overnight. Young girls copied her hairstyle and waited for hours outside her home in order to get her autograph; a ski resort in the Chouf Mountains bought the rights to bear her name; she was offered contracts to appear in full-length films and advertisements for the Lebanese Tourist Authority; she was appointed the chief hostess of Casino de Liban, where society personages and wealthy Arab tourists gambled away astronomical sums of money; she opened an exclusive fashion boutique together with her sister and was the guest of honor at every social function.

Georgina appeared at Beirut's exclusive restaurants and night-clubs with escorts who changed frequently, as duly noted in local gossip columns. She became used to enjoying life in the limelight and planned to open a chain of fashion boutiques all over Lebanon. She received several marriage proposals but didn't accept any of them: she still had so many things that she wanted to accomplish before settling down with one man.

She couldn't have imagined that she was soon to meet the man who would totally transform her life.

On November 28, 1971, in a private dining room on the second floor of the Cairo Sheraton Hotel, waiters were dancing attendance around members of the Arab Defense Council, who had taken a break in their deliberations to partake of a festive luncheon. The defense council, which functioned under the auspices of the Arab League, met frequently to discuss security matters common to its member states.

The Nile flowed lazily past the large glass windows of the hotel dining room. Here and there could be seen brilliant flashes of sunlight reflecting off the sails of the *feluccas* (fishing boats) on the water. In the dining room and outside it were posted armed security guards, whose job it was to ensure the safety of the council members.

At the age of fifty, Wasfi al-Tal was the Jordanian prime minister and the chairman of his country's delegation. He finished eating, chatted for a few minutes with his table companions, and rose to make his way back to the conference room, where decisions were about to be made concerning various plans of action against Israel.

Tal was a personal friend and confidant of King Hussein. He was among those who had pressed the king to destroy Fatah and had personally directed the interrogation and torture of key members of the organization who had been arrested by the Jordanian Armed Forces. With gritted teeth, Arafat heard of Tal's involvement in the execution of Fatah operatives and demanded his immediate assassination. Black September was chosen to carry out his command.

Tal crossed the elegant lobby accompanied by his bodyguards. He shook hands with acquaintances as tourists regarded him curiously, and his wife announced that she was about to go on an organized tour around the city with some of the other delegates' wives. She parted from her husband, saying that she would return that evening and wishing him luck with the conference. The bodyguards surveying the lobby noticed nothing suspicious.

They soon realized that they hadn't been watchful enough. A dark-skinned youth sitting in a corner of the room ostensibly reading a newspaper raised himself slowly out of his armchair and walked slowly in Tal's direction, shouting "Traitor!" He pulled out a revolver and shot Tal five times before the bodyguards managed to respond. Tal collapsed, and the shooter, twenty-three-year-old Manzur Khalifa, got down on the floor, avidly licking the blood of the murdered minister. "This is my lunch," he shouted. "I've never eaten so well."

Wasfi al-Tal died of his wounds an hour or so later. The Egyptian secret service arrested the assassin and led him to the interrogation cell in the basement of one of its bases. None of his interrogators took pity on him. Covered in blood, in terrible pain and close to death, Manzur divulged the identity of his associates, who were arrested the same day while attempting to escape from Egypt. It was established that they were all members of Black September; it was the first time the name of that organization had appeared in the headlines.

King Hussein was horrified by the news that his prime minister had been assassinated. The bloody event took him back to the day when his grandfather, King Abdullah I, had been assassinated. Hussein had been sixteen years old on July 20, 1951, when he accompanied his grandfather to prayer in the Al-Aksa Mosque in Jerusalem, where a Palestinian assassin, an envoy of the Mufti of Jerusalem, shot the king and his grandson. Abdullah died instantly, and Hussein was only spared due to a gold pin he was wearing on his chest that stopped the bullet. From that day onward, he realized that the Palestinians wouldn't cease their efforts to kill him as well.

After Tal's assassination, all the information that had been collected up till then about Black September was retrieved from the Mossad archives in Tel Aviv. In fact, the file was almost empty. All they knew was that the organization had been formed in order to avenge the butchering of Fatah activists in Jordan, and that the man who had formerly served as chief of intelligence, Salah Khalaf (Abu Iyad) was appointed to be its commander. It wasn't only the Mossad that knew nothing about the organization. Hardly anyone in Fatah itself knew how many members there were and who stood at its head. Very few of them knew that the brains behind the operation, the man who had recruited the shooter and had planned Tal's assassination down to the last detail, was none other than Ali Hassan Salameh, Abu Iyad's right-hand man.

But even with the scanty information they possessed about Black September, it was clear to the Israeli intelligence services that the organization was liable to become a danger. Information sources in Lebanon and Jordan were urgently instructed to collect every detail about the organization's chain of command, plans of operation, and the location of its headquarters, training facilities, and arsenals. The people working for the Mossad rushed around Beirut and Amman collecting all the information they could. Using sophisticated bugging devices, they tapped additional sources. But all the data they managed to gather only revealed that Black September consisted of a team that had been trained a few years earlier in an Egyptian secret service base and that Ali Salameh was the most senior officer among them. The heads of the Mossad carefully studied reports detailing Ali's biography and personality. They reached the undeniable conclusion that Ali would be a tough opponent.

The man and woman met on a clear spring evening in a little restaurant in Vancouver, far away from the elegant, busy restaurants opposite the pier from which the huge passenger ships set off on long-term and short-term cruises. There were only two other couples in the restaurant, who took no interest in them. They spoke English.

"I wanted to inform you that you are about to be promoted," Yizhak smiled at Sylvia over a plate of steaming salmon. It was exactly six months since she had arrived in Vancouver.

She gazed at him with shining eyes.

"Tell me about it," she urged him.

"Not so fast," Yitzhak said, curbing her enthusiasm. "Up till now, you've only passed the first stage of assuming a new identity. You've assimilated into new living conditions, adopted a daily routine, and become popular with your neighbors. Now you are moving on to the next stage, whose purpose is to put your new identity to a test that is far more complex. You will need to be quick-witted and adaptable, and you will again have only yourself to rely on while proving that Patricia Roxenburg is ready to set out on her first true mission."

Yitzhak told Sylvia that the operational unit had decided to plant her in an international photographic agency located in Paris. He explained that the decision was based on the fact that this could be a convenient base of action that would arouse no suspicion.

"Which agency are you referring to?" she asked. Since assuming the guise of a news photographer, she had collected considerable information about international photographic agencies.

"I still have no idea," Yitzhak admitted. "I only know that Paris is the best location for you to work from."

He warned her that getting accepted by such an agency wouldn't be easy. Hundreds of French photographers, who were far more experienced than she was, were constantly knocking on the doors of such organizations. Only the very best had a chance of being hired, those whose news photographs could be marketed internationally.

Yitzhak told Sylvia that he was flying to London the following day for a meeting with a British businessman who had helped the Mossad in the past to make the right connections in the right places. It would become clear at the meeting if this man would be able to make contact with French photographic agencies. Yitzhak promised to report the outcome of the meeting to Sylvia as soon as possible.

When they parted, Sylvia was too excited to sleep. The moment she had been waiting for was finally here. She would go to Paris under a new identity, where she would surely receive her first assignment as a Mossad clandestine combatant.

For over an hour she walked through the empty streets of her neighborhood, occasionally checking to see whether anyone was following her. Caution had become an integral part of her being.

The meeting with the British businessman took place in an opulent men's club near Trafalgar Square. Yitzhak told him that he was seeking work in Paris for a female relative, a Canadian photographer. The businessman didn't ask unnecessary questions. He wasn't in contact with photographic agencies, but he promised to look into the matter. He telephoned Yitzhak the very next day.

"I've organized a meeting in Paris with someone who has better connections than I do."

"What's his name?"

"Michel de Carson, a film producer. Does his name ring a bell?"

"No."

"He's Jewish and supports Israel—a wonderful man."

Michel de Carson turned out to be cordial and willing to help. He recalled that one of his friends ran an international photographic agency in Paris and asked the name of the photographer to be recommended to him.

"Her name is Patricia Roxenburg."

"Is she really talented?" asked the Frenchman.

"Very."

Louis Dalmas, Carson's friend, was the owner of the Dalmas Photographic Agency, which operated out of a roomy office near Orly Airport in Paris. He was a gifted photographer and an experienced businessman. Photographs from his agency were distributed to all corners of the globe, and all the major newspapers were among his clients.

At Carson's request, Dalmas asked to meet Sylvia. She bought a plane ticket and arrived in Paris with an impressive portfolio of her work. There wasn't a single photo that disclosed her true identity; none had been taken in either South Africa or Israel.

It was December 1971, and Paris aroused her curiosity—the ancient houses, the scent of fresh croissants and baguettes that wafted from the bakeries on the streets, the elegant women, the jets of water used by the street sweepers at dawn and the swish of their brooms scouring the cobblestones and the asphalt of the streets, the intoxicating odor of crepes and roasted chestnuts near the Arc de Triomphe, the lovely bridges over the calmly flowing River Seine, and the riverboats leaving a thin wake of foam behind them.

France was a major international crossroads. It was easy to cross the border into other European countries, and it was encouraging to know that French public opinion at that time was very supportive of Israel. Sylvia was thrilled to be there.

Louis Dalmas received Sylvia a bit dubiously. He had learned from experience that when a friend or acquaintance tried to convince him to accept a photographer into his company, it was generally someone lacking in professional skill. In heavily accented English, he asked to see her portfolio. She spread out in front of him portraits and shots of landscapes, sporting events, demonstrations, strikes.

"Not bad," he mumbled.

He asked her to tell him where she had acquired her professional training. If she told him the truth, it would disclose her Israeli background.

"I studied in Vancouver," she said.

"When can you start work?"

"I just need a few days to rent an apartment. After that I can start."

He gave her two weeks to get settled in.

After she parted from Dalmas, Sylvia visited a few real estate offices offering apartments for rent and, with the approval of the operational unit, rented a one-room apartment on a quiet side street in the heart of the city, close to the French Television building. She phoned Yitzhak, the man who had coached her through her Vancouver period and had helped her secure employment at the Dalmas Agency. He was pleased to learn that she had managed to rent an apartment and gave her the number of a public telephone booth. "You will be able to call there every day between noon and two o'clock in the afternoon," he told her. "The man waiting for your call is your case officer. Be prepared for a surprise."

When she called at the agreed hour, a familiar voice answered. She couldn't believe her ears.

"Is it really you?" she asked with emotion.

"Yes, it's me, and no other."

It turned out that her case officer in Paris was to be Abraham Gemer, her former instructor at the School for Special Operations. Even now she didn't call him by his real name, but only by his code name, Oded. In France she still wasn't allowed to know his private number, visit him at home, or meet his family. He, along with her commanders, would be responsible for giving her instructions and receiving her reports. It was also his job to supply Sylvia with whatever she required.

In effect, the case officer has complete control over the combatant's life. He knows exactly where she is at all times and may be contacted immediately if necessary. They meet in cafés and restaurants under the guise of a social meeting, but their conversations center only on operational missions. In many cases, an interdependent relationship develops between combatant and case officer. The case officer decides, while the combatant acts. The case officer's instruction is an unequivocal command. It must be fulfilled, except in cases of illness.

Despite their limited relationship, the case officer and the combatant get to know each other in shifting circumstances. When the case officer is assigned to another post and a different case officer takes over, he, as well as his combatant, must undergo a period of adjustment to the character traits and work style of the other, including tone of voice and degree of attention to detail. This is not always a smooth process.

Two weeks later, Sylvia phoned Dalmas.

"I'm ready to start," she said.

"Excellent. I have an interesting assignment for you. Come quickly. I'm waiting for you."

She took the Metro to his office. As usual, she checked that she wasn't being followed. As a precautionary measure, she changed trains a few times before reaching her destination.

"Do you know where French Somaliland is?" Dalmas asked when she entered his office.

"In East Africa."

"Exactly. Prepare to go there."

"Why?"

"Tensions are building up that are liable to lead to civil war."

"When should I go?"

"As soon as possible."

She phoned Abraham and put him in the picture. He reported to Special Operations Unit headquarters about Dalmas's offer. They approved the journey and sent Sylvia a long list of safety regulations to be followed.

Despite the intense heat of its climate, French Somaliland, a country with a population of half a million located in East Africa (which was granted independence in 1977 and is now called Djibouti), could have been an almost exact copy of the Garden of Eden. It had lofty mountains, deserts, and wild animals, and Tejora Harbor near the capital offers tempting bathing beaches. In its turquoise waters may be found some of the most famous diving locations in the world. At one segment of the coast are sharks, but they present no danger to humans, so it is possible to swim alongside them without fear.

Sylvia arrived there at a period the country would later prefer to forget. About a third of its inhabitants were members of the Afari tribes, which had arrived from Ethiopia in the third century BC. The Somalis arrived later, bringing the Islamic religion with them. The French built the capital city, Djibouti, and as was their custom, disseminated French culture and language, turning the region into a French colony. A few decades later, a referendum was held, in which most of the inhabitants supported continued French control. The objectors to a continued French presence, most of them Somalis, opened hostilities whose purpose was to establish Muslim rule. France had a particular interest in the country due to its strategic location at the entrance to the Red Sea and its straits. The French Army was called upon to quell the disturbances and restore order. Naturally the matter was arousing considerable interest in France, and the French press was giving it front-page coverage.

The capital city was under curfew when the Air France plane from Paris touched down at the small airport. The passengers were conveyed into the city accompanied by a French military escort, and on the way Sylvia saw rotting corpses lying at the roadside. She booked into the Miramar Hotel in the heart of the city and, despite the warnings of the hotel receptionist, left the Miramar armed with two cameras.

She photographed demonstrators confronting army personnel, captured photos of the two camps shooting at each other, and interviewed French merchants who were entrenched, heavily armed, in their homes. Bullets whizzed past her, yet Sylvia felt no fear; she simply laid down on the ground and continued taking pictures.

She spent a day at a French army camp outside the city. She met officers and soldiers, accompanied them to skirmishes, and witnessed arrests of Somalis who were later expelled from the country. As arranged by the Dalmas Agency, she sent her photos to Paris via military aircraft.

On the last day of her stay, she went swimming in the Red Sea. The beach was deserted, and the echo of gunfire could be clearly heard. She hired diving equipment and took an underwater tour of the coral reefs. When she returned to Paris, her photos were still appearing on the front pages of the newspapers. She was the only photographer sent from France to document the disturbances, and Louis Dalmas, her boss and the director of the photographic agency that sent her there, gave her a special bonus in thanks for her good work.

Ali Salameh traveled all over Europe on a false passport. He visited Munich, Brussels, Amsterdam, Paris, and Madrid. Everywhere he went, with the help of Arab embassies, especially Libyan ones, he set up new cells of Black September. He gathered around him hand-picked men to whom he supplied weapons and ammunition that were stashed in agreed-upon hiding places.

Ali Salameh's tour of Europe had an additional purpose. He was looking for people who could carry out a mega-attack that was then only at the planning stage, and he wasn't looking only for men.

Ali wanted Black September to occupy first place in the world ranking of terrorist organizations. His aim was for the organization to present a constant threat to governments and individuals, especially Israelis. For this purpose, he was planning on a large scale. He would put an end to limited terrorist attacks and sporadic assassinations, instead staging mega-attacks that would echo around the world, causing widespread fear and admiration.

The more Ali delved into the details of his planned attack, the more enthusiastic he became. If it succeeded, he thought, the whole world would hear about it.

He knew that success depended on the expertise of those involved. The more professional the hit team, the less likely that something would go wrong.

The head of the team, Abu Sneina, the son of an orthodox Muslim family that was one of the largest and most respected in Hebron, was chosen by Ali without hesitation. Abu Sneina had commanded the hijacking to Algeria of an El Al plane four years previously. He was experienced not only in hijackings but also in conducting negotiations for the release of hostages in exchange for terrorists imprisoned in Israel. Ali could think of nobody more suitable for the present mission.

Next he selected a Druze by the name of Abed al-Aziz al-Atrash, an active member of Black September. Al-Aziz had a young girlfriend, Rima Tanos, an orphan who had been brought up in a convent in Bethlehem and later moved to Beirut. She lived there alone and penniless and on several occasions was a victim of rape and assault. Rima also agreed to join the team and recommended her friend Therese Halsa, who was also a Christian, a former student at the Acre Nursing School, who had escaped to Lebanon with her Muslim lover after her family had refused to allow them to marry. Therese was an avid supporter of the Muslim struggle, and when Al-Aziz approached her to join the hit team, she agreed readily.

The four were given false passports and plane tickets to Brussels. They were not worried about security checks, since a previous reconnaissance tour of the airport had revealed that these were perfunctory. From the airport they went in separate taxis to the railroad station, where in safety deposit boxes they found revolvers and explosives that had been smuggled into Belgium via diplomatic pouch to the Libyan Embassy. The women wore wigs.

On May 8, 1972, the terrorists returned to the Brussels airport and took off on a Sabena flight headed for Ben Gurion Airport after airport security had failed to detect their concealed weapons. There were ninety-nine passengers on board. At noon, a short time after the flight attendants had finished serving lunch, one of the terrorists burst into the flight deck with a drawn revolver and announced, "This is a hijacking." He demanded to convey to the Israeli government that the team would release the passengers and crew if it would release imprisoned terrorists and promise to return the hijackers safely to Lebanon. After landing at Ben Gurion Airport, negotiations began, but in a daring operation, a commando unit of the IDF High Command, disguised as ground crew, broke into the plane, killing the two men, arresting the two women, and releasing the unharmed passengers and crew.

The two women were immediately taken for interrogation. Their questioners demanded to know who had sent them on the hijacking mission. Both women, Therese and Rima, in separate interrogation rooms, repeated the same version: they had been sent by activists of Black September.

"We want names," demanded the investigators.

They named Al-Atrash and Ali Salameh.

"What do you know about Salameh?" they were asked.

"Hardly anything. We only met him once, when he briefed us about the operation and supplied us with passports and tickets."

"Where does he live?"

"We have no idea."

They stuck to their stories even after a particularly long and grueling interrogation.

The hijacking of the Sabena plane came as a shock to the Israeli intelligence community.

None of the participants in an emergency meeting at the office of the director of the Mossad, Zvi Zamir, could have foreseen that it would happen. After a long period of Fatah attacks on Israelis in the occupied territories, the chief of the Southern Command, General Ariel Sharon, with the help of crack army units, had managed to establish a strong military presence in the Gaza Strip, causing the attacks to cease almost completely. It appeared as if the terrorist organizations had decided on a cease-fire; but, as always, the quiet was deceptive, and the sense of security that had spread through Israel in wake of Sharon's success was short-lived.

The Israeli intelligence services were still groping in the dark regarding Black September. They had taken into consideration the possibility that Israeli planes would be hijacked, or even blown up in midair, but assumed that there was only a slight possibility of this actually happening. The hijacking of the Sabena plane to Ben Gurion Airport established a whole new reality.

From the point of view of the Mossad, Ali Salameh was the main focus of interest. Until that moment, very little information had been entered into his file. From the time he had been recruited for action as head of Black September, Ali had been a man shrouded in mystery. He had sold his Mustang, and now he didn't even own a car. He avoided visiting public places of entertainment, surrounding himself and his family with armed bodyguards. Only the head of intelligence, Abu Iyad, knew exactly where he was and what he was doing.

The Mossad's information-gathering agencies, the Intelligence Branch of the IDF and the Israeli Foreign Ministry, who were all ordered to expand the search for information regarding Ali Salameh, sketched a portrait of an evasive, wily, and intelligent terrorist who spoke fluent English and German, a man who could be violent when necessary, who could torture suspects to death and commit cold-blooded murder. He appeared to be a lone wolf who had no close friends, told his wife nothing, and rarely spent the night at home. Nothing more about Ali was known to Israeli intelligence— nothing about his connections with the Libyan and Algerian embassies, which supplied his men with arms, explosives, and vital information about possible targets; nothing about where he resided in Europe; and nothing about his daily habits. There was limited information concerning Ali's cooperation with the Stasi and his recruitment of Palestinian students in Western and Eastern Europe.

The Israelis were also unaware of the most important fact about Ali. While they were attempting to reveal his weak points, he was already putting all his efforts into planning a terrorist attack that would completely overshadow the Sabena plane hijacking. The plan was Ali's brainchild, and Abu Iyad embraced it eagerly.

On May 30, 1972, at ten o'clock p.m., an Air France plane from Paris landed in Ben Gurion Airport. During a stopover in Rome, three young members of a Japanese terrorist organization (the Red Army) had boarded the plane. They were carrying false passports, and nobody checked their luggage.

At Ben Gurion they calmly collected their suitcases, opened them up on the floor of the terminal, pulled out machine guns and hand grenades, and opened fire on passengers, while also throwing hand grenades in their direction. Twenty-four passengers, most of them Christian pilgrims who had come to visit the Holy Land, were killed instantly. One of the Israelis killed was Professor Aharon Katzir, an international chemical expert and one of the founders of the Scientific Corps of the IDF. Among the terrorists, only one remained alive, a confused youngster named Kozo Okamoto, who exhausted his interrogators with his strange theories about how human beings turned into astral bodies after their death.

In an all-out effort and using various methods, Israeli intelligence discovered that the Japanese terrorist team was acting according to a plan that had been devised by Black September. It became clearer than ever that in order to prevent this deadly viper from striking again, there was an urgent need to cut off its head.

Sylvia Rafael. At lower left is her signature in Hebrew.

All photographs courtesy of Keshet Publishing

Sylvia (seated, in front row) in Arab dress in the Jordanian refugee camp.

Headquarters of the School for Special Operations, Allenby Street, Tel Aviv.

Moti Kfir, head of the School for Special Operations.

Abraham Gemer, Sylvia's instructor and case officer.

Georgina Rizk, Ali Hassan Salameh's second wife and former Miss Universe.

The arch-terrorist Ali Hassan Salameh.

Ali's father, Hassan Salameh, commander of Palestinian forces.

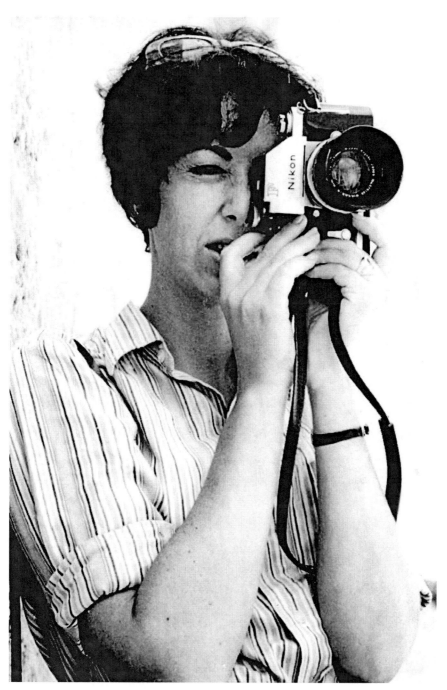

Sylvia in her identity as Canadian news photographer Patricia Roxenburg.

Yasser Arafat and Ali Hassan Salameh's eldest son at Salameh's funeral in
Beirut.

Bredveitspenal Women's Prison in Oslo, where Sylvia was incarcerated.

Sylvia meets with Israeli writer Ephraim Kishon in the Norwegian prison.

The last photograph: Sylvia and her husband, Annæus Schjødt, on a cruise a few months before her death.

Sylvia Rafael's grave at the military plot at Kibbutz Ramat Hakovesh.

5

Imprisoned in a Refugee Camp

Beirut was aptly called "Paris of the Middle East." The former French occupation had left behind a fragrance of elegance and style that lingered long after French political influence ended. Beirut boasted many wealthy residents and large Arab banks, pleasure-seeking tourists, fabulous nightclubs, and beautiful women who could be purchased for the right price. During the day, Beirut was a bustling commercial city. Carefree vacationers sunned themselves on its golden beaches, and passengers disembarked from cruise ships on their way to sightseeing tours around the city. In the evening the restaurants and clubs opened their doors, and the dance floors were packed with lively crowds moving to the sound of loud music. In the entertainment district, traffic jams were rife and drunks swayed their way down the streets.

But behind the bright lights of Beirut in the 1970s, behind the frivolous, unbridled revelry, another type of activity altogether was taking place. Equipped with false passports, trained terrorists were arriving from abroad and meeting secretly in the refugee camps with their Palestinian hosts, planning ways to strike out at Israel and shake its confidence. They included members of the German Baader-Meinhof gang, experts in assassination and explosives from the Japanese Red Army, and top members of the Italian terrorist organization, the Red Brigades. Even the arch-terrorist Carlos, who had won an international reputation for murder and destruction, arrived in order to contribute his expertise.

A carefree atmosphere reigned at the exclusive restaurant on Sif a-Din al-Ketaib Street in Beirut. Georgina Rizk was sitting at a table with a group of friends. The waiters danced attendance on them, and the owner of the restaurant arrived in person to serve them their meals. They dined and laughed, joining the crowds on the dance floor between courses and moving to the strains of the band.

Georgina and her friends weren't facing the entrance to the restaurant, so they didn't notice that Ali Hassan Salameh had come in. Together with two companions, he approached a table being cleared by the waiters, surveying with interest the pretty women sitting at the surrounding tables. When he noticed Georgina, a shiver of excitement went through him. He recognized her immediately from her frequent appearances on the front pages of the newspapers.

She was more beautiful than any other woman in the restaurant, and when she returned to her table, he approached her, bowed, and asked if he might invite her to dance.

Georgina looked up at him. She didn't recognize him; what she saw was a handsome man wearing a black shirt stretched over a muscular torso. Ali smiled his most charming smile, which had already conquered endless female hearts, offered his hand, and led her to the dance floor.

The handsome couple immediately became the center of attention. They danced well together. His arm circled her shapely back, her hand rested on his shoulder. "My name is Ali," he said. "Ali Hassan Salameh."

"The name sounds familiar," Georgina replied.

"That's probably due to my father," he said, adding boldly, "His name was Hassan Salameh, the leader of the Palestinians in the 1948 war."

She vaguely remembered that she had learned about him at school.

"What do you do?" she asked.

"I have a position in Fatah, alongside Yasser Arafat."

A momentary shiver went through her. She had never met anyone from Fatah before, and none of her friends had any contact with extreme Arab organizations. All that she knew about Fatah was from the newspaper headlines, but that was enough to arouse her antipathy.

"Do you kill people?" she wanted to know.

"Only bad people."

"Women and children, too?"

Her question embarrassed Ali.

"Only if there is no choice."

"There's always a choice." Her voice held a touch of reproach.

"Look," he said apologetically. "The Jews were the first to kill women and children. They wiped out entire Arab villages in 1948, drove the residents from their homes, and didn't let them return. Qula, the village where I was born, was also occupied and destroyed, and the villagers were driven out. We are at war, Georgina. In war innocent bystanders also get killed."

It seemed strange to Georgina for her to be listening to what he was saying in the calm, pleasant atmosphere of the restaurant. It wasn't the time or the place to speak of such things.

"I'm sorry I dragged you into this conversation," she said. "I prefer to talk about other things."

"About what, for example?"

"About you."

"What do you want to know?"

"The important things."

"Ask me and I'll tell you."

"Are you single?"

"No, I'm married."

Her eyes opened wide with surprise.

"Is your wife here with you?"

"No."

"Why not?"

Again he was embarrassed.

"Our relationship isn't very good," he mumbled.

"I understand."

The music stopped. Ali accompanied Georgina back to her table.

"Can I see you again?" he asked.

She turned away from him and said, "I don't think that will be possible."

Ali returned to his table, disappointed and downcast. A woman had never refused him before. He was used to having them fall at his feet without the slightest effort on his part. Georgina was different. Her refusal just served to make him more determined than ever to win her over.

He called the waiter and stuffed a wad of bills into his hand. The waiter disappeared and returned with a bottle of select champagne. He brought it to Georgina's table and placed it in front of her.

"From the gentleman at the next table," he said, pointing at Ali.

She bowed her head in thanks. The waiter released the cork from the bottle with a pop and poured a glass for Georgina. She asked him to fill her friends' glasses as well. After a while, the group got up and left the restaurant. Georgina didn't give Ali a backward glance.

The Dalmas Photographic Agency and the French Foreign Office were impressed by Sylvia-Patricia's photos from Djibouti and suggested that she have an exhibition in Paris. She reported this to her case officer, Abraham, and asked what she should reply. The question was passed on to the headquarters of the Special Operations Unit, where deliberations took place about whether or not to authorize such a highly publicized event. On any occasion involving so many participants, there was always a danger that someone who knew Sylvia would turn up and recognize her. But after weighing the pros and cons, it was decided that the proposed exhibition should proceed, that it would establish Sylvia's image as an international news photographer and so make it easier for her to gain access to Arab countries.

Her photographs were hung on the walls of the elegant Ritz Hotel on Place Vendôme, and at the opening hundreds of lights were twinkling in the chandeliers suspended from ceilings decorated with gold leaf. The elite of Paris society, journalists, and representatives of foreign embassies in evening dress filled the hall, anxious to meet the photographer whose name was unknown to most of them. The exhibition was entitled "Living Proof from Djibouti: The Photography of Patricia Roxenburg." A representative of the French Ministry of Culture praised both the exhibition and the photographer in his welcoming speech, which was loudly applauded.

The color and black-and-white photographs had been mounted in identical wooden frames. Some of them had already been published in the French press, but others were being shown for the first time. They depicted the disturbances at Djibouti—the dead in the streets, crying children in their mothers' arms, an angry mob attacking a French business establishment. Alongside these disturbing scenes were impressive portraits of local types captured by Sylvia's camera lens: Affari dignitaries in colorful costume, Somali farmers tilling the arid soil in depressed areas, French military personnel, a family sitting down to a frugal meal in a rural hut, widows, orphans dressed in rags begging in the streets, fishermen netting their catch in the turquoise waters of the gulf.

Sylvia circulated among the guests, who were eager to hear about her experiences. She was wearing a long black dress with no jewelry or makeup. Despite this, she stood out in the crowd, not only due to her height, but also because of the charm she radiated. Many guests asked to exchange calling cards with her.

One of the visitors who seemed particularly interested in her was a senior diplomat from the Jordanian Embassy. He introduced himself and said that he was very impressed by her photographs.

She took the opportunity to tell him that her fondest dream was to photograph portraits of famous personalities and ordinary people in Arab countries. "The exotic atmosphere of such places attracts me very strongly," she said.

"Have you ever visited Jordan?" the diplomat inquired.

"Not yet."

"Would you like to pay us a visit?"

"Gladly."

He was quite a bit older than she, his black hair already showing traces of silver, and she sensed that the interest he expressed in her went beyond a merely professional one. She listened attentively to his stories about the Jordanian nation and government. When the crowd began to disperse, he suggested that she join him for dinner. She couldn't find any reason to refuse. He chose the Ritz Hotel restaurant, one of the most expensive in Paris.

During dinner the Jordanian was interested in learning everything about her, including her background and her career. She told him that she had been born in Canada, lived in Vancouver, and had published photographs there in the local press before moving to Paris.

"I will investigate the possibility of inviting you to our country as a guest of the Government Information Bureau," he promised. He wrote down her telephone number. When they finished eating, he offered to drive her home in the embassy limousine. She refused politely.

"I live nearby," she lied, carefully concealing her home address.

"May I invite you to dinner again?"

"Of course."

Sylvia reported her conversation with the Jordanian to her case officer. He indicated that if invited, she would need special permission from headquarters to visit Jordan.

Louis Dalmas, her boss at the photographic agency, was thrilled by the idea.

"None of our photographers has ever been to Jordan," he said. "If you manage to capture interesting subjects, such as refugees, soldiers, and local leaders, I'm sure we will be able to sell your photographs to news agencies around the world."

The Jordanian diplomat phoned Sylvia two days later and told her that the information department had approved her visit to his country. "Consider our home to be your home," he said in Arabic, translating immediately into English. "When we meet for lunch, I'll give you further details."

He asked her to meet him at Le Spadon Bleu, a famous seafood restaurant. When she arrived, he was already waiting for her at a table by the window. He rose to his feet, shook her hand warmly, and said, "I'm so glad you've come."

"So am I," she said, and it was the truth. The trip to Jordan aroused both her excitement and her curiosity. The Special Operations Unit approved the journey without hesitation, since making contact with influential people in Arab countries was a vital step toward turning Sylvia into a bona fide clandestine combatant. She had every reason to feel satisfaction. The difficult path she had followed until now—constructing her new identity in Vancouver, becoming accepted at the Parisian photographic agency, and establishing her reputation as a prominent news photographer—had gone as smoothly as possible. She was feeling optimistic about the future, whatever difficulties might be in store for her.

The Jordanian diplomat told her that she could depart for his country in a few weeks. He was gratified to inform her that he would be her guide on the trip. "I promise you an unforgettable experience," he said fervently.

Before they flew to Jordan a few weeks later, Sylvia received instructions from Abraham about how to communicate with him, even though she wouldn't actually be there for the Special Operations Unit. In fact, if the need arose, she might be called upon to perform some service. She wasn't the kind of combatant who was destined to perform one defined task (for example, surveillance of a particular target). Her talents would allow her to fulfill various functions, but her commanders didn't expect her to do anything for them in Jordan, at least not on that occasion.

Her companion arranged an entry visa for her at the airport in Jordan and accompanied her through passport control. An official car with a Jordanian flag was waiting outside; the chauffeur opened the door for them. A room had already been reserved for her at the luxurious Regency Hotel in Amman.

Amman, "the city on seven hills," is the capital of Jordan and the seat of the government. The ancient part resembled the Old City of Jerusalem, while the modern part, with its stone houses, gardens, and busy streets, resembled modern Jerusalem. The diplomat she had met in Paris was to act as her guide. He took her on a tour of the

Medina Quarter in the center of the city, where most of Amman's historical sites are located. They visited the Ummaya Palace, which overlooked the city, visited the Roman amphitheater and Hercules's Temple, and ate *mansaf*—a dish made out of lamb, rice, and yogurt—at the fashionable Khan Zaman restaurant. A team of waiters in traditional Bedouin dress treated them like guests of honor, loading the table with the finest delicacies served by the restaurant and plying them with *tamarindi*, a sweet date wine.

For the next three days, Sylvia and her companion traveled the length and breadth of the country, from Aqaba in the south to Gerash in the north, from Wadi Rum to the amazing red rock city of Petra. Sylvia photographed every interesting character that came her way: vendors selling pita bread on the beach at Aqaba (from which she stole homesick glances at Eilat across the bay), drivers of the horses and carriages that carried tourists to Petra, desert dwellers, peasants, and students in school uniforms in Amman. She captured scenes depicting local and family customs. Apart from military installations, she was allowed to photograph freely.

Memories of his brief meeting with Georgina Rizk continued to haunt Ali Salameh. Her image accompanied him everywhere he went, distracting him and affecting his concentration. No woman had ever excited him so much.

In his head he replayed their short conversation on the dance floor a thousand times. He felt that he had lost control and blurted out things that were better left unsaid, at least at such an early stage in their relationship. He was certain that he had startled her with the information that he was a member of Fatah. She had caused him to admit against his will that he was connected with activities in which blood was spilled. He recalled the expression of disgust on her face when she learned of this.

But despite everything, like a diamond miner searching for the most precious gem, Ali swore that he would ultimately win Georgina at any cost. He phoned her the very next day after their first meeting in the restaurant and again invited her to have dinner with him. She refused.

"Why?" he asked for an explanation.

"Because there are things about you that disturb me."

"Does it disturb you that I'm a member of Fatah?"

"Yes."

"Does it disturb you that I'm married?"

"That, too."

"Well, those are two good reasons to meet and have a talk."

"Actually, those are two good reasons for not meeting."

He mustered all his powers of persuasion to get her to say yes, but he didn't succeed.

But that didn't mean he was going to give up. That afternoon he sent a huge bouquet of roses to her house, signing the accompanying card: "From a man who isn't accustomed to being refused." Together with the flowers, he sent letters pouring his heart out and quoting the poems of Lebanese poet Goubran Khalil Goubran (for example, the poem with the line "Love has no desire but to fulfill itself"). Two weeks later, a messenger arrived carrying ten vases in which to place the bouquets he sent her daily.

He tracked down the nightclubs where Georgina spent her evenings and arrived there as well. Two or three times, he managed to invite her to dance, but she remained silent while they were dancing and broke contact the minute the band stopped playing. Ali arrived a few times at the casino where she worked and tried to engage her in conversation, but she totally ignored him. His only reason for hope was that Georgina didn't banish him from her sight but only rejected his advances.

Before his trips abroad, Ali arranged to have flowers sent to Georgina every day while he was away. Upon his return, he would send mutual acquaintances to her home to plead his case.

Six months after Ali started courting Georgina, she finally consented to have dinner with him. He had a haircut, put on his best designer suit, and waited anxiously until she entered the restaurant. She approached his table regally, looked him straight in the eyes, and said, "You always get what you want, don't you?"

"I get what's important to me."

She smiled.

"I've been collecting information about you," she said. "People who know you tell me that you are very stubborn, intelligent, and quick-witted. They say that you're not afraid of anything."

"I'm afraid of people who are smarter than I am."

"Are there any?" she raised her eyebrows in mock surprise.

"Unfortunately, there are too many."

In the background, the restaurant was playing songs by Umm Kulthum.[1] Ali ordered a bottle of wine and toasted their continuing friendship.

"To you," Georgina added. "I wish you a long and happy life."

"Thank you."

"I've heard that your life is in danger."

"Sometimes."

"Couldn't you find other, safer, employment?"

"I've never tried. I'm committed to what I do."

"Doesn't it bother you to leave your wife a widow and your children orphans?"

"It bothers me very much, but I've chosen a certain path and I can't change it. I act in my father's memory and in the name of my people."

"I understand," she said, and her eyes reflected sadness. Ali was thrilled to see that she was concerned about the risks he was taking. He saw this as a sign that she cared about him.

They ate Lebanese delicacies prepared in the French style. After dinner, he drove her home. She noticed that they were being followed by an open Jeep in which sat three armed men.

"We're being followed," she said, trembling.

"Don't worry. Those are my bodyguards."

When they stopped near the gate to her parents' mansion, he asked her if they could meet again. This time she didn't refuse him. He wanted to take her into his arms and kiss her, but he didn't dare.

"I had a lovely time this evening. Thank you," she said, and ran quickly through the heavy iron gates.

Caution was ingrained in Sylvia's nature. Her instructors had repeated over and over that good clandestine combatants must take into account that they might arouse suspicion at any moment. She planned her every move, took into consideration every eventuality, prepared for whatever might occur. Every time she went out on a photographic expedition in Jordan, she used a well-tested method that would tell her if someone had gone through her things while she was absent from her hotel room: she placed a hair on her suitcase, checking upon her return to see if the hair was still in place.

Two days before the end of her stay in Jordan, Sylvia asked to visit a refugee camp in order to photograph scenes of daily life in the camp. Her companion didn't see any reason to prevent her from doing this. He accompanied her to the Al-Wahdat Camp. Wearing a long black dress with a scarf covering her head, she walked with him through narrow alleys where sewer water flowed in the gutters, visiting clay huts and wooden shacks that were built haphazardly. She spoke with the residents by means of an interpreter and photographed those adults and children who were willing to be her subjects.

Her visit attracted a large crowd. Grown-ups eyed her curiously. Children begged for coins. Everything was going smoothly until two men carrying machine guns arrived on the scene, pushing their way through the crowd and approaching her. They pointed their weapons at Sylvia and her companion and demanded to know what they were doing there. The Jordanian diplomat explained that he had been appointed by the Ministry of Information to accompany a photographer from Paris. This didn't convince the two armed men. Threatening with their guns, they directed the visitors to a nearby stone building. They seated Sylvia and her companion on the floor and demanded to see the Jordanian's papers. He whipped out his wallet and showed them his identity card. Sylvia took out her passport and her press card.

"This won't be passed over lightly," threatened the diplomat.

"Silence!" shouted one of the armed men.

They sent for someone who could speak English, and a man arrived who could translate the questions they were firing at Sylvia.

"What have you been photographing?"

"Residents of the camp."

"Did you photograph armed men?"

"No."

"Why did you choose this camp?"

"Because I'm preparing a series of photographs for my agency."

"Have you ever visited Israel?"

"Never," she answered calmly. Her passport didn't bear a single Israeli stamp.

"Do you have Israeli friends?"

"Not a single one."

"Are you married?"

"No, I'm not."

"Do you have a boyfriend?"

"No, I haven't."

"Is photography your only source of income?"

"Yes."

They asked for her address in Jordan and her future travel plans and threatened to kill her if they found out that she was lying. She looked them straight in the eye and answered all their questions. During her training for the Mossad, she had undergone tough interrogations, whose purpose was to prepare her for the real thing. She had learned to stand up to questioning without losing her head and to stick to her cover story.

The interrogators confiscated the films she had photographed. One of them left the room with the film, leaving Sylvia and the Jordanian with the other one. "I apologize," said the diplomat to his companion. "This wasn't supposed to happen." The armed man shouted at them to be quiet, gesturing menacingly with his weapon. The room was oppressively warm, and nobody had even bothered to bring them a glass of water.

The man who had left with the exposed film finally returned. He handed the developed photographs to Sylvia.

"Now we believe that you aren't an Israeli agent," he said. All the photographs were portraits of the camp's residents; not a single one showed anyone carrying a weapon. "I'm sorry for the inconvenience," said one of the men apologetically, "but you must understand why we must be careful. We are being persecuted by the Jordanian authorities and constantly threatened by the Israelis."

Sylvia's companion deposited her outside her hotel. Immediately upon entering her room, she checked if the hair she had left on her suitcase was still there. It was. Now she was positive that nobody suspected her or had gone through her things during her absence.

Israel's clandestine combatants, a select group of men and women operating in enemy territory and among concentrations of Arabs in other countries, are the spearhead of the Special Operations Unit. They are trained to act courageously in unexpected circumstances. One of their responsibilities is to supplement information obtained by Israeli intelligence, the air force, and other bodies. It is their job to provide information for special operations and details regarding terrorist organizations, their commanders, training bases, and explosives experts. They carry out surveillance and man observation posts, ready to respond to every unforeseen situation. The combatants are liable to be detected at any moment. If they are caught by non-Arab security forces, they are liable to be arrested, imprisoned, or deported from the country in question. Getting caught in enemy territory could easily result in death.

Danger accompanies the combatants on all their missions, but in the course of their training—and even more so after its completion—they learn to cope with it, among other ways, by means of their ability to convince themselves that "it won't happen to me." This mantra echoes in the subconscious of every operative. It helps them devote all their energies to their mission, whatever dangers are involved.

The agreed-upon signal was four knocks on the door of the safe house where Sylvia would meet her case officer when circumstances prevented them from meeting in a café or a restaurant. Operatives' apartments in Paris were generally rented in buildings without a concierge, since the latter were liable to present a risk, and they weren't the only ones who posed a risk: hotel receptionists, drivers, or nosy neighbors might wittingly or unwittingly give help to local security authorities. They generally presented no direct threat, but their interference could seriously imperil a sensitive operation.

Sylvia heard two consecutive knocks, a pause, and then another two knocks. She opened the door of her apartment and found Abraham standing in the doorway. He had phoned an hour earlier and informed her of his arrival in a previously agreed code. She was waiting for him, but she didn't know the purpose of his visit, since he obviously hadn't discussed it with her over the phone.

Abraham sank into the sofa in the living room of the small flat. Sylvia offered him coffee, but he declined. Someone else knocked on the door. It was Moti, who had been recently appointed director of the advanced headquarters of the Special Operations Unit in Europe and had also asked to participate in the meeting.

"You're about to take a trip," Abraham said in his deep baritone. Sylvia waited to hear more.

"It's a very complex assignment," he continued. "Somebody must be eliminated."

This was no longer a test. It was the real thing, a real assignment, which would be both complicated and dangerous. From every angle, it was the kind of assignment that was only given to experienced combatants. Despite her limited experience, Sylvia was considered capable of performing it.

"Where is this person located?" she asked.

Abraham named a hostile Arab country.

She remembered with horror the Lavon Affair (known as "The Mishap"), in which a dozen dedicated young Egyptian Jews were asked to spy for Israel against the country in which they were born. They were caught by the Egyptian authorities, tortured, and imprisoned. Skilled attorneys defended the accused young Jews, who had been trained in Israel, but the Egyptian judges didn't have the patience to listen to legal arguments. It was of utmost importance for them to impose harsh sentences in order to deter any such incidents in the future, and that is what they did. Two of the accused, Dr. Moshe Marzouk and Shmuel Azar, were sentenced to death; the others were incarcerated in Egyptian prisons, only to be released fourteen years later. A short time later, an Israeli clandestine combatant by the name of Max Bennett was also imprisoned in Egypt on charges of espionage. He committed suicide in his cell.

"Is it liable to end like the Lavon Affair?" Sylvia asked quietly.

"I sincerely hope not," Abraham answered expressionlessly. The Lavon Affair had shaken the ground under the feet of the Israeli intelligence community. Abraham preferred not to speak of it.

The presence of clandestine combatants in enemy countries lengthens the operational arm of the State of Israel, which relates to them as a strategic asset. There are activities that the combatants execute on their own and others that are carried out by them in conjunction with special IDF detachments. A case in point is the "Spring of Youth" operation, in which combatants of the operational unit assisted the IDF detachment that attacked and killed prominent Fatah operatives in Beirut.[2] Sending combatants into enemy territory almost always raises a fundamental question: should only unmarried people be sent, or might those with families also be called upon? The decision is always made taking the specific circumstances into consideration.

During Sylvia's briefing session, Abraham mentioned the name of a terrorist leader residing in the Arab country to which Sylvia was about to be sent. He was an educated, wealthy man who had strong ties of friendship with police and army personnel. He had purchased large amounts of weaponry that was being used by his men for mega-attacks and suicide bombings meant to weaken and dishearten Israel.

It was a country in which the secret service was everywhere and travelers entering the country by air or by sea were thoroughly checked. Every foreign resident was automatically considered a suspect. But every intelligence operative knows that even the most perfect defense network is not without its loopholes. There are ways of infiltrating even the most closely guarded country, and the Mossad had discovered one.

"We've devoted considerable time to planning this operation," said Abraham. "We've checked all the means of access to the country and have decided that the seaports are the safest for our purposes. You will be teamed up with an experienced combatant, and the two of you will disguise yourselves as a honeymooning couple. A used car has been especially prepared for this operation, which you will load onto a ferry. The car is full of explosives that have been hidden so carefully that they are almost impossible to detect. According to our sources, the security checks at the seaports aren't too strenuous."

Abraham went over Sylvia's cover story with her, giving her operational instructions in case they encountered mechanical difficulties with the car. ("On no account are you to leave it behind for repair, even if the breakdown is serious. Insist that you are in a hurry, and must have it back immediately. Pay as much as necessary in order to speed up the process.") She and her partner would be given maps indicating an accepted tourist route. "Be careful not to exceed the speed limit," he warned her.

"On a specified date, a few days after your arrival," he said, "you will park the car in a central square in the capital city, outside the target's residence. The next day is a national holiday. The man is planning to leave his house at eleven o'clock that morning in order to participate in a mass rally. When he comes out, you will blow up the car with a remote control device and immediately exit the country."

"What will happen if they catch us?"

"We will do everything in our power to rescue you."

That very day, Abraham introduced Sylvia to the combatant who was meant to impersonate her husband. They were the same age, and she knew nothing about him, except that he spoke a few languages, mainly English, and had previously been a student at the Sorbonne in Paris. They went over their cover story several times and were given detailed instructions regarding the operation and ways of communicating with their case officers if it became necessary. They personally arranged entry visas for the country they would be visiting.

The car was handed over to Sylvia and her partner, and they took it for a few practice runs, being careful to stay within the permitted speed limit and avoiding the thought that they were sitting inside a death trap. It reminded Sylvia of a French film she had once seen called *Le salaire de la peur* (The Wages of Fear), in which the hero, played by Yves Montand, is required to drive a tanker filled with nitroglycerin over a bumpy dirt road.

"But there's one big difference," she said wryly to her fellow combatant, who was driving.

"Yeah, what is it?"

"That was a film, and this is for real."

They planned their journey very carefully, buying wedding rings and equipping themselves with cameras and proof of the car's ownership. They put on casual clothes and received last-minute instructions for activating the explosive device. The remote control device that was meant to detonate the explosion was well hidden inside the car.

When they arrived at the port, they realized that they had overlooked one small detail: to reserve places on the ferry. It turned out to be full to bursting, and no tickets were available for the next few days. Sylvia's partner took the initiative. He approached the captain, stuffed a few hundred dollars into his hand, and a few minutes later, places were miraculously found for them.

As was anticipated, no difficulties arose at the port of destination. The port officials were used to foreigners who arrived with cars to visit well-known tourist sites. They made a superficial check of the couple's papers and personal belongings, and when they discovered nothing amiss, wished them a pleasant stay and stamped their passports and the entry permit for the car.

The two combatants booked a room in a modest hotel and behaved to all intents and purposes like a honeymooning couple.

They waited for a message to arrive from Paris announcing any last-minute changes of plan. They were required to wait for a coded phone conversation in their hotel room on a specific date and time, as well as a day before or after it. The call didn't arrive. Sylvia and her partner found the silence unsettling, and they knew that the longer they stayed in their room, the greater the chance that they would arouse suspicion among the hotel staff. They needed to find some occupation that would justify their remaining in the room. Sylvia's ingenuity was now put to the test. None of her instructors had prepared her for such an eventuality. She racked her brains to find a convincing solution and eventually came up with one. She approached one of the hotel employees, told him that she and her husband were professional painters who were enchanted by the view from their window, and requested that he buy them two easels, drawing paper, and paints. The hotel employee searched for hours until he managed to purchase the equipment at an outrageous price from a local artist who specialized in painting landscapes for tourists.

Sylvia and her companion set up the easels next to the window and began painting the view: the mosque, the streets, and the adjacent houses. Within a short time, the room was filled with paintings. They showed them proudly to every hotel worker who entered the room. Some of the workers asked to have their portraits painted, and the "artists" promised to do so when they had time.

The awaited phone call took place on the third day. It was short and concise: the operation would be carried out as planned.

The easels were abandoned; the time had come to prepare for action. The two combatants left the hotel to stake out the site where the explosion was supposed to take place and plan access and escape routes. When Sylvia's partner stopped at a kiosk to buy cigarettes, a veiled woman approached him and asked him in English what time it was. He knew that it was unacceptable for a Muslim woman wearing traditional dress to approach a strange man in the street. He replied to her question, whispered to Sylvia that they were apparently being followed, left her standing there, and ducked into a side street. To his dread, he noticed that the veiled woman was walking behind him. He went into a shop; she entered after him. When he emerged from the shop, she approached him again. "Do you need any help?" she asked. "No," he answered. "I'm fine." He started walking faster, employing the avoidance tactics he had been taught by the Special Operations Unit, until he finally managed to shake the woman off. Afterward, he entered the hotel lobby, attempting to hide his anxiety, and sent Sylvia out to complete the reconnaissance that had been interrupted. She returned an hour later. "I don't think I was followed," she said, but her companion hadn't calmed down yet: he was certain that somehow or other they had aroused suspicion.

Only later did they discover that it was a false alarm. The woman who had approached Sylvia's partner was apparently a local prostitute. It appeared that some of the prostitutes in that city wore veils and accosted tourists with casual questions in order to arouse their interest.

The next morning Sylvia and her partner went out on a final expedition to the place where the car was supposed to explode. They made their way through the busy streets, checking carefully if anyone was following them. When they arrived in the square opposite the terrorist leader's home, they surveyed the area carefully. Sylvia went pale.

"Do you see what I see?" she asked.

"Yes, I do," he answered. "I see that we have a problem."

As part of the holiday celebrations, dozens of stands had been set up around the designated victim's residence, and hundreds of people were already crowding the area, eating, drinking, and waving flags and enlarged portraits of the leader, completely blocking the road and causing serious traffic jams.

"An explosion would kill dozens of people," whispered Sylvia.

"You're right. We'll have to report it."

They phoned Paris. Their contact listened to them quietly and said, "I'll call you back within the hour." He transmitted the information to the commanders of the Special Operations Unit, who had estimated that the square would be much less crowded and that the number of casualties would be minimal.

The contact in Paris phoned the same day. His message to Sylvia was clear and concise: "Mother is ill. Return home immediately."

This was a coded message meaning "The operation is canceled."

It wasn't the first time the Mossad had canceled a planned operation at the last minute. An unexpected development sometimes makes it necessary to reassess the situation, resulting in either calling off the operation altogether or delaying its execution.

Sylvia and her partner reloaded the car onto the ferry and returned the way they had come. In mid-voyage, standing by the railing, they smiled at each other, took off their wedding rings, and threw them into the sea.

Sylvia's partner told her that it was the second time one of his operations had been canceled at the last minute.

"For the same reason?"

"Exactly. They try to avoid the death of innocent bystanders at all costs."

According to the security code of the Special Operations Unit, it was forbidden for combatants to tell the other members of their team about their involvement in previous operations. But Sylvia's companion found it hard to resist telling her about one of his first missions as a combatant, which was to track down Zayid Mukasi, an

Athenian merchant and one of Greece's chief Fatah operatives. It was suspected that the terrorist was about to send a shipment of raisins to Israel containing a large amount of explosives, which were meant to be detonated upon docking at the port of Haifa. The Mossad discovered the plot in time. An ambush was set up near the merchant's home, and he was shot down as he left for his place of business.

The story had a sequel. A short time after that liquidation operation, it turned out that the initiator of the shipment was the head of the Athens branch of Fatah. The order was given to take care of him as well.

Members of the Special Operations Unit arrived at his apartment when he was out and managed to plant an explosive device under a coffee table in the middle of his living room. One of the combatants was stationed at an observation point outside the building, from which he had a clear view of the apartment and the table. The combatant waited until the target arrived and entered the living room, at which time the device would be activated by remote control. The plan seemed uncomplicated enough, but the reality wasn't so straightforward. It turned out that the Fatah member had a lover who visited him often. Whenever she came to call, they would make love on the coffee table in the living room, the very table under which the explosive device had been placed.

The combatant waited patiently until the man was alone in his apartment. Unfortunately, each time it appeared that the coast was clear, the girl reappeared. Since the instructions were to kill the man and nobody else, the operation was canceled. The Fatah member was eventually eliminated while driving in his car.

When Sylvia and her companion disembarked from the ferry, a contact was waiting to relieve them of the car. The two combatants boarded a train and traveled to Paris in separate compartments. Abraham met them both at a small restaurant in Montparnasse and received a full report of what had happened.

Sylvia looked at him admiringly.

"I'll never forget," she said, "that you canceled an operation so as not to harm innocent bystanders. I'm so impressed by your moral standards."

The woman entering the large apartment building in western Beirut had covered her face with a black veil. She wasn't an orthodox Muslim, but in this instance the veil was imperative. She wanted to avoid being recognized.

An armed guard stopped her and asked her to identify herself. She said that she had no means of identification. "The chief is waiting for me," she announced. "My name is Zeinab." She had phoned him the previous day and asked for an appointment.

The guard rang Arafat's apartment.

"It's okay," said Arafat. "I'm waiting for her."

The guard suppressed a knowing grin. This wasn't the first woman who had gone up to the Fatah leader's apartment. Arafat was a forty-two-year-old bachelor and had prolonged affairs with his secretaries and other women, some of whom stole into his apartment secretly while others arrived openly. For a long time, rumors were rife that all these encounters with women were meant to hide the fact that he actually preferred men.

Ali Salameh's wife knocked on the door, and Arafat opened it himself. She took off the veil, revealing her sad expression.

"Thank you for agreeing to meet with me," she said softly. "I hope I'm not intruding."

"I'm glad to see you," he said, smiling paternally. "I greatly admired your relative, Abed al-Kader al-Husseini. He was a brave fighter for the Palestinian cause."

She nodded in acknowledgment. At that moment Arafat's words of praise didn't interest her in the slightest. Her thoughts were somewhere else entirely.

"I wanted to speak with you because you are the only one who can help me," she said.

Arafat looked at her expectantly. He had met her only once, at her wedding. Ali had never discussed his wife with Arafat or with other Fatah leaders. She herself never appeared in the places frequented by Arafat. Thus he was surprised when had she called and requested an urgent meeting.

He gestured for her to be seated, and she sat on the edge of the sofa. He settled into an armchair facing her.

"I hesitated a long time before approaching you," she began, "hoping that the problem would solve itself, but it hasn't. That is why I am here."

"What problem are you referring to?"

"To Ali. He's the problem."

"Tell me all about it. I'm listening."

"When I married him," she said, "I felt that it was the right thing to do. Our families strongly supported the marriage. It was arranged, and in such cases there is usually no talk of love, but I fell head over heels in love with him anyway. I was captivated by his manliness. I enjoyed seeing him surrounded by men who adulated him. I was happy for him when he was promoted to more senior positions. Of course, from the very beginning there were signs that it wouldn't be easy being married to him. Of course I was aware that he was very different from me, loving to have a good time, enjoying the pleasures of life, dancing in nightclubs. I hoped that he would change after the wedding, but that didn't happen. He disappeared from home often, arriving only in the morning. At times he disappeared for days on end. I suffered it all in silence out of love for him. I hoped everything would change after we had a child, but after Hassan was born, Ali continued as usual. When our second son, Osama, was born, it again made no difference to his behavior. Ali took no interest in me or in his sons. They know that their father is a well-known hero, and they both ask me all the time when he's coming home to spend a little time with them. But Ali is only interested in what is going on outside his home, not in his family. He probably has another woman, or more than one."

"I'm sorry to hear about this," said Arafat. What she had told him about her husband didn't surprise him. He was aware that Ali loved chasing women and enjoying life.

"We've had endless discussions and arguments about our relationship," Zeinab continued. "I beg him to stay at home more, to spend more time with his children. He promises to do so, but he doesn't keep his word."

Yasser Arafat offered her a glass of water. She sipped it slowly.

"His work is his whole life," she continued. "He takes more and more responsibilities upon himself, disappearing from home for weeks at a time."

"What can I do to help you?" Arafat asked sympathetically.

"I know it's a lot to ask, but I have no choice. I would like . . . if possible . . . for him to have more regular work hours, so that he can devote more attention to his family. Could you lighten his burden of responsibility? It might help me rehabilitate my family life."

Arafat thought for a moment.

"I can understand why you've come to see me, and I don't hold it against you," he said finally, "but you must get used to the fact that your husband isn't just another Fatah member. He is one of my top people. He carries out assignments that are capable of bringing a revolution to the Middle East. This is a holy objective, Zeinab, and it is important that a man with such responsibilities be given full support. It is imperative for him to fulfill his role without any unnecessary worries."

"He's not the only top man in Fatah," she retorted. "Most of them have families and still manage to do their jobs."

Arafat got up and walked around the room, looking for words that would express what he wished to say.

Finally he turned to her and said angrily, "You and I have no right to distract Ali from his work. I suggest that you wait patiently. Perhaps someday, when we achieve our goals, we will all finally be able to sit quietly and devote time to family."

Zeinab Salameh left feeling more depressed than she had when she arrived. Yasser Arafat, Abu Amar, her last hope, wasn't willing to help her. Fatah was more important to him than her family's future. She was more certain than ever that Ali would eventually be lost to her forever.

At times, between operations, on quiet days after the pleasure of action and the excitement of danger, loneliness—like an elusive viper with a deadly bite—would sneak up on Sylvia. Age was showing its signs, and it was difficult for her to ignore that the years had passed without allowing her to devote time to her own needs. She was still young and attractive, but she had remained alone, and it sometimes worried her.

On days when loneliness loomed large, she looked for ways of keeping as busy as possible. She requested additional photographic assignments from the Dalmas Agency, read books, painted on the banks of the Seine, went to the cinema, wrote birthday poems for family members, and dined in small local restaurants. But alone, always alone.

She had assumed that her thirtieth birthday would be spent in the usual way, but it turned out differently than she had imagined. In the morning, the producer from the Dalmas Agency phoned and asked her to cover the launching of a modern tourist boat on the Seine. It sounded like an undemanding assignment, but the promise of a luxurious spring cruise on the river in the company of new people sounded to Sylvia like an ideal way to celebrate her birthday.

The cruise boat shone white in the sun. Comfortable seating had been arranged on the lower and upper decks behind shining windows. The crew, in white uniforms trimmed with gold, received the guests with a smile, a bow, and a glass of select champagne.

Sylvia circulated among the guests, snapping photos while sipping champagne and nibbling caviar canapés. A tall, elegant, pleasant-looking man was also taking photographs using a large professional camera. He introduced himself as Hans Rauch, from the Magnum photographic agency. He was younger than she and spoke fluent English with a slight German accent. Sylvia was pleased when he complimented her on the shooting angles she had chosen. She noticed that he didn't move from her side and began suspecting that he was following her. Her suspicions were aroused even more when he directed his camera not only at what was happening aboard ship, but also at her. She wondered if he was also using his camera as a cover-up for other activities.

The boat was launched, moving away from the pier and setting a course toward the middle of the river. Hans invited her to lunch with him on deck, and she couldn't refuse. Against a background of breathtaking views of the city, Hans told her about himself. He had been born in Germany to a Catholic family, moved with his family to Greece, had worked as a news photographer in Athens, and was now employed in the same profession in Paris. She told him whatever she could about herself within the confines of her cover story. Apart from her case officer and her partner on the operation that was canceled at the last minute, Hans was the only nonnative resident Sylvia had spoken to in a long while.

She asked herself again if he was actually a spy and if the story he had told her was part of a subterfuge concocted by some anonymous intelligence outfit. Hans could be a representative of an enemy organization following Mossad operatives who were responsible for recent attacks. Could he have followed her onto the boat disguised as a news photographer? She studied Hans Rauch carefully, trying to detect something that might give him away, but she found nothing. He was behaving politely, cordially, maybe a bit nervously, like a would-be suitor on a first date.

At the end of the cruise, before they went their separate ways to develop and print their photos, Hans invited Sylvia to join him for a drink that evening at a bar in his neighborhood. She hesitated. She really wanted to accept his invitation but still hadn't shaken off a slight suspicion that he was setting a trap. Scenarios ran through her head, each one more terrifying than the last. She feared that Hans might drag her to some dark place, murder her, and escape without leaving a trace. During her training, she had constantly been reminded that such things could happen even to the most cautious clandestine combatants.

"I'm busy this evening," she lied. "Give me your number and I'll phone you when I'm free."

"We can meet after you finish whatever you need to do," he insisted. "I don't go to bed early."

She promised to be in touch but was still alert to possible danger.

At her insistence, she met Abraham a few hours later at one of the cafés at Place Chaillon. She told him about her encounter with Hans.

"Did he do anything that looked suspicious?" her case officer asked.

"I don't think so."

"Did he ask you for your address?"

"No."

"Did he follow you after you parted?"

"No."

"What was your impression of him?"

"He seemed to be a very nice person."

"Do you want to have a relationship with him?"

"I think so."

"Okay," he said. "Wait a few days until we find out who he really is."

Abraham would have been happier for Sylvia not to get romantically involved while she was serving in the Special Operations Unit. He knew that intimate attachments could seriously compromise operations by causing unwanted complications. But there was nothing he could do to prevent Sylvia from developing a friendship with a man. Like other combatants, there was no clause in her contract forbidding her to become involved in personal relationships, as long as they were reported. Sylvia was a healthy woman with needs and emotions that couldn't be ignored. It was obvious that sooner or later she would meet someone and fall in love.

But Hans, like any foreign resident, represented a risk. Abraham told his superiors about him, and they approached the German intelligence services via the channels that dealt with such things, requesting that the Germans check up on this man, without explaining why they needed the information. The Germans examined the matter with their characteristic thoroughness. They bugged his phone, listening in on one conversation that aroused suspicion. Hans was telling an unknown listener about his sick grandmother: "Tell her that I'm doing my best to obtain the medicine," he said. "I'm sure I'll succeed."

It sounded like a coded message.

The undercover investigation of Hans Rauch by the German secret service was conducted quickly and efficiently. Information was gathered about his family and associates. Interpol checked if he had a criminal record and how his work was evaluated by the agency that employed him. The final conclusion was that Hans was not connected in any way with an enemy organization. It seemed that the young man had told Sylvia the absolute truth about himself and that there was no reason to suspect him. The Mossad received the Germans' report without raising any objections. "Your guy is okay," Abraham announced to Sylvia. Her face brightened and her heart skipped a beat. She was delighted to be free to pursue her friendship with Hans.

She immediately phoned him. He sounded pleased when she identified herself.

"I'm sorry it took me so long," she said. "I had lots of work to finish and didn't have a second."

"Never mind," he reassured her. "I was busy, too. I was looking for a special medicine for my grandmother in Athens."

"Did you find it?"

"Yes, but it took a long time. I sent her the medicine yesterday, and she wrote me that she's already using it and it's helping her."

"I'm glad to hear it."

She asked when they could meet.

"Are you busy this evening?" she dared to ask.

"Not really. I'd like to have dinner with you."

They decided to meet at a family restaurant behind the Opera building, whose owners Hans knew. Sylvia devoted considerable time to deciding what to wear. It had been a long time since she had made an effort to look her best.

"You look wonderful," Hans complimented her when they met. She noticed with pleasure the attention she was getting from the other diners.

Afterward Sylvia couldn't decide if the evening was wonderful due to the food or to the company. Hans was a delightful person with wide horizons and interesting conversation. She listened with fascination to accounts of his extensive world travels and about his favorite pastime, rock climbing.

He asked her about her life, where she lived, where she had learned photography, and Sylvia felt uncomfortable having to hide the truth from him. Having to deceive a man she liked so much put a damper on her spirits.

"Do you intend working as a photographer much longer?"

"I think so."

"I don't," he said, surprising her.

"Why not?"

"Suddenly it doesn't interest me anymore. I feel as though I've done it all. Another photo of politicians at an international conference, a new cruise ship, the first snowfall in Paris. I'm really tired of it all."

"Does that mean that you'll stop working for Magnum?"

"I already have. I told them this week that I'm quitting."

"What will you do?"

"I have some savings that will keep me going for a while. After that I'll look for something else."

"In what direction?"

"I don't know yet, but it must be something interesting, exciting. I'm incapable of working at a humdrum job."

"Good luck, Hans."

He changed the subject: "Next year I'm planning on climbing Mt. Everest. I'd love it if you'd come with me."

"If we're still friendly by then," she smiled.

Sylvia couldn't avoid comparing Hans with Avery, her ex-fiancé in South Africa. Hans was completely different. He made her feel like a young girl who has just discovered romance. Avery had been a good friend a long time before she had even realized that she was in love with him, but now it seemed that meeting Hans had revealed to her what love really was. She could see from his eyes that he felt the same way about her.

"It's been a long time since I met a girl like you," he said, confirming her intuition.

They walked hand in hand to his apartment, where they drank wine and made passionate love. Hans fell into a deep sleep, but Sylvia forced herself to stay awake for fear that she might divulge secret information in her sleep. When she saw it was getting light outside, she was seized with dread. She had forgotten to tell Abraham where she was. For the first time she had broken one of the basic rules of her profession: to report her whereabouts at all times in case she was urgently needed. She apologized to Hans that she needed to rush to work, and phoned Abraham from a public telephone in a nearby café. No, he hadn't tried to reach her during the night.

"Where were you?" he asked.

"With Hans," she replied.

"You sound like a woman in love," he commented.

"You're right—that's exactly what I am."

From the latest reports pieced together by Israeli intelligence, it seemed that Ali Hassan Salameh was paying frequent visits to West Germany. Small Black September cells were being formed, trained, and prepared to carry out orders in various German cities. The reports revealed that Ali was meeting them secretly, but he consistently managed to elude the Mossad agents sent to track him down.

This scanty information wasn't sufficient to allow the Mossad commanders to send a professional team after their most wanted man, but it was at least a start. They decided to concentrate their efforts in Germany, but it soon became clear that this wasn't so easy. Ali Salameh generally traveled under a false passport and frequently changed his appearance. Sometimes he grew a beard; at other times he appeared wearing a wig or dark sunglasses. He generally introduced himself as a Lebanese businessman and refrained from using public transportation, preferring to be driven from one place to another in the cars of those he could trust. He often carried a loaded weapon and was accompanied by bodyguards. He didn't doubt for a moment that the Mossad was looking for him, and he did whatever he could to elude its grasp.

Apart from maintaining surveillance and paying large sums of money to various individuals who could help the Mossad track Ali down, more sophisticated, creative, and indirect methods were needed in order to locate him.

The various branches of the Israeli intelligence community increased their efforts to find him, following suspects who were known members of Black September, spending days and nights gathering information about Ali Salameh's whereabouts. Frankfurt, a bustling commercial city, was a major center of Arab activity in Germany. The heads of the Mossad decided to concentrate a significant part of their efforts there. They set a clever trap in Frankfurt that seemed innocent enough on the surface and that had at least a chance of succeeding.

They built a cover story that seemed totally convincing. A Jordanian businessman called Samir al-Eyni, whose chief enterprises were in Arab countries, lived in a well-appointed apartment in the heart of the city. Samir was a charming bachelor in his forties with a pleasant, open personality, who acquired many friends, especially in the Arab community. He often held high-spirited parties in his apartment and gladly put his spare bedrooms at the disposal of young Palestinians, many of whom were members of Fatah, who wished to spend the night. Rumors of his hospitality spread like wildfire among young Arabs, who came and went, spending a night or two in the apartment and enjoying his lavish table. He generously contributed to Palestinian charity funds and regularly sent food parcels to refugees in the Lebanese and Jordanian camps, but took no interest in politics.

However, Samir's commercial activities were no more than a ruse: he had a deep, dark secret that he revealed to nobody. His real name was Moshe Levy, and he was a clandestine combatant from the Special Operations Unit. It was hoped at the Mossad that terrorists directly involved in Ali Salameh's European operations or their friends would inadvertently divulge information about Ali's whereabouts while spending time at Samir's apartment. As the search for Ali Salameh intensified, the commanders of the operational unit hoped that information overheard at the apartment would finally lead them to their prey.

Samir al-Eyni did everything he could to make his visitors feel at home. On the walls he had hung photographs of the Al-Aksa Mosque and Muslim lucky charms called *hamsas* studded with semiprecious stones.[3] His kitchen offered a constant supply of Arab coffee seasoned with cardamom, food in abundance, and even fresh pita bread that he would buy every morning from a bakery in one of the city's immigrant neighborhoods. Every visitor was free to prepare food for himself according to his personal tastes. Samir al-Eyni never complained about the dirty dishes that were left in the sink or the overflowing ashtrays. He offered to drive his visitors anywhere they had to go and even lent them money if they needed it.

The visitors felt free to bring friends to the apartment and invite them to stay without the host's permission. Their conversations were carefully monitored by the Mossad when Levy was absent. They yielded a considerable amount of information, but not a single detail that could lead them to Ali Salameh.

Every Mossad operative bearing a false identity lives with the constant feeling that at any moment something is liable to interfere with his plans. A slip of the tongue, a temporary lapse of attention, or an unfortunate incident is enough to sabotage the most successful cover story. But as time passed and Moshe Levy became more deeply involved in Frankfurt's Arab society, it seemed as though nothing could go wrong. Fate decided differently.

One day a regular visitor, a young Palestinian with Jordanian citizenship who was responsible for recruiting volunteers for Black September in Europe, brought his mother along to the apartment. She was a Jewish woman who had become a Muslim in order to marry an Arab from East Jerusalem. The middle-aged woman wearing traditional Arab dress stayed in the apartment for a few days, cooking for the young guests and not saying much. On the third day of her stay, the Mossad listened in on a conversation she had with her son.

"Your host looks suspicious," she said.

"What makes you think so?" asked her son in surprise.

"I think he's a Jew."

Her son laughed. "That's impossible," he said. "I've known him for a long time. He's a Jordanian born and bred, a staunch supporter of Fatah, and a sworn enemy of Israel."

"For all that," his mother insisted, "something in his accent is unconvincing. I can smell a Jew a mile off. Don't forget that I was born Jewish."

Other young men joined the conversation. Some of them jeered at the woman's comments, while others took them seriously.

"We'll find out when Samir returns," the woman's son promised her.

That was enough for Levy's case officer, who summoned him to an emergency meeting.

"Your cover has been blown," he said curtly. "Follow me."

Levy was shocked, finding it hard to understand how his secret had been exposed. He was immediately rushed to the airport and put on a plane bound for Israel. He never returned to Germany.

A secret file was kept at Black September headquarters for every member of the organization in Arab countries, Europe, and Asia.

The file didn't only contain updated information about the operative, but also full details of his activities outside the organization. Most of Black September's activists in Europe used their professional lives as a cover story, making it very difficult for the Mossad to locate them.

Ali Salameh would look through these files frequently in order to select suitable people for operations demanding professional knowledge in various fields. That was how he discovered Mohammed Masalha.

Twenty-seven-year-old Masalha was born in Haifa. In the 1948 war, when he was three years old, his family escaped to the West Bank; when he grew up, he went to study in Germany and remained there after getting his degree. Masalha led a double life. On the surface, he was a prominent architect with an office in Munich, whose photograph often appeared in the newspapers. In secret, he was a Fatah operative, a member of Black September.

On a clear afternoon on July 18, 1972, less than two months after the bloody attack at Ben Gurion Airport, Ali met with Mohammed Masalha in Munich. They met in a secret apartment in a vacation resort outside the city. Salameh's two bodyguards, armed with revolvers hidden in their clothes, guarded the apartment and only allowed Masalha to enter after they ascertained that he was unarmed.

This was a crucial meeting for Ali Salameh. It was going to lay the foundation for the biggest operation Black September had ever carried out. Its success would not only be a huge accomplishment for the organization, but also an impressive feather in Ali's cap.

"I read in the newspaper," Ali began, "that you are involved in building the Olympic Village near Munich."

"Exactly."

"Does that mean you have free access to the buildings where the athletes will be housed?"

"Of course."

We need you, Masalha," Ali said. He revealed his intention to appoint Masalha commander of a well-trained unit of Black September fighters. Its assignment would be to attack the Israelis' rooms in the Olympic Village and take them hostage, holding them until terrorists imprisoned in Israel were released. He asked his visitor to maintain absolute secrecy regarding the mission.

Masalha's job was to plan the team's route into the Olympic Village, marking the exact location of the Israelis' quarters, and when the time came, lead the attack and the retreat.

"I am honored to fulfill your request," Masalha told Ali with emotion.

After his return to Lebanon, Ali hurriedly recruited fifty hand-picked young Fatah members and sent them to the Nahar al-Bard training camp in the north of the country, several miles from Beirut. There they were trained by members of international terrorist gangs and East German intelligence agents, who taught them the effective use of various types of weapons and how to activate explosive charges, fight in built-up areas, take hostages, and conduct negotiations with the enemy. None of the trainees knew the nature of the mission they were being trained for. They could only guess that it was a particularly important one, since Ali Salameh arrived every day at the camp to personally monitor their progress.

At the end of a month of intensive training, most of the participants were sent home, leaving only the eight most successful trainees. Ali Salameh met with every one of them individually and told them that very soon they would receive information about the operation in which they were to participate.

In order to smuggle the necessary arms from Beirut, Ali appointed a man and a woman from the ranks of Fatah. They were supposed to carry machine guns and ammunition in their luggage, and Ali arranged it so that they would go through customs without a problem. One of the chief customs officers in Cologne airport was regularly paid large sums of cash by Fatah to turn a blind eye to smuggled arms.

On August 23, 1972, the smugglers boarded a Lufthansa plane from Beirut to Cologne. The man wore an expensive suit, smelled of aftershave, and exuded self-confidence. The woman with him was trim, attractive, and dressed impeccably, looking as though she had stepped out of the pages of a fashion magazine. They had brought with them four suitcases and were received by the customs officer at the German airport. He instructed his workers to open one suitcase only for inspection. The travelers were allowed to choose which one would be opened. It contained hundreds of women's brassieres. They didn't bother opening the other three, which contained submachine guns, hand grenades, and ammunition.

The travelers went by hired car to Munich and hid the luggage in rental lockers at the railway station. They were met by Ali Hassan

Salameh's representative, who took the keys in order to hand them over to Ali upon his arrival in Munich.

The date of the operation was drawing near. Ali Salameh gathered together the eight outstanding trainees in Beirut and equipped them with plane tickets to Rome and Belgrade. They left on separate flights carrying false passports and student cards from European universities. At Rome and Belgrade, the eight boarded planes bound for Munich. Masalha and his aide, a student who was an expert in guerrilla warfare, met them in Masalha's apartment and gave them full details of the operation. Masalha alerted them that attacking the Israelis' living quarters might involve quite a risk. "First of all, the Olympic Village security guards might notice you," he warned. "It could also happen that the Israelis will open fire. Be careful."

Ali Salameh arrived in Munich and spent the remaining days until the operation heavily guarded in a rented apartment together with his associate in planning and commanding the operation, Mohammed Uda, nicknamed Abu Daud. They both thoroughly briefed the terrorist team.

On September 6, 1972, at 4:30 a.m., after collecting the weapons and the ammunition, the eight terrorists jumped over the fence surrounding the village, broke into the Israelis' quarters, and after killing two of the athletes, took the nine remaining ones hostage.

Ali Salameh and Abu Daud also arrived at the Olympic Village to observe the attack from outside the fence. When they heard gunfire, they realized that the operation was in full swing and it was time to escape. They got into a car that was waiting for them nearby and were taken immediately to the airport. They had reservations on an Alitalia flight to Rome. After presenting false passports at the check-in counter, they were soon on their way to Rome. From there Ali Salameh flew to Beirut and Abu Daud took off for Belgrade and Warsaw, where he hid out for a few years before finally settling in Jordan.

German security forces were summoned to the village immediately after the first gunshots were heard, but only on arrival did they understand exactly what had happened. Their evaluation of the situation was that any attempt to overpower the attackers was liable to endanger the lives of the Israeli hostages. Meanwhile, until they found a more creative solution, they began negotiating with the kidnappers. The director of the Mossad, Zvi Zamir, who was urgently rushed to Munich, offered to participate in the negotiations between the Germans and the terrorists. He had a rich military background (among other things as the chief of the Southern Command), but had no experience with hostage negotiations. The Germans replied unequivocally that they didn't require any outside assistance. Zamir had to make do with observing events from afar, and what he saw was totally unsatisfactory.

In the course of the negotiations, the Germans offered to put a plane located at one of the German Air Force bases at the disposal of the kidnappers, which would transport them wherever they wanted to go. In fact, the plane wasn't going to take off to anywhere. This was a trick that was meant to save the hostages.

The kidnappers accepted the offer, but the moment they got off the bus with the hostages and walked toward the plane, the Germans opened fire on them. The terrorists became furious and opened fire on the hostages. In the exchange of fire with the Germans, five terrorists were killed. The ones remaining alive were arrested and interrogated.

When Ali Salameh arrived at Black September headquarters in Beirut, he found a hive of furious activity. His men told him about the gun battle between the German security forces and the terrorists, and Ali smiled with satisfaction. He didn't place much importance on the fact that the hostages had been killed and that there was to be no exchange of prisoners with Israel. He was much more interested in the event's attracting wide media, which he believed would focus world interest on the Palestinian struggle. His wish was granted.

Late that night, while the residents of the refugee camps were still celebrating the murder of the Israeli athletes, Arafat convened the Fatah high command and praised Ali in their presence. They shouted, "We all are Black September!" while Arafat hugged Ali joyfully and repeated over and over, "You are my son . . . you are my son . . ."

Ali returned to his office bursting with pride and longing to strike while the iron was hot. His brain was filled with ideas for additional terrorist attacks.

On the television screen in her small Paris flat, Sylvia carefully followed the events in Munich. The terrible scenes haunted her: masked terrorists on the verandah of the Israeli athletes' quarters negotiating with German security officers; the hostages arriving with their captors at the military air base; their getting off the bus and starting toward the plane under threat of the terrorists' machine guns . . . Suddenly the German forces surrounding the base open fire. One plane goes up in flames. Some of the lights go out as a result of the shooting. For a few moments, only gunfire from the terrorists' and the Germans' weapons may be seen; then, silence. The announcer appears on the screen and states that the broadcast from Germany has been interrupted, and that he doesn't know when it will resume.

Sylvia couldn't believe what she was seeing. Terrorist attacks in Israel and abroad had been multiplying at a fast rate, but this was the first time the assailants had demonstrated such daring. They had not hesitated to stage an attack at an international venue at the height of a world-class sporting event and take Israeli athletes hostage. Sylvia asked herself where the Israeli and German security guards were when the terrorists broke into the Olympic Village. She didn't know if Israeli security personnel had attempted to stop the terrorists on their way to the air force base. She had so many questions, and the television broadcast didn't answer a single one.

The next morning she got up early and went out to buy the English newspapers. She read with horror about the murder of the Israeli contestants as a result of the German attack on the kidnappers. It reminded her of the slaughter that the Nazis perpetrated on her relatives in the Ukraine. Now it had happened again: innocent people had been murdered just because they were Jews.

A smaller headline in the *Herald Tribune* stated that Black September, headed by Ali Salameh, had taken credit for the operation. The article outlined the activities of the organization and presented a biography of its leader, who was described as "a determined, experienced terrorist, who has no fear of dying."

Sylvia went on to read articles in other newspapers, and they left a bitter taste in her mouth. In her mind's eye, she saw Israel wrapped in deep mourning. The Mossad high command must surely be convening emergency meetings in an atmosphere of tension and heightened alertness.

She desperately needed to talk to someone, express her feelings, and be given support. She couldn't turn to her lover, Hans, since she was forbidden to reveal her connection with Israel, and he was in effect her only true friend in Paris. Apart from Abraham, she wasn't acquainted with any Mossad operatives in the city, and he was busy arranging his return to Israel with the completion of his period of service in Paris. Her new case officer, whom she knew as David, had already arrived to take over from his predecessor.

Too upset to remain alone with her thoughts, Sylvia phoned David and asked him to meet her. When they met, David noticed that her eyes were red from crying. He didn't have to guess why: he was also grief-stricken by the terrible tragedy.

Sylvia showed him the article about Ali Salameh in the *Herald Tribune* and commented, "I assume that Salameh is our chief target now."

"I suppose so," her new case officer responded, although nobody had yet informed him of this.

"I hope that when it happens, I will be part of it," she added.

"You know that isn't my decision, Sylvia. If there is such a plan, it might very well take place in an Arab country, not here."

"I've already been to an Arab country. The prospect doesn't frighten me."

He searched for an answer that would satisfy her.

He finally said, "I hope you will be considered."

"That isn't good enough, David. You have connections with the bosses of the Mossad. Report this conversation to them."

From the report he had received from his predecessor, David understood that despite Sylvia's extroverted personality, she was a very disciplined operative and never asked for anything.

"You're probably not used to a member of the organization asking anything for himself," she said, reading his thoughts, "but most of my father's family perished in the Holocaust. The Germans wouldn't have managed to exterminate so many Jews if the victims had defended themselves. One of the main reasons why I came to Israel and eventually joined the Mossad was because I decided to defend the Jews in order to prevent what happened in the Holocaust from ever happening again. Salameh is responsible for killing Jews. He won't stop until we cut his hands off. I want to be the one to do it."

"You are a very brave woman," said David. "I'll do whatever I can so that when the time comes, your request will be seriously considered."

The psychological evaluation in Sylvia's file stated, "There is a lack of quiet in Sylvia that craves for action. . . . She knows that she is special and that she possesses unusual and varied abilities."

It was clear to the Israeli government that it must respond quickly and resolutely to the slaughter of the eleven athletes at Munich. The air force was put into action. Israeli planes bombed terrorist camps in Lebanon and Syria, killing and wounding a large number of men training there. However, it was clear that this wasn't enough to deter the terrorist organizations. Meanwhile, information had reached the Mossad revealing that Black September's headquarters in Beirut had been totally abandoned for fear of an Israeli attack. Most of the organization's leaders and the heads of other terrorist organizations had gone underground. Arafat himself was also carefully guarded, so there was no immediate chance of curtailing Arab terror. Israel was trapped in a no-win situation. It was obvious that only an operation big enough to deal a death blow to the terrorists would achieve anything. But at the same time, it was necessary to respond immediately, even if the response was ineffectual and far from intimidating. The air force was again put into action, taking off for Lebanon and broadening the extent of the bombing to include various infrastructures and installations. This resulted in many dead and wounded, and very few newspaper headlines. The Israeli press was strongly critical of such operations, and the general consensus was that Israel was not achieving its objective.

Ali Hassan Salameh was intoxicated by victory and more self-confident than ever, interpreting the Israelis' response as a clear sign of confusion and weakness. He felt that the time was ripe for another attack on Israel that would deal a death blow to its national morale. Sometime after the Israeli bombings, he returned to his headquarters, pulled out old and new contingency plans, placed his operatives in Europe on high alert, and commanded them to carry out a series of missions.

A few days later, a terrorist unit hijacked a German passenger plane, announcing that if Germany didn't release the three murderers who had survived the Munich massacre, then they would kill the hostages on the plane. The Germans gave in. The prisoners were released and flown to Libya, where they were warmly received at a mass demonstration. People were crushed to death in an effort to shake hands with the three murderers, as though they were God's messengers on earth.

This success motivated Black September to strike again a few days later at various locations. Ami Schori, the agricultural attaché at the Israeli Embassy in London, was opening his morning mail as usual, when a letter bomb that was supposedly sent to his office by an academic institution exploded in his hands. Schori was killed instantly. Zadok Ophir, a Mossad operative in Brussels, waited at a café in the center of town for an Arab who had promised to sell him information about terrorist gangs in Europe. What he didn't know was that the man he was about to meet was a double agent (and a Black September operative) who had prepared a bitter surprise for him. The Arab approached Ophir and pulled out a revolver, shooting the Israeli and seriously wounding him. He was on the critical list in a Brussels hospital for several months, until he finally managed to get back on his feet and return to service.

As a result of these attacks, Israelis and Jews everywhere began to feel threatened and insecure. Safety measures against terrorism were instituted at every concentration of Israelis and Jews abroad. Especially tight security measures were initiated at Jewish synagogues and educational institutions. In Israel and in the Jewish world, it was obvious that only an appropriate Israeli response would serve to restrain the terrorist organizations.

Against this backdrop, Israel's prime minister, Golda Meir, convened an emergency meeting of her cabinet. Her sad face expressed her pain. "This situation is intolerable," she said, and requested the ministers to come to an unequivocal decision to expand the war against terror, recruit more clandestine combatants, and initiate more operations. She promised the director of the Mossad unlimited funds for this purpose and expressed the hope that he would do everything in his power not to put his combatants at unnecessary risk.

At Mossad headquarters, an urgent plan was formulated to eliminate all those involved in the Munich attack, wherever they might be. The combatants of the operational unit were commanded to prepare for action, as they would momentarily receive orders to launch the operation.

Ali Salameh was well aware that Israel was about to expand its activities against his organization. "There is going to be a war," he declared to his men without a trace of apprehension, "but we will be victorious. We will overpower them, exhaust them, crush them."

Ali convened a meeting of Black September's commanders at his headquarters, which was located in a well-guarded office building in western Beirut. He realized that he couldn't sit back and do nothing in the face of the imminent Israeli attack, but he was also aware that the possibilities of action had recently been severely limited.

This was due, among other things, to the fact that the airline companies had tightened up security against hijacking, especially regarding security checks at airports, which had become much more exhaustive and sophisticated. As a result, it was practically impossible to stage elaborate terrorist attacks on the scale of Munich by landing Black September units in Israeli airports. But Ali knew that he mustn't delay. Black September had won widespread admiration throughout the Arab world, but this might quickly fade or be transferred to another terrorist group if his organization showed any signs of weakness in its war against the Mossad.

For several hours the commanders of Black September discussed various plans of action. Someone suggested sending terrorist units from Lebanon to Israel in commando boats or by means of motorized air gliders. They also weighed the idea of assassinating an Israeli ambassador to a foreign country. But the most daring suggestion was raised by Ali himself: "We'll show them that, despite security checks at the airports, we are capable of blowing up an El Al plane."

It was an extremely ambitious plan, and Ali knew he was working against tremendous odds. At El Al counters all over the world, airline security officers—under orders from the Shabak (Israeli Security Agency), which was responsible for Israeli security at home and abroad—operated a concentrated defense network that no passenger could penetrate without undergoing a thorough security check.

"Blowing up an El Al plane is an impossible task," said one of those present at the meeting.

Ali laughed. He replied, "The term 'impossible' doesn't appear in our lexicon."

He commanded his men to obtain an El Al flight schedule from Europe to Israel for the next three months and information regarding the type of plane that would be used for each flight.

"We are going to blow up a plane," he promised confidently. "We have already demonstrated that we are capable of carrying out even the most impossible missions."

Excited about his plan, Ali took off for Rome in the disguise of a religious dignitary and met secretly with one of his most reliable and ardent admirers, Aadel Wail Zuitar, Black September's representative in Italy. Ali was filled with admiration for Aadel Zuitar, due to his rich cultural background. He was the son of a family of respected intellectuals who had immigrated to Rome from Nablus fourteen years earlier. His father was a historian who had translated works of the French philosophers into Arabic. Aadel was thirty-eight years old and, like his father, also worked as a translator of books and articles into Arabic. He worked for a pittance at the Libyan Embassy in Rome as a translator, lectured before intellectual Muslim groups, and was a connoisseur of fine art and music. He was a slightly built bachelor, who dressed with monk-like simplicity, kept a strictly vegetarian diet, and was extremely frugal with his meager earnings.

Ali explained his plan to Zuitar, and six hours after their meeting, he was on his way back to Beirut. He breathed a sigh of relief when the plane touched down. He always felt much more secure at home.

Aadel Zuitar took his assignment seriously. He recruited two young Arabs of his acquaintance, students at Rome University who were prepared to do any deed in the name of Black September, and offered them a tempting proposition: to find two innocent European girls and win their hearts. He gave them a free hand in choosing the girls, and they immediately went out hunting. The objective was to win the girls' trust and get them and their luggage onto an El Al plane headed for Israel. Their luggage would be filled with well-hidden explosives that would detonate when the plane was in midflight, with the objective of killing or injuring as many Israeli passengers as possible.

It was summertime, and Sperlonga Beach near Rome was crowded with vacationers both young and old. The two young Arabs wandered around the beach for an hour or so, until they spotted two girls sunbathing on the yellow sand. One of them was radiantly beautiful, and both were a bit overweight. They would be easy prey.

The two young Arabs approached, carrying bottles of cold soft drinks, and offered the drinks to the girls. They accepted gladly. In the ensuing conversation, it emerged that the girls were English students who were spending the summer in Italy. The boys introduced themselves as the sons of wealthy families in Ramallah, who were studying in Rome.

In the evening the two couples went to a packed restaurant near the railway station. They ended up in the boys' apartment. Passionate attachments soon developed, at least on the part of the girls, who were wooed with presents, flowers, declarations of love. The two couples spent every waking hour together, and the English girls gladly agreed to accompany the boys on a visit to their families in Ramallah. The Arab men purchased four tickets on an El Al flight from Rome to Ben Gurion Airport and, to the girls' delight, also planned extensive tours around Israel that the four would take together. But two days before the planned trip, the two Arabs announced that they would be delayed in Rome for a few days by unforeseen circumstances. They suggested that the girls go on without them, stay in a hotel in Tel Aviv that had been booked beforehand, and go sightseeing around the city until they arrived. The girls were glad to comply, and they also agreed to take a tape recorder with them as a present for one of their boyfriends' brothers. "He will come to the hotel to collect his present," they told the girls. They didn't suspect that the innocent-looking tape recorder contained a powerful explosive charge. Aadel Zuitar had attached a detonating device and an altimeter to the bomb, which would explode when the plane reached a specific altitude.

The suitcase containing the tape recorder passed through the security check at Rome Airport and was loaded onto the plane, which was scheduled to take off at noon. The flight attendants were about to serve a hot meal to the passengers, and the two English girls sat together, talking excitedly about their new boyfriends.

Ali Salameh and Aadel Zuitar had planned the operation down to the last detail. What they didn't know was that, due to previous bombing attempts, the walls of the plane's baggage hold had been fitted with reinforced steel plates, which formed an effective shield between the hold and other parts of the plane. The explosive charge was detonated as planned while the plane was flying above the Mediterranean, but it caused no damage whatsoever. The passengers heard a muffled, indistinct noise from below, and continued with what they were doing, completely unaware; but the pilots immediately understood what had happened. A red light lit up on the instrument panel, warning them of an explosion in the baggage hold. The warning system indicated that, despite the explosion, there was no danger to the plane or its passengers. In fact, everything was functioning normally when the plane landed at Ben Gurion Airport.

The passengers were detained on the plane until security officers had completed their investigation of the baggage hold. When they located the remains of the tape recorder and the baggage checks attached to it, the two young English passengers were arrested and interrogated. Only then did they realize that they had been the victims of a well-conceived plot.

The Italian police received a report from Israel that explosives had been smuggled onto a plane at Rome Airport. They immediately went in pursuit of Fatah operatives in the city, and arrested Aadel Zuitar, among others, whose brother had been deported from Germany a short time earlier on suspicion of being connected with Black September. Aadel was thoroughly interrogated but was released, since the police had no proof that he had taken part in the attack. The two young Arabs who had tempted the girls to smuggle the explosive charge onto the El Al plane had disappeared without a trace.

Aadel returned to his job at the Libyan Embassy in a good mood. Nobody could prove what he had done, and he didn't think anybody would try to go after him for his role in the bombing. The concierge at his apartment in Piazza Annabelliano welcomed him with a calm smile. No, nobody had been looking for him in his absence. There were no letters, either.

Aadel went up to his apartment, finished writing an article, and went to bed.

Sylvia Rafael was on a photo assignment behind the scenes at the Olympia Theater in Paris. Her subject was Yves Montand. She was photographing the entertainer in his dressing room as he was being made up for a performance, engaging in conversation with the orchestra conductor, and giving autographs to fans who had managed to infiltrate backstage. Working in the theater gave Sylvia hours of pleasure. She loved rubbing shoulders with great artists, and her profession often provided her with the opportunity to meet them in their natural surroundings. In fact, she enjoyed every assignment given her by the photographic agency. It was convenient for her and her case officer that she was employed as a freelancer, as it meant that she was always available for assignments from the Special Operations Unit.

She brought the films of Yves Montand's performance in a taxi to the offices of the Dalmas Photographic Agency, where they would be developed and distributed to major French and European newspapers. She got back to her apartment after midnight.

The phone rang before she even managed to make herself a cup of coffee. David, her case officer, was on the line.

"I'm sorry to tell you that your sister has been hurt in an accident," he said, carefully sticking to the message code. "The situation is critical, and I suggest that you remain in Paris for the time being. Something is liable to happen in the next few hours."

"Is her situation that critical?" she asked.

"Yes, Patricia. Perhaps we'll pay her a visit tomorrow."

She put down the receiver and felt her heart beating in her chest. The meaning of the code was clear: the Special Operations Unit had an assignment for her. When David said that the next day they would go visit her injured sister, it meant that very soon Patricia would know exactly what the assignment was. What came immediately to mind was Black September.

Sylvia was no less excited now than she had been when she was sent to eliminate a terrorist leader in an Arab country. Now, as then, she lay awake all night. The new assignment aroused her curiosity and her enthusiasm. It was easy to imagine that the target would be a senior terrorist, but which one? And where would the operation take place? Would she yet again be sent behind enemy lines, or would the operation take place in Europe?

The Special Operations Unit of the Mossad is organized for action in both enemy countries and friendly ones. Their major goal is to attack terrorists wherever they may be found. Each operation demands careful planning and a basic assessment of the situation. Intelligence information is gathered and analyzed, on the basis of which decisions are made. Teams of well-trained experts determine the most effective and safest means of approaching the target, the operational procedure, and the escape routes to be followed after the mission is completed. The possibility that the mission will fail is also taken into consideration; thus decisions are made in advance regarding what should be done in case of arrest and diplomatic complications. Such precautions proved to be unnecessary in regard to Sylvia Rafael's new assignment.

Early the next morning, Sylvia met with David and was briefed for the mission. She was to travel to Rome immediately and join a team that was attempting to locate Aadel Zuitar. He was described to her as a forty-five-year-old native of Nablus, a graduate in literature and philosophy from Baghdad University, and a resident of Libya who had immigrated to Rome. He was fluent in English, French, and Italian and was a translator of books from Arabic to Italian. He had an apartment near the Piazza Annabelliano in Rome but was accustomed to spending most of his time in the homes of his numerous female friends. She carefully studied a photograph of Zuitar sitting on a park bench reading a book.

On the night train from Paris, Sylvia didn't feel the least bit tired. She stared at the towns passing by in the dark, thinking about her lover, Hans Rauch, and their last meeting, remembering that they had eaten the dinner that Hans had prepared and had shared an excellent bottle of wine. She didn't tell him that in the next few days she would be traveling to Rome, since he might start asking questions that she couldn't answer. Sylvia only mentioned in passing that she would be busy the following day. She knew that as long as she was involved in the present mission, she wouldn't be able to make contact with her lover. She wondered how he would react when he discovered that she had disappeared and thought about how she would explain her absence when she returned to Paris.

When she didn't succeed in falling asleep, she went out to roam around the train. A young couple was drowsing in one of the compartments, the woman's head on the man's shoulder, a faint smile on her lips. The young woman looked as if she had nothing to conceal. Unlike me, thought Sylvia.

On the platform of Rome Central Station, a man from the Special Operations Unit who had arrived in Rome the previous day was waiting for Sylvia. As previously agreed, she identified him by the tie he was wearing, which was blue and decorated with stars. He shook her hand briefly and led her to a waiting car that he had hired from Avis. During the journey, they synchronized their cover stories; then he handed her a simple gray women's handbag. Inside it a camera had been installed that was meant to take photographs through a hidden opening in the bag. Sylvia was familiar with such operational tactics.

In the interest of security, the car stopped a short distance from the hotel where Sylvia had reserved a room under the name of Patricia Roxenburg. She put her bags in the room and rejoined the combatant who was waiting for her below. After a short journey through the streets of Rome, her companion pointed out a large gray building. "That's the Libyan Embassy," he said.

That same day, in Beirut, Ali Hassan Salameh received a message from Aadel Zuitar. "I was interrogated by the police, but they found nothing," Zuitar wrote. "I'm ready for the next mission."

Ali had big plans for his man in Rome but had decided to put them on hold for the moment. He was worried that, despite Aadel's release due to lack of evidence, the Italian police might still be trailing him and, even worse, the Mossad might be taking an interest in him. Ali's answering telegram contained a few words only: "Daddy's looking for a new flat." The coded message meant: "Get out of your present apartment, find another place to live, and go underground until further notice."

Sylvia took the bag containing the hidden camera, bought a sandwich, and sat down to eat it on a public park bench, from which she could easily observe the entrance to the embassy. Her partner was not far away, guarding her from among the bushes.

Other people sitting on benches nearby were scattering bread crumbs for the pigeons, so Sylvia did the same, while checking to see whether the man she had been sent to photograph was leaving the embassy. She finally spotted him that afternoon emerging from the building holding some books. She photographed him with her hidden camera and began following him. Aadel Zuitar went by bus to the offices of the Petrinelli Publishing Company, stayed there for a while, and afterward bought some food items at a grocery and paid a visit to a woman with whom he had intimate relations. Sylvia and her partner were parked in their rental car not far from her building, pretending to be a loving couple.

Meanwhile, a messenger arrived at Aadel's flat to deliver Ali's telegram. Since he didn't find him at home, he left a message on the door and went off to deliver additional telegrams.

An hour later, Zuitar left his girlfriend's house. Sylvia and her partner followed him in their car. He got onto a bus, got off at a stop near his flat, and walked at a leisurely pace toward home. It was 10:30 at night. Two trained clandestine combatants of the Special Operations Unit were waiting in a nearby alley. They saw the lights of the hired car go on and off twice. That was the sign to go into action.

Aadel Zuitar removed his door key from his pocket and walked toward the elevator. He didn't manage to reach it. The two combatants aimed Biretta 0.22 handguns equipped with silencers at him, shot him twelve times, and fled.

Zuitar was the first senior terrorist to be eliminated after the Munich massacre. Many others had already been targeted.

The ability to lie without blinking an eye, to stick to a cover story and a false identity while being totally truthful to one's case officer—these are vital characteristics of clandestine combatants of the Special Operations Unit. The truth can at times place them in grave danger.

Lying had become an integral part of Sylvia's nature. The Mossad instructors had taught her how to hide the truth effortlessly, but it was a different story when she was obliged to lie to the man she loved, the person who was closer to her than any other. Like other combatants in a similar situation, she was faced with a dilemma: who should be lied to and who should be told the truth? How was it possible to lie to those one loved? How could one tolerate a situation where the heart longed to reveal everything, but reason forbade it?

Immediately upon her return from Rome, Sylvia knocked on Hans Rauch's door. They had not seen each other for a few days, and he asked the one question she was dreading: "Where were you?"

"Working," she said quietly. It wasn't a lie.

"Couldn't you call me?"

"I wasn't near a phone." That also wasn't far from the truth.

He studied her carefully, and she felt as though she were being interrogated.

"You're a very mysterious woman, Patricia," he said. "Has it occurred to you that I know nothing about you?"

"I haven't got such deep secrets," she answered. That was a lie. Her entire past life and true identity were exactly that: a closely guarded secret.

He invited her out for dinner. During their conversation, she asked him, "What did you do while I was away?"

"I loafed around, went for walks, drank wine."

"Did you look for work?"

"I tried to, but nothing came of it."

She felt distressed all through the meal by the thought that she would have to continue hiding the truth from him.

When they returned to his apartment, she finally dared apologize: "I'm sorry, Hans. I must go back to work very soon, and I'll probably be away for a few days."

He was again surprised.

"Where will you disappear to this time?"

"Dalmas is preparing to send me on an assignment."

"Where to, exactly?"

"It's a secret."

He wasn't convinced.

"I didn't know that the Dalmas Agency had secret assignments."

"They asked me not to discuss it with anyone."

"That's strange—I don't understand."

"Drop it, Hans. I have nothing to add."

Rather than continuing to lie to him, Sylvia left Hans's apartment and went roaming around the Paris streets. It was a clear summer night. Crowds of tourists were being photographed near the Arc de Triomphe and sitting in cafés along the Boulevard de Champs Elysees. She saw smiling faces, heard cries of amazement from people on their first trip to Paris. It seemed as though she was the only one with a heavy heart, a mind in turmoil. Her lover haunted her thoughts. She was worried that if he didn't manage to find work soon, he might seek his fortune elsewhere, far away from her. The enforced distance between them, and the fact that she would often have to disappear from his life on urgent missions, guaranteed that their relationship would suffer, might even come to an end. She could of course quit the Special Operations Unit in order to be with him—this was not the first time such a thought had crossed her mind—but she knew that the timing was terrible. Activities in Europe were at fever pitch, and Sylvia was a significant part of it all. She was experienced and able, and she had won the unconditional admiration of her superiors. They had provided her with the most exciting years of her life and had made it possible for her to realize her potential, her ambitions, and her dreams. It would be unfair to abandon them now. And what exactly would she do if she quit? Almost anything else would seem insignificant compared to her work for the Mossad, and far less satisfying. Still, quitting had its advantages. She would have Hans at her side. She would live with him, marry him, bring children into the world. She wanted Hans to be the father of her children. It would be so painful to give him up now.

She sat in deep reverie on an iron bench under a weeping willow tree whose branches hung down like long braids of hair. She returned to her apartment after midnight and called her case officer, despite the late hour.

"I must meet with you," she said.

He arranged a time and place to meet her the next morning.

"What's happened?" he asked in alarm when they met.

She told him about her conversation with Hans.

"Tell me about your relationship with him," he said. "Is it serious?"

"Very. I love him and he loves me. I don't want to lose him, or give up the Mossad because of him. My relationship with him is important to me, but I also love my work. I can't lie to him any longer. What do you think about recruiting him to the Special Operations Unit?"

"I don't know what to say," David replied. "I'll talk to my superiors."

The commanders of the Special Operations Unit found Sylvia's suggestion surprising, and it was the first time they had had to deal with such a situation. Furthermore, as a result of the Lavon Affair of 1954, in which a group of Egyptian Jews who were active Israeli intelligence agents were imprisoned for years, with two members of the group executed by the Egyptian authorities, the decision had been made not to recruit or employ combatants who knew each other. But they respected Sylvia and needed her now more than ever. The siege on Arab terrorist leaders was at a critical stage. Her accomplishments spoke for themselves and held the promise of much greater achievements in the future. They knew that Hans was liable to break off the relationship if he discovered that Sylvia had been lying to him. This would cause a major crisis in her life, and there was no way of knowing how long it would take her to overcome it. They found themselves facing a serious dilemma.

On the surface, the idea of recruiting Hans Rauch to the Special Operations Unit seemed ridiculous, but the more they turned it over in their minds, the more they came to realize that it did have its positive side. After all, Hans had already unknowingly passed all the security checks and had been found to be spotless. His acceptance into the Mossad, especially into the Special Operations Unit, would certainly strengthen his ties with Sylvia. He would finally know the truth, and she could continue to serve them free of the shadow hanging over her.

When David informed Sylvia that the Special Operations Unit commanders had theoretically approved her idea, she was amazed; she hadn't believed that this could really happen.

"You can't imagine how happy this makes me," she finally said. "I know that it wasn't an easy decision, and I'm aware of the possible dangers. That's why I so appreciate what you have done. I'll never forget it."

"We just wanted to make it clear to you how important you are to us."

Sylvia was near tears.

"This is the greatest thing that anyone has ever done for me," she whispered.

David and Sylvia had a lengthy discussion about how to break the news to Hans.

"Don't mention the Mossad. Only tell him that you know people who run a company that collects different types of information. Tell him that the company has connections with Israel and that they are looking for European representatives and might be interested in him. We'll put him through a series of tests, and if he passes them successfully, he'll be informed about the true nature of the work. At that stage, he will also be told that you work for the Mossad, but that there is a very slight possibility that you will both be assigned to the same location."

"That shouldn't be a problem."

That same day Sylvia presented the suggestion to Hans. He listened attentively and asked for additional details about the company and the kind of work they were offering. Sylvia said that she had no idea. She hoped that it was the last lie she would ever have to tell him.

After he met with representatives of the unit in Paris, Hans Rauch was invited to undergo tests in Israel. He was informed that he was being offered a secret assignment and consequently had to arrive in Israel under a false identity. He was handed an Israeli passport bearing a fictitious name. The security officers at Orly Airport in Paris let him onto the plane after having received orders not to detain him.

At Ben Gurion Airport he was collected by a man he had never met and taken to an apartment on Bloch Street in Tel Aviv. That evening he was taken out to dinner and on a sightseeing tour of Tel Aviv and Jaffa at night. Hans took in the sights and studied the people carefully, trying to understand what it was about this country that touched the hearts of so many people.

The next day Hans was driven to a small office in the center of town in order to undergo some tests. In the room were two English-speaking functionaries from the Special Operations Unit and an independent psychologist. They shook his hand and told him that the tests would continue for a few days, and only upon their completion would they be able to discuss employment opportunities. During the days remaining until the tests were set to begin, Hans was taken on sightseeing tours of Jerusalem and the Golan Heights.

For three days, from early in the morning until late at night, Hans underwent exhaustive tests and interviews to determine whether he was suitable for the job. He was interviewed in English about his childhood and his relationship with his family. He was asked to offer solutions to complex situations and to answer questions that tested his degree of self-confidence and his ability to cope with stress, make an impression, and adjust to unfamiliar social situations. He was also interviewed about his relationship with Sylvia.

At the height of the tests, Hans commented with a smile, "I've had several job interviews in my life, but I've never been put through anything like this. Don't you think you're exaggerating?"

"That's how we operate," replied one of the team members shortly. "Thanks to tests like these, we hardly ever hire unsuitable candidates."

When the tests were completed, the team met to make a decision about Hans Rauch. The majority were favorably impressed. It was finally decided to recruit Hans to the Special Operations Unit, train him, and infiltrate him into a port city in an Arab country. A cover story would be devised for him that would allow him to perform the tasks assigned to him without arousing suspicion.

After undergoing training in Israel for undercover work, he was informed of his acceptance to the unit. Only then did Hans finally realize which organization had recruited him, and only then was he informed that Sylvia was serving in the same unit.

He smiled.

"I had my suspicions," he told Sylvia later, "but I had no proof."

It was decided to send Hans to an enemy country disguised as the agent of a European import-export company. His assignment was to provide information about army movements, security installations, and terrorist activity in a major port city.

He returned to Paris and told Sylvia about his being accepted for the job. She wasn't allowed to know anything about his planned destination, and although he didn't say so, she understood that they would now be separated by a great distance. Of course she would have preferred him to be stationed in Europe, but obviously his assignments would be dictated by the needs of the Mossad.

Sylvia and Hans met almost every day, gathering sweet memories to take with them when they were apart. They strolled hand in hand through the park, ate in restaurants, visited exhibitions, and bought one another small parting gifts.

Ostensibly, the private life of a Mossad operative doesn't necessarily influence his or her work, but in reality this is not the case. The constant switch between leading a normal life and being involved in missions under conditions that are anything but normal can only be withstood by the very determined. It is difficult to devote attention to spouse or family when you are obliged to be totally immersed in a faraway, sometimes life-threatening, mission. The fear that you will lose your life or be arrested or kidnapped hangs over your loved ones like a menacing shadow, even if they have no idea where you are or what you are doing. It is not rare for families to break apart in such circumstances.

The last meeting between Sylvia and Hans was emotionally charged. He brought her a bouquet of flowers and spent the night in her apartment. In the morning, they found it hard to say good-bye and looked for excuses to stay together a little longer. As Sylvia prepared breakfast, Hans said, "When it's all over and we are together again, it will be my turn to fix breakfast." Sylvia accompanied him to the Metro station, and they embraced for a long time on the steps leading down to the platform.

At first Sylvia had hopes that Hans would contact her, but it soon became clear that this was not to be. It was of course out of the question to use the phone or correspond. Months passed, and Hans knew nothing about Sylvia, nor did she receive a sign of life from him.

Disappointed and lonely, Sylvia felt as though she were facing a blank wall and that nothing could be done about it. It was clear to her that her lover had entered a cul-de-sac, and this was shaking her foundations and clouding her future. There were days when her longing for Hans was unbearable, but there were others when he didn't even enter her thoughts. As time passed, what was bound to happen in such circumstances really did occur. Hans was busy acclimatizing himself to a new country and making an effort to win credibility. Sylvia found herself drawing away from him more and more, being deeply involved in her work and in the new missions that were assigned to her. She knew a long time would pass before they met again. When that finally happened, would they be able to reignite their passion?

She had nothing to complain about regarding the Mossad. Quite the opposite: they had accepted her lover to work for them at her request. They had made it possible for her to tell Hans the truth about her job, believing that by doing so, they would strengthen her commitment to the organization. But the outcome was quite different. Hans's image was fading quickly from her memory, and she missed him less and less.

Her case officer later informed her that Hans would soon be transferred to another assignment in an even more distant country. Sylvia received this information indifferently, only asking for further details out of politeness.

"What's happened to your enthusiasm?" asked David with a smile.

"It seems to have evaporated."

"Do you have any regrets?"

"I regret that I might have missed the opportunity to raise a family."

"Never mind. I'm sure that you'll still find the right one."

"Don't forget that I'm almost forty. Chances are that I'll end my life without a man at my side."

That was one of the rare occasions when Sylvia was totally mistaken.

"Do you remember this person?" asked David. He showed her a photograph of a man in his fifties.

The man in the photo looked familiar, but Sylvia didn't remember where she knew him from.

"He was at the opening of your exhibition at the Ritz," her case officer reminded her.

Then she remembered. She had submitted the calling card handed her by Dr. Mahmoud Hamshari to the Special Operations Unit, together with the cards of other prominent Arabs who had attended the exhibition.

"What about him?" she asked.

"Today he is one of the key Black September activists in Europe. Officially he's a history lecturer and acts as the Fatah representative in Paris. In reality he is in constant contact with Ali Salameh, organizes the smuggling of arms and ammunition to Black September operatives in Europe, and coordinates terrorist operations. We know that he was involved in blowing up the Swissair plane from

Zurich to Tel Aviv in 1970, which resulted in the deaths of forty-seven passengers and crew. Hamshari was apparently also involved in the attempt on Ben-Gurion's life during the prime minister's visit to Copenhagen in 1969. As if that wasn't enough, we also know that he is stockpiling weapons in his Paris apartment."

"Let me guess: he's on our hit list."

"Exactly."

"What's my part in the mission?"

"We're hoping that Hamshari remembers you from the exhibition. If he doesn't, remind him that you work for the French press. Offer to interview and photograph him. All you need to do is make an appointment to meet him outside his apartment and spend two hours with him."

"Is he married?"

"His wife is a Frenchwoman named Marie Claude, and they have a daughter. His wife goes to work every morning, and his daughter goes to school. His apartment is empty until noon, so we should be able to break in then."

"What do I tell him if he asks what newspaper I work for?"

"Tell him that you work for the Dalmas Agency, which acts as a distributor that will sell the interview to various papers."

David handed Sylvia an issue of *Jeune Afrique* that had appeared a year earlier, in which Hamshari was interviewed by the journal's editor, Bashir Ibn Yahmad. Sylvia knew enough French to read the article in the original. In the interview, Hamshari spoke about the Palestinians' right to rule their own country, criticized Israel's attitude toward the Arabs, and expressed the opinion that if the Arab world were united against Israel, a Palestinian state would have been established long ago. In the article Hamshari denied any connection with terrorist organizations.

"Okay," said Sylvia, putting down the article. "When should the interview take place?"

"Phone him today. Make an appointment to meet him either tomorrow morning or the day after, and let me know what you've arranged, when, and where."

"Excellent."

A deep voice answered Sylvia's call, and she introduced herself. Hamshari remembered her.

"What are you working on these days?" he asked. "Are you planning a new exhibition?"

"Certainly."

"What will it be about?"

"Portraits, mainly. I've been to Jordan. I photographed dozens of interesting characters."

"I'll be glad to receive an invitation."

"I won't forget to send you one."

She asked how he was and what he was doing.

"I'm very well," he replied, "lecturing, writing . . ."

Sylvia suggested interviewing him.

"On what topic?"

"About your academic work and your political opinions."

"I've already been interviewed by *Jeune Afrique*."

She had assumed that he would mention that.

"But that was a year ago, sir," she responded promptly. "Since then there have been so many developments in the world in general, and in the Arab world in particular. Your opinion is highly valued."

"Really?"

"Really."

"You've convinced me."

They arranged to meet the next morning, December 8, 1972, at a café on the ground floor of Hamshari's apartment building at 175 Elysees Avenue.

"I'm meeting him at ten in the morning," Sylvia informed her case officer.

"We'll be ready," said David.

Hamshari arrived exactly on time. When he entered the café, he took a quick look around. There were only a few customers, and none of them looked suspicious, not even the well-dressed gentleman reading a copy of *Le Monde*—who was in fact a member of the Special Operations Unit, sent to guard Sylvia.

Hamshari made his way to a table at the back of the café, where Sylvia was waiting for him, and planted a polite kiss on both her cheeks.

"You look wonderful," he complimented her. "How do you do it?"

They ordered coffee, and the interview began. Sylvia asked for Hamshari's forecast regarding developments in the Arab world, the influence of terrorist organizations on Arab countries and the world in general, about his career and his family. Hamshari answered eloquently, in clear, concise sentences. He expressed anger at Arab leaders who did not give enough support to the Palestinian cause. He advocated the Arab refugees' right of return and declared that the struggle against Israel would continue until the Palestinians achieved all their objectives. Most of his answers were what Sylvia would have expected, but she continued questioning him. She had been instructed to keep her interviewee with her for a specific length of time, and her endless questions were meant to ensure that she would succeed in doing this. She wrote down every word Hamshari said in her notebook, photographed him, and promised to send him a copy of every newspaper that published the interview. They parted at 12:15. "Don't forget to quote me word for word," was his last request.

Sylvia walked quickly through the narrow streets leading away from the café. The sky was gray, and the pedestrians hurrying by didn't pay any attention to her. She felt pleased. She had succeeded in keeping Hamshari away from his apartment without arousing suspicion. Although she knew what fate awaited him, it didn't distress her. He was a criminal who had done unforgivable things. It was inevitable for him to be punished.

When she was sure that nobody was following her, she took a cab to the Dalmas Agency. Dr. Mahmoud Hamshari went up to his apartment. His wife and daughter weren't home yet. He sat down at his desk. The telephone rang. He picked up the receiver, detonating an explosive device that had been planted at its base while he was being interviewed by Sylvia in the café.

Hamshari was seriously wounded and died shortly afterward in the hospital.

The strenuous, dangerous work, the frazzled nerves, the need to constantly take safety precautions, and the eternal loneliness—all of these were taking their toll on Sylvia. She felt as though her patience was running out, as though her work was no longer giving her a sense of satisfaction. Almost every night she awoke with nightmares, and she suffered from chronic stomach trouble.

"I don't know what's happening to me," she confessed to David. He smiled.

"You simply need a vacation," he said.

Frequently, after a period of intense, exhausting activity, combatants are sent on vacation to Israel. David, Sylvia's case officer, thought she was working too hard and that a trouble-free vacation would renew her depleted energies. He recommended this to the commanders of the Special Operations Unit, and they gave their approval. Sylvia also suggested that Hans be allowed a vacation at the same time, so that he could join her, perhaps allowing them to bridge the gap between them. Unfortunately, he was embroiled in a complex mission in the country where he was stationed, so there was no possibility of this happening.

Sylvia was given an Israeli passport. In order to ensure that nobody was following her, she took a train from Paris to Brussels, wandered around that city for several hours, and only then boarded a plane for Israel. Upon her arrival, she was astonished by what she saw. In the years that had passed since she had been sent abroad by the Mossad, new neighborhoods had sprung up, parks had appeared everywhere, and broad highways had been constructed.

A small, furnished apartment had been rented for her in Tel Aviv opposite the promenade that stretched along the coast connecting Tel Aviv and Jaffa. She enjoyed sitting on her balcony facing the Mediterranean and watching the fishing boats passing by on the turquoise waters. Early every morning, she went down to the sea and swam for hours.

She took trips all over the country and wrote long letters to her family in South Africa, telling them that she was happy working for the company, which had offices in many foreign countries. She also visited the family that had adopted her in Kibbutz Gan Shmuel, painted landscapes in oils and watercolors, and managed to put her other identity on hold for the time being.

Part of Sylvia's vacation was devoted to meeting with her commanders. She was updated regarding the relentless pursuit of terrorist leaders, especially Ali Hassan Salameh, and was introduced to new intelligence techniques. She beamed with pleasure at being complimented on the fine work she was doing. The director of the Mossad himself shook her hand and wished her similar successes in the future.

The commanders of the operational unit spoiled her from the moment she landed in Israel and did their best to make her vacation memorable. They took her on trips and invited her out to restaurants. One of them invited her to join him at a philharmonic concert and at an exhibition at the Tel Aviv Museum of Art. She told old friends that she met about her job with a large commercial firm in

Europe, her generous salary, and her plans to return to Israel after her contract expired. None of them knew how far this was from the truth.

During her vacation, Sylvia made contact with Abraham Gemer, who after his return from Paris had assumed a senior post in the operational unit. For the first time, she learned the true identity of the man who had been her first case officer. She was invited to visit his home and meet his wife, Dina. Abraham told her that he had begun law studies at Tel Aviv University parallel to working for the Mossad.

"I've always dreamed of studying psychology," Sylvia said, "but I don't think I'll be able to do so in the near future."

By the time her vacation ended and she parted from her friends, she was filled with renewed energy and couldn't wait to get back into action. She had begun to miss the adrenalin rush of suspense and danger that were an integral part of her secret life.

Sylvia flew back to Brussels and boarded a train to Paris. David was waiting for her at the Gare du Nord.

"What's going on?" she asked.

"I haven't had time to breathe," he replied.

"A lot of work?"

"Tons."

"Anything for me?"

"Especially for you."

The Mossad's struggle with Black September was tough and brutal, but as 1972 drew to a close, the Israelis were gaining the upper hand. Ali Salameh was still at large, but several junior officers of his organization had been eliminated. In the months since undercover Israeli combatants had launched their antiterror operations, not a single Mossad combatant had been killed. Black September had lost almost a dozen.

Yasser Arafat was sunk in deep depression. He summoned Ali Salameh and demanded that he step up operations, stage a spectacular terrorist attack on the scale of the Munich massacre, and put as many Mossad agents out of action as possible. Ali hung his head in shame and embarrassment. Even though he wasn't really being openly rebuked, it was clear that Arafat meant to do just that. Suddenly the paternal, understanding leader had been replaced by the tough Fatah boss demanding results.

"You can rely on me," said Ali in his own defense. "I will still surprise you."

He returned to his office in a despondent mood. Somehow, the Mossad had taken the initiative and was delivering a death blow to his organization. Ali knew that he must gather all his strength in order to turn the situation around and win back Arafat's favor and the respect of his men.

Just then, one of his henchmen burst into the room.

"They got al-Hir!" he shouted.

Ali's eyes opened wide in amazement. This was not what he needed at that moment.

Hussein al-Hir, the organization's representative in Cyprus, had maintained strong ties in Nicosia with East German intelligence. Terrorists passed through Nicosia on their way to training camps in East Germany, and arms, ammunition, and explosives were conveyed from East Germany through Nicosia into the hands of Black September. Ali had considered al-Hir to be one of his key operatives.

"How was he killed?" asked Ali.

"He dined with a friend from the Soviet Embassy, then returned to his hotel. At one in the morning, he went to bed. Shortly afterward, a large explosive charge went off in his room. The ceiling caved in, the room was demolished, and al-Hir died before he managed to call for help."

Ali held his head in his hands and sank into a deep silence. It was obvious to him who was responsible for al-Hir's death. He hoped to be able to strike back before the Mossad launched yet another successful operation.

But he didn't move quite quickly enough.

The next in line was Professor Basil al-Khubaisi. He was a native of Iraq, a lecturer in law at Beirut University, and a veteran expert in terrorist activity. He was forced to escape from Iraq in 1956 after having been involved in an antigovernment terrorist attack. A few years later, with the help of another Iraqi who was smuggled into the United States, Khubaisi dreamed up and planned the assassination of Israeli prime minister Golda Meir during a state visit there. A car bomb that was supposed to blow up next to the prime minister's plane was detected in time by American security officials. FBI investigators mounted a search for the perpetrators of this operation, but never discovered the link with Khubaisi.

Khubaisi moved on to Paris, living in a small hotel near the

Madeleine. He was in the habit of drinking coffee every morning at a nearby café, spending the day at the Sorbonne library, and conducting late-night meetings with Black September activists who arrived from all over Europe to confer with him.

At the conclusion of one of these meetings, Khubaisi was on his way back to his hotel. When he passed by the Madeleine Church, two men blocked his way, shot him nine times, and ran off without leaving a trace.

Ali Salameh received the terrible news the next morning in Beirut. He urgently summoned the organization's high command, but before they managed to convene, more shocking information arrived: al-Hir's second in command was killed in Nicosia. He was killed in his hotel room by a sophisticated bomb that went off after he went to bed.

At this point, Ali Hassan Salameh knew that if he waited any longer, he would be replaced as the head of Black September. Arafat craved a relentless war of attrition, accompanied by numerous retaliatory attacks, and Ali knew that he had to deliver the goods, and the sooner the better. He felt like a boxer whose legs were giving way under him and whose eyes were swollen shut due to his opponent's constant punches; but that didn't mean he was out for the count. The challenges now facing him made him more determined than ever. Despite this temporary slump, he would recover his strength and reign victorious.

Following the murder of the Israeli athletes in Munich and the twenty-four passengers at Ben Gurion Airport, Prime Minister Golda Meir held a series of urgent meetings with the director of the Mossad, Zvi Zamir; the defense minister, Moshe Dayan; and the vice–prime minister, Yigal Allon. The prime minister was concerned about the possibility that additional serious attacks were in the offing against Israelis and Jewish institutions abroad. Her greatest source of worry was Black September, which had already demonstrated its ability to strike extremely sensitive targets. She was well aware that as long as Ali Salameh was in charge, the bloodshed would continue.

As if to confirm her fears, at a meeting in her office in February 1973, the director of the Mossad presented Meir with a newly received secret document. The prime minister paled as she read it. It stated that information-gathering sources in Europe had uncovered a major terrorist plot personally initiated by Ali Salameh himself. According to the plan, a team of Black September activists would hijack an El Al plane in Paris or Vienna, booby-trap it with explosives, force the pilots to fly the plane to Tel Aviv, and blow it up over the heart of the city. The suicide bombers would be chosen from among Arab students who were members of the organization in France and Austria.

"Can this plan actually be carried out?" demanded the security minister.

"It would have been possible in the past, but now it's unlikely," answered Zamir.

"Is there still a chance that it will succeed?"

"There's always a chance."

Golda Meir had other things to worry about, too. Black September had finally succeeded in murdering a Mossad clandestine combatant in Europe in retaliation for eliminating its men. His name was Baruch Cohen, and he had been stationed in Spain under the fictitious name of Moshe Cohen Yishai. Cohen had run a network of Palestinian agents, who supplied him with information about the activities of Arab terrorist organizations in the area. When Salameh learned of this network, he sent a double agent to infiltrate it and supply Cohen with false information. Cohen's name topped the list of Mossad combatants that Ali most wanted to get rid of.

On a cold winter's morning, Cohen was sitting at the back of a Madrid café, deep in conversation with the double agent. He didn't suspect that he had walked into a trap. When he left the café at around eleven o'clock, two men approached him, shot him three times in the chest with revolvers equipped with silencers, got into a car with fake license plates, and drove away before the ambulance and the police arrived. Baruch Cohen died before he could receive medical treatment.

"Gentlemen," said the Israeli prime minister in a firm voice, "this cannot be allowed to continue. It is imperative to stop Ali Salameh before disaster strikes again."

"In our estimation," said the Mossad chief, "we are getting closer to him than ever before. We have eliminated most of his key men in Europe. The organization's cells in Paris and Rome are in chaos, and despite Salameh's intentions, no new ones have been established during the past year—"

"What does that tell us?" Golda Meir interrupted.

"It tells us that Ali Salameh will probably be leaving Beirut very soon in order to fortify his organization's European presence. We're keeping a watchful eye and planning toward such a possibility."

He told the prime minister that Ali's code name in the Mossad was the "Red Prince," because his hands were covered with blood.

"A suitable choice," replied the prime minister.

Apart from his telephone number and the fact that he spoke perfect French, Sylvia knew nothing about her case officer, David. She had no idea whether he was a native-born Israeli or how many years he had been serving in the Mossad. She didn't know his address or if he was married or had children. She had never asked him for any details about his private life because she knew that she wasn't going to get any.

The relationship between case officer and combatant is based on mutual trust and personal closeness, on understanding and rapport. It is, however, complicated by the fact that the case officer knows everything about the combatant, whereas for security reasons the combatant knows absolutely nothing about the case officer.

Sylvia wasn't personally acquainted with any of the combatants of the Operational Unit in Europe. Even when they worked together in the same team, she didn't know their real names, nor did they know hers, apart from the one she used as part of her cover story.

On a few occasions she had observed hit teams in action, but they usually performed their task under cover of darkness, so it was impossible to identify them. The ones she had seen performed their mission with consummate skill and drove off in their getaway cars as though they were professional racing drivers. As far as she knew, none of them had ever been caught by the security forces of the countries where they served. She was proud of the fact that, with her help, they managed to reach the right people at the right place and the right time. She assumed that in unexpected circumstances, if reinforcements arrived or there was unexpected resistance that would endanger the operation, she might have to join them in their escape and help them cover their tracks. She had been trained in the use of weapons and was confident that she would be capable of driving quickly through winding streets and of escaping to safety if the need arose.

Although at first it had seemed difficult or nearly impossible, living with a double identity became part of Sylvia's daily routine.

She spent her spare time improving her French, reading, painting, and visiting museums and small art cinemas that screened high-quality films. Her neighbors were accustomed to seeing her carrying a baguette under her arm every morning from the local *boulangerie*, like a Frenchwoman born and bred. She always went out with a sophisticated camera slung over her shoulder. Her correspondence with her parents was conducted by registered mail at one of the post offices in the city. The concierge, who lived in a flat on the ground floor, took pride in knowing everything about the tenants of the building. She was well aware that the pretty lady on the third floor never brought a man home to her flat and sometimes left with a small suitcase and was absent for days at a time. When she once asked Sylvia where she went so often, the tenant answered briefly, "To take photographs."

Sylvia always took care to avoid any encounters with Israelis or South Africans, for fear of bumping into someone who might recognize her. She generally spent evenings in her flat, cooking for herself, drinking the wine she loved, or editing the Dalmas employees' satirical newsletter, which had been her idea and which included humorous caricatures that were her handiwork. She bought numerous photograph albums, which filled her bookshelves. At the flea market she bought flowered drapes and hung them over the windows of the flat, serving partially to hide the apartments facing hers in the next building. On her days off, she would set up her artist's easel near the Seine and paint views of the river.

She received a modest salary and expenses according to monthly reports she submitted to the Mossad. Most of her money was spent on essentials and on secondhand art books that she bought from the stalls along the Seine. She didn't buy expensive clothes at fashionable boutiques or go to beauty salons, and she kept in physical shape by taking long walks around Paris.

She didn't worry about being exposed, because by now she was certain that her cover story was airtight; but whenever she left her flat, she still made sure she wasn't being followed. This was a basic security measure that became second nature to every clandestine combatant of the Special Operations Unit.

The winter of 1973 gradually came to an end, and spring arrived. The first green buds appeared on the naked branches of the trees on the Parisian boulevards, people began leaving their coats at home, and young couples could be seen embracing on the benches by the river.

At times Sylvia felt a twinge of nostalgia when she thought about her lover, Hans. She longed to experience the coming of spring with him and stroll through the streets of Paris arm in arm, but she somehow managed to pull herself together. Hans had become a distant memory, and she felt destined to go through life without him.

Easter in Paris was supposed to be a time of enjoyment and relaxation. Although she was usually careful not to develop close personal ties, Sylvia accepted an invitation to dine with the family of one of her work colleagues. The Dalmas Agency hadn't given her any new assignments over the holiday and she hadn't heard from David for a few days, so she assumed that he had nothing for her at that moment. She drank coffee in the small kitchen of her flat and decided to spend the day visiting the Louvre. The telephone rang before she managed to leave the flat, and her case officer was on the line. "I must meet with you immediately," he said.

She hurried to the designated meeting place, assuming that she would again be asked to participate in locating a wanted terrorist. She hoped it would be interesting.

David received her with a smile.

"Guess where we're sending you," he said.

"To sunbathe on the Riviera," she smiled.

"Guess again."

For the first time she saw his eyes shine. David's gaze was generally cold and businesslike when he gave her assignments.

"Enough! Don't keep me in suspense any longer."

"Salameh," he said almost in a whisper.

"Really? Are you serious?"

"Absolutely."

At last the moment she had been waiting for had arrived.

"You see," he said, "I took your request seriously."

"Wonderful!"

"You'll need to leave immediately."

"Where to?"

"Beirut."

He continued, "I'm not allowed to give you more details as yet about the operation itself, but it looks as though it's going to be a really large-scale one. You will be arriving in Beirut as a news photographer. Make a reservation today at the Sands Hotel on the Corniche, the Beirut promenade along the seacoast. After you settle in at the hotel, rent a car that can hold five or six passengers in addition to the driver. At ten o'clock in the evening go down to the bar. Someone will introduce himself as James Morgan of London. Be nice to him—he's one of our clandestine combatants. The next day you will go out on a tour of Beirut. Together with other combatants, you will trail leaders of terrorist organizations, including Yasser Arafat, Ali Salameh, and George Habash, who are scheduled to meet in Beirut during the next few days in order to expand operations against Israel. Some of them are staying in a house on Verdun Street, and Salameh also lives on that street. You will receive further instructions from James Morgan. Take into account that Beirut has two faces, one visible to the naked eye and the other hidden beneath the surface. Lebanon is currently being ruled by two governments: an official one in Beirut and a Palestinian terrorist government, which is gaining power and influence. It is imperative for us to obtain detailed information about these terrorist leaders."

David instructed Sylvia to arrange an entry visa into Lebanon and buy an airline ticket to Beirut. She did so immediately. Two days later, she boarded an Air France 3:30 p.m. flight to Beirut. Her Canadian passport, in the name of Patricia Roxenburg, was valid and stamped with an entry visa to Lebanon. There was no reason why anyone would prevent her from entering the country.

She arranged to take a leave of absence from the Dalmas Agency and rushed back to her apartment to pack. At 1:30 in the afternoon, she took her small suitcase, went out into the street, and hailed a cab. While standing on the pavement, she was attacked by severe stomach pains. She ignored them and instructed the driver who had stopped for her to take her to the airport; but in the course of the journey, her condition worsened, and she lost consciousness. The driver rushed Sylvia to the hospital, where it turned out that she was suffering from a severe appendicitis attack. "We'll have to operate immediately," the surgeon told her. She begged him to delay the operation, because she had to get on a plane very shortly. He regarded her dolefully.

"I very much doubt, madame, that you will be able to fly today, tomorrow, or the next day. If we don't operate immediately, your condition will become critical."

The hospital clerk wrote down her health insurance particulars.

Sylvia asked that a telephone be brought to her. She phoned David and told him what had happened.

He quickly dispatched another surgeon to give a second opinion. Later on, when visiting her in the hospital, he was informed by both surgeons that there was no choice but to operate and that it would take a full week for her to recuperate fully.

He wished her a speedy recovery.

Sylvia turned her head away from him and cried into her pillow as she was wheeled off to the operating room.

6

A Man in Women's Clothing

After Sylvia was hospitalized, another combatant from the Special Operations Unit was recruited to take her place. He arrived in Beirut on April 4, 1973. On that same day, he was joined by five more combatants from the Special Operations Unit. They arrived on separate flights from various European locations and rented cars from Avis and Hertz at the airport. They booked into three different hotels on the Beirut promenade, where rooms had been reserved for them by European travel agencies. Along with the combatant who had taken Sylvia's place, they left their luggage in their rooms and set out to reconnoiter the roads in the area in order to determine possible access routes to residential areas and beaches.

Five days remained until the operation was to take place. The six clandestine combatants continued circling the streets of Beirut and observing what was going on in two buildings, one on Madame Curie Street and the other on Verdun Street. The first building housed representatives of the Popular Front for the Liberation of Palestine (PFLP); the second, operatives of Black September. By means of coded broadcasts, the six Mossad combatants transmitted detailed reports about the structure of the buildings and their security systems.

Back in Israel, the commanders of the General Staff Reconnaissance Unit carefully studied the details of the buildings on Curie and Verdun Streets and looked for a residential neighborhood that closely resembled the one where the terrorist leaders were living. They found one in north Tel Aviv, and in the days that followed the commandos staged practice nocturnal attacks on the neighborhood. They told the startled tenants that there was no cause for alarm: they were simply practicing army maneuvers in built-up areas.

On April 9, four Israeli Navy missile boats sailed from Haifa to the coast of Beirut. On their decks were about forty commandos of the General Staff Reconnaissance Unit and paratroopers, all equipped with arms and explosives. They were all dressed as civilians; some wore wigs. One of them, Ehud Barak, who was later to become the chief of staff of the Israeli Army and subsequently prime minister of Israel, was disguised as a woman.

Shortly after midnight, the missile boats put down anchor off the coast of Beirut, opposite Dove Beach, and motorized rubber boats transported the soldiers to shore. On the road bordering the seacoast, six cars were waiting that had been hired by the Mossad clandestine combatants.

Without a sound, the soldiers piled into the cars and set out for the city. A short distance from the buildings housing the terrorists, the cars stopped and the soldiers got out. The force split into two. Some of the soldiers ran toward the building on Curie Street, which was accommodating senior officials of the Popular Front for the Liberation of Palestine. The others headed for the building on Verdun Street, where the Black September commanders were staying. All the soldiers had previously been shown photographs of the terrorist leaders who were expected to be in the buildings earmarked for attack. Before setting out for Lebanon, the group that was meant to attack the building on Verdun Street had been given four photographs of the commanders of Black September, including the most wanted terrorist of all, Ali Hassan Salameh. The operation was given the code name "Spring of Youth."

The forces moved quickly and efficiently under cover of darkness. The route had been planned in advance by the Special Operations Unit after preliminary surveillance of the area. As in many other cases, its clandestine combatants had given invaluable assistance to the operational force.

When the soldiers neared the Popular Front's building, two guards posted at the entrance spotted them. The guards were surprised to see a group of civilians approaching and didn't suspect that they were carrying weapons and explosives. Before they realized what was happening, rounds were shot at them at close range, and they were killed instantly.

At that same moment, paratroopers and commandos also attacked the second building. The soldiers went from room to room, surprising the terrorists in their sleep and shooting them. Some of those attacked managed to return fire. Two paratroopers were killed, and some were wounded, but the others continued fighting. Some of the key activists of the two terrorist organizations were killed, including three commanders of Black September. Only one, the most sought-after of all, was spared. Ali Hassan Salameh was spending that night not far away, in a building surrounded by bodyguards. When he heard the gunfire, he assumed that a shooting match had broken out between two warring factions of Fatah.

After intense fighting with additional terrorists who had come to join the gun battle, and an attack on machine shops that were used by Fatah to manufacture weapons, rockets, and underwater mines, the Israeli forces gathered up their wounded, returned to the automobiles waiting for them, and raced to the seashore. Once there the soldiers, along with the six clandestine combatants of the Mossad Special Operations Unit, abandoned the rental vehicles, boarded the rubber boats, and made their way back to the missile boats.

The Israeli Navy vessels immediately raised anchor and returned to the coast of Israel.

Sylvia was amused to read popular spy stories in which female undercover agents were depicted as glamorous temptresses who managed to get heads of state and army generals into bed, intoxicate them with passion, and squeeze vital state secrets out of them. She also smiled to herself when reading about charismatic male spies who formed romantic attachments with their victims. From experience she knew that in reality the secret world was far more humdrum than it might seem to outsiders, and that real spies were never as attractive and good-looking as they were in books. For that reason she was taken by surprise when a short time after her recovery, David showed her a photograph of a tall, handsome, broad-shouldered man who was destined to be her next target.

"Who's this good-looking guy?" she asked, studying the photo of a man who resembled a film idol.

"You've probably never heard of him. His name is Mohammed Budya."

"French? Arab?"

"Algerian."

"Black September?"

"Yes."

"What else do we know about him?"

"Women are crazy about him, and he knows how to recruit them for terrorist operations."

David told her that in April 1971, it became known just before the Passover holiday that Black September was planning a huge terrorist attack in Israel. The plan was that a few men and women who were French nationals would arrive in Tel Aviv on separate flights carrying a new type of explosive that couldn't be detected by airport X-ray machines.

An intelligence source passed on the information to the authorities, resulting in more stringent security searches at airports. Among other suspect items, the luggage of two Parisian girls who had ostensibly arrived in Israel on vacation was carefully checked. A white powder was discovered inside their suitcases and in the hollow heels of the shoes they were wearing. The powder was immediately sent for testing and found to be highly explosive material. Both young women broke under interrogation.

Nadia and Madeleine Bradley, the two women taken into custody, were the daughters of a wealthy Moroccan businessman living in Paris. They claimed that a man they had both been romantically involved with had sent them to Israel on an all-expenses-paid trip. Apparently, he was the one who had planted the explosive powder in their suitcases and shoe heels. They said they were supposed to meet up with other French tourists who had arrived in Israel before them. As a result of this disclosure, Israeli security forces arrested an elderly French couple who were staying at a hotel in central Tel Aviv. A search of their room turned up a radio containing fuses for detonating explosive charges. The next day another arrest was made: a young woman named Evelyn Burj had arrived from Paris in order to put together the bombs that were supposed to be detonated on Passover Eve in the packed dining room of a large hotel on the beach. The link connecting the Bradley sisters, Evelyn Burj, and the wife of the elderly Frenchman was Mohammed Budya, who had been romantically involved with all four of them. "This is that man," David told Sylvia, as he pointed at the photograph.

"He does have an impressive record, doesn't he!" exclaimed Sylvia.

"Here are a few more facts about Budya," continued David. "He was sent by the F.L.N. Algerian underground—the National Liberation Front—to perform terrorist operations in Paris, but was caught and sent to prison for three years. After his release from prison, he returned to Algeria, but couldn't fit in there and eventually emigrated to France. In Paris he was appointed the director of a small theater. He's been married and divorced three times. Evelyn Burj was the cashier at his theater.

"Budya maintained close ties with Palestinian terrorist groups and Russian intelligence agents before joining Black September. He is a very active terrorist, acting as a liaison between secret cells of Black September in Europe, smuggling arms, and planning large-scale attacks against Israel and concentrations of Jews all over the world."

"What is my role in all of this?"

"We know where Budya lives. We also know that since Hamshari's elimination, Budya has been carefully avoiding crowded places and meetings with strangers. He has only one weakness: beautiful, intoxicating women. If you follow the women he is involved with, there's a good chance that they will lead you to him. Find out which women he's seeing, when and where he sees them, when he stays at home, what kind of car he drives, where he eats."

Later David informed Sylvia that she would be joined by a young woman combatant.

"She is very talented, but inexperienced," he said. "Give her easy assignments, and let me know your impressions."

He introduced Sylvia to an energetic, determined young woman of twenty-eight, a graduate of the Political Sciences Department of Tel Aviv University.

David provided them with a list of six Parisian women who were currently romantically involved with Budya, including their addresses and long-range photographs that had been taken of them.

The two combatants spent the next few days collecting information about Mohammed Budya's lovers. One of them was a university lecturer, another was active in a relief organization for Palestinian refugees, yet another had recently arrived in Paris from Algeria, two of them were store managers, and the remaining one worked as a clerk in a law firm. After two weeks of surveillance, Budya was observed going up to the Algerian woman's flat.

The two-woman combatant team set up an observation post opposite Budya's house. This was a good opportunity for them to become acquainted. They discovered that they had a lot in common. They were both attractive women, courageous, and fired with motivation. They had a mutual love of art and classical music and were proud of being able to contribute to the State of Israel. They were equally well informed regarding terrorist organizations, especially Black September.

One morning, they spotted a large-breasted blonde woman with heavy makeup emerging from Budya's house. Something about her brisk, confident step aroused suspicion. Sylvia studied the woman carefully, then cried out in surprise. Mohammed Budya had disguised himself as a woman.

Sylvia and her partner followed him to a café in the Gare St. Lazare, where he met up with two young girls of Middle Eastern appearance. Afterward, he set out on foot for Haussmann Boulevard.

In the early evening Budya returned home, still dressed as a woman. The next morning he left his house sporting a blue beret and dark glasses. He walked to a restaurant in Saint Germain, where he dined with a beautiful woman. After they parted, he made a few purchases at a nearby bookshop and returned home on foot.

In the days that followed, Sylvia reported frequently to David about the results of their surveillance. When it became clear that Budya was spending his nights at home and leaving every morning at 7:00 a.m., the commanders of the Special Operations Unit immediately started planning the hit operation. When preparations were completed, an operational unit was sent to Mohammed Budya's house. They identified his car near the building and planted an explosive charge in it. The next morning, when Budya started the motor, the detonated charge blew him to bits.

His funeral was attended by an inordinate number of beautiful women.

Finally, like a light shining through heavy darkness, the Mossad received the information that it had been waiting for. One of its sources in Germany, the friend of a young woman who was in love with Salameh, heard from her friend that the arch-terrorist was soon to arrive in the city of Ulm in northern Germany. The source didn't know exactly what business Salameh had in the city, but he was apparently planning to spend a few days there.

Four clandestine combatants of the Special Operations Unit were immediately dispatched to Ulm, and they set up observation posts in pairs at the intercity bus station and at the railway station. After a few days, one of them sighted a man whose build and facial features matched Salameh's. The combatant followed the man until he arrived at an apartment on the second floor of an old building on the west side of the city, where he remained all night. Taking shifts, the combatants watched the building all through the night. When morning came, people began to enter and exit the building, but the man they were watching was not among them.

At noon one of the combatants bought a hot pizza in a box and knocked on the apartment door, posing as a pizza delivery boy in order to find out if Salameh was still in there. But when he knocked on the door, there was no reply. The surveillance of the building continued all through that day and the ones that followed. After awhile, the team came to the inevitable conclusion that Ali had managed to slip through their fingers yet again.

It was a bitter disappointment. An exhaustive search for Salameh continued in the city of Ulm and the surrounding area, but with no results. Ulm was a relatively small city on the banks of the Danube, and there were a large number of exit routes by car or train. It was thus not possible to place lookout posts next to every escape route out of the city that Ali Salameh might take.

After it had become absolutely clear that Salameh had succeeded in slipping away from the Mossad's grasp, another lead turned up that raised new hopes. Information had arrived from sources close to Black September that explained Salameh's presence in Ulm. It seemed that he was trying to put together a team that would assassinate the Israeli ambassador to Sweden in Stockholm in retaliation for the murder of Mohammed Budya in Paris.

All efforts were now concentrated on Sweden. The security system guarding the embassy was tightened, the Swedish police were placed on high alert, and members of the Special Operations Unit left for Stockholm in an effort to locate the terrorists who were meant to carry out the assassination. They were hoping that Ali Salameh would be among them.

Meanwhile, more pieces of information had arrived about Salameh's whereabouts. They all had a common denominator: Salameh had left Germany and was heading for Scandinavia.

The headquarters of the Special Operations Unit went on red alert. It seemed that there was finally a real chance to get to Salameh and destroy him. But what was his exact location? Would he make a stopover in another Scandinavian country?

One announcement followed another, complicating matters even further. It finally emerged that Black September had abandoned the Stockholm plan entirely, due to the strict security measures that were being taken by the Swedish security authorities to ensure the safety of the Israeli ambassador. Simultaneously, according to information conveyed by the intelligence agencies, it was learned that although Salameh had given up on Sweden, he had decided to mount an operation in another Scandinavian country, but which one was as yet unclear.

The high command of the Special Operations Unit prepared itself for this new development. Combatants were dispatched to various destinations with instructions to make every effort to pick up the trail of Salameh's contacts, locate the man, and discover what he was plotting.

A team of clandestine combatants was sent to Geneva in order to follow Kamal Benaman, a mysterious twenty-eight-year-old Algerian who was married to a Swiss woman and was one of Salameh's associates. They discovered some interesting details about him: during the day Benaman, wearing overalls, worked at a factory on the outskirts of Geneva and took a bus to work and back. In the evening he would leave home and drive to an outlying pub, where he would drink beer and flirt with women. It didn't take the team long to discover that on those occasions Benaman would meet European contacts of Black September. At other times, Benaman would reveal another, totally different, aspect of his existence: dressed elegantly, he would attend receptions held by Arab diplomatic attachés and hobnob with visiting Arab dignitaries. On such occasions, he carefully concealed his connection with Black September.

On July 14, 1973, the combatants stationed in Geneva sent an urgent message to the Special Operations Unit command: Kamal Benaman had left the building of the Saudi delegation to the United Nations and had driven to Geneva Airport in a car bearing diplomatic license plates. Carrying a small traveling bag, he had rushed to the SAS check-in counter and shortly afterward boarded a flight to Copenhagen.

No one at Special Operations Unit headquarters knew the purpose of the Algerian's journey. Among other possibilities, they conjectured that he was on his way to meet members of Black September in preparation for a terrorist attack. Another possibility was that Ali Hassan Salameh was in Copenhagen, and that Benaman, one of his key men in Europe, was on his way to meet Salameh there. In any case, it was vital that the Israelis keep on Benaman's trail. His flight number was relayed to Special Operations Unit representatives in Copenhagen, who rushed to the airport.

There was a chance that Benaman would lead the Special Operations Unit to Ali Hassan Salameh; this made it essential for the Mossad to send a combatant team to Scandinavia.

David, Sylvia's case officer, phoned her urgently. "Cancel all your plans," he said, "and prepare for a journey."

She didn't ask him about her destination, since they never discussed work over the phone, but something told her that this was no routine mission.

"Is there anything else I need to know?" she inquired.

"Not for the moment." He himself didn't yet know the details of the plan.

Zvi Zamir, the director of the Mossad, whose top priority was eliminating Ali Hassan Salameh, assigned Mike Harari, the commander of the Special Operations Unit, to put together a list of combatants to be sent to Scandinavia. Harari was fifty-four years old, tall, and suntanned, with many years of experience in intelligence work. He was well acquainted with all of his combatants. He met with them often and knew everything about their training and achievements, their strong and weak points. Within two days, he had assembled a list of his most experienced combatants, including Abraham Gemer; Dan Arbel, who was a native of Denmark; and Sylvia Rafael, who had exhibited resourcefulness and persistence on a countless number of missions. Harari searched everywhere for other combatants who could speak Scandinavian languages. He added Marianne Geldinkof, who had been born in Sweden and was just starting the Operation Unit's training program. She was added to the team due to her Scandinavian background, despite her lack of experience in field intelligence.

Meanwhile, events were developing rapidly. An Arab agent working for the Mossad in Beirut transmitted new information to Tel Aviv, which confirmed the assumption that Ali Hassan Salameh was within reach. The man reported that Salameh was about to arrive in Norway in order to activate a team that would launch attacks on Israeli targets. All the parts of the puzzle began rapidly falling into place. The intelligence branch of the Mossad was now aware that, first of all, one of Salameh's associates, an Algerian by the name of Kamal Benaman, was on his way to Denmark; and, second, that Ali himself would be momentarily departing for Norway. It seemed almost certain that the two were supposed to meet. But where—in Denmark or in Norway?

Denmark was quickly ruled out. It appeared that Benaman had no intention of arriving there. The SAS plane took off from Geneva and did in fact land in Copenhagen Airport on the afternoon of July 14. However, Benaman didn't make his way toward the terminal exit, but instead hurried to the transit passengers' lounge and headed toward the exit gate of an additional SAS flight. The flight attendants checked the tickets of a small number of passengers who began boarding the plane. The combatant who was following the Algerian saw that the sign above the counter indicated that the flight was to Oslo.

The combatant phoned his case officer on a hidden walkie-talkie and reported the destination of the man he had been following. The case officer passed on the information, which aroused considerable enthusiasm in the Mossad. Now everything was clear: Benaman and Ali Hassan Salameh were about to meet in Norway. This looked like the golden opportunity that they had awaited so long.

The team of clandestine combatants that was to track down Salameh quickly completed its preparations and departed for Oslo from Israel and various European countries. Sylvia took off from Paris and met up with Dan Arbel in the Norwegian capital. The two shook hands coolly. Three years previously, they had participated in a mission disguised as a couple. They had been sent on an information-collecting mission that involved sailing in a hired boat along the coast of a hostile Arab country. After a few hours of smooth sailing, a patrol boat apprehended them before they had a chance to reach their destination. Their captors removed the film from their cameras and interrogated them for hours. They both stuck to their cover stories, claiming repeatedly that they were a couple who had chosen that country because it seemed like a good place to spend an exotic vacation. The investigators didn't succeed in forcing them to reveal the true purpose of their trip and eventually released them, with a strict warning never to return to that country.

In Oslo the combatants met the head of the team, a stocky, short man of about forty, whom Sylvia had never met before. He was an experienced operative, a Holocaust survivor who had withstood the horrors of World War II thanks to his resourcefulness and bravery. He told Sylvia that he had been twelve years old when they had taken the Jews of his city to a pit in a thick forest and mowed them down with machine guns. He had exploited a moment when the guards weren't paying attention and escaped to a nearby wheat field, ducking the bullets that the Germans fired at him. He hid in the field but was located by hunting dogs that were sent after him.

The Germans beat him cruelly with the butts of their rifles and stood him on the edge of the pit with a group of Jews. The order was given to fire, and the Jews fell lifelessly into the pit. The boy jumped into the pit before the German bullets hit him and pretended to be dead. Under cover of darkness, he crawled out of the pit and escaped yet again.

He found refuge in a work camp whose inmates did maintenance on a German Air Force landing strip. They were responsible for sweeping the runway and removing any obstacles that would interfere with landings. One day he saw a German plane falling in flames from the sky and crashing onto the runway. The lad ran to the site of the crash, where he spotted an unconscious pilot with his head leaning forward on the controls. The boy pulled the man out of the cockpit minutes before the plane exploded. The pilot, a squadron flight commander, was hospitalized, and when he recovered, sent for the lad who had saved his life, appointing him his personal servant. The boy survived the war due to the officer's protection. After the cease-fire, he managed to escape to safety with the help of a Russian officer of Jewish extraction. He immigrated to Israel and fought in the War of Independence. Later he was recruited to the Shabak, transferring from there to the Mossad, where he participated in countless missions as a Special Operations Unit clandestine combatant in Europe.

In Oslo he explained the details of the mission that had been assigned to the fighting team. He handed every team member a photograph of Ali Hassan Salameh, announcing, "This man is the reason why we are here. Please note that he may not resemble his photograph, since he is a master of disguise. Take into consideration that he may be wearing a wig, a beard, a mustache, or unusual clothing."

Sylvia studied the photograph carefully and with evident excitement. The man most wanted by the Mossad was within reach, and she was determined not to let him slip out of her grasp this time.

Sylvia and Abraham Gemer finally met up in Oslo after a long period of separation. They were both surprised and pleased to learn that they would be working together. "It's lucky that we have been chosen to participate in the same mission," Sylvia said to Abraham, remembering that they had worked together so well when he was her instructor at the School for Special Operations. They and the other combatants were gathered together for an initial briefing, during which they were instructed to pay cash only while on the mission, in order to avoid the possibility of being traced due to a telltale credit card number.

Sylvia and Marianne were the only women in the group. Marianne told Sylvia that despite being deeply intrigued by the task ahead of them, she felt unprepared for it. When Sylvia asked why, Marianne explained that this was to be her very first mission.

Sylvia was shaken. Until that moment she had trusted her superiors to know exactly what they were doing. It seemed to her that they would have sent only the most experienced combatants on such a complex and delicate mission, but suddenly doubts crept into her mind. "There must be something that you do exceptionally well," she probed.

"I speak Swedish," said Marianne.

"But we're in Norway," said Sylvia. "Do you know any Norwegian?"

"A bit."

It was obvious to Sylvia that Marianne might be a weak link on the team and that she might interfere with the success of the mission. She worried that Marianne might encounter difficulties that she herself and her case officers would be totally unprepared for. "I wish you success," Sylvia replied with a heavy heart. In other, calmer, circumstances, she might have appealed to the commanders of the Special Operations Unit to reconsider their decision to include Marianne in the team. But it was the eve of a vital mission, the team members had already been chosen and had arrived at their destination, and such a last-minute change in the makeup of the combatant team could adversely affect the operation.

Sylvia didn't allow herself to sink into pessimism. She had no choice but to look on the bright side: apart from Marianne, the team that had been sent to Norway consisted of experienced, trained combatants who were capable of improvising solutions to any problem that might arise in the field. Sylvia hoped that the quality of the team as a whole would compensate for its one inexperienced member.

In the hours and days to come, however, Sylvia's peace of mind was disturbed even further, shaking her absolute trust in her commanders for the first time. When she inquired how the team members were meant to behave in the event anything upset the plan, it turned out that the combatant team had received no instructions about how to act in such circumstances. Furthermore, to her knowledge, there was no clear plan of retreat. She asked Abraham Gemer if he knew if such a plan existed in case anything went wrong. He shrugged his shoulders.

"As far as I know, they didn't consider that," he said.

"Why not?" she asked in astonishment.

"Because nobody believes that anything unexpected will happen to make retreat necessary."

Gemer admitted to Sylvia that he too was uneasy about this.

This gap in planning seemed to Sylvia to be a sure recipe for disaster. She was used to going out on missions whose every detail, especially retreat routes, had been meticulously thought out.

Three combatants were immediately assigned to search for Benaman, on the assumption that he would lead them to Salameh. None of them knew where the Algerian was staying. They hoped to find him at one of the hotels in the city. They didn't think this would be too difficult, as there weren't that many places to stay in Oslo. Marianne and Dan Arbel, who also knew some Norwegian, made a list of all the hotels in the capital by means of a local telephone directory. They divided between themselves the task of phoning each hotel and asking if Benaman was a guest there. All the hotels they contacted, from the cheapest to the most expensive, answered in the negative. Finally, after hours of inquiries, they tried the student residence hall of Oslo University. The receptionist at the desk confirmed that Benaman was indeed staying there.

At daybreak, Dan Arbel took up a post near the building, keeping his eyes fixed on the main entrance. A few hours later, he saw Benaman leave the residence hall, buy a sandwich and a bottle of juice at a small food stall on the corner, and return to the building. Arbel didn't budge but remained at his lookout post, ready to follow the Algerian anywhere he decided to go. Hours passed, but there was no sign of Benaman. Arbel began suspecting that something was amiss and decided to investigate. He strode confidently toward the main entrance and approached the receptionist, a young student who raised her eyes from the book she was reading. Arbel introduced himself as a friend of Benaman's and asked for his room number.

"Room 114, first floor," the girl answered.

Arbel cautiously ascended to the first floor and located the room. To his astonishment, the door was wide open and the room was empty.

Arbel realized that his man had apparently escaped through a side door. He entered the room and searched for clues as to where Benaman might be headed. The room contained a narrow bed, a clothes closet, and a small sink. There were no clothes hanging in the closet, nor was there a suitcase in the room, but on the bed lay an open schedule for trains leaving for the town of Lillehammer. A circle had been drawn in pencil around the train departing at 11:55.

Arbel found it hard to imagine that Benaman would have deliberately misled him by circling a false item on a train schedule. The man was apparently in such a rush to catch the train to Lillehammer that he had forgotten to take the schedule with him or to destroy it. The time was 10:40 a.m.

Arbel ran out of the building, stopped a taxi, and asked to be taken to the railway station. The journey took twenty minutes. Less than an hour remained before the train left for Lillehammer. Arbel rushed to Platform 7, and then passed through the cars of the train waiting there, but didn't find the man he was looking for. He descended from the train and hung around the platform waiting for Benaman's arrival. A few passengers made their way to the train—a few elderly people, a young couple, a woman carrying a baby, a porter carrying a few suitcases and packing crates.

After a long wait, Arbel spotted Benaman nearing the entrance to the station. He hesitated and retraced his steps. Arbel tailed Benaman. The Algerian didn't notice Arbel, although he seemed to be taking precautions to ensure that nobody was following him. He darted into a narrow side street, stopped at a small café, and gulped down an espresso while standing at the counter. He glanced at his watch, went out, had a good look around, returned hurriedly to the railway station, bought a ticket, located Platform 7, and entered one of the railway cars. An electronic sign above the platform indicated the train's destination: Lillehammer. The train left a few minutes later with Benaman on board.

Arbel immediately phoned the unit's command post and conveyed the new information. A few minutes later, the report reached the Special Operations Unit in Israel. Mike Harari, who was about to leave for Norway himself, was now certain that Benaman was traveling to the small resort town for a secret meeting with Ali Salameh. He gave the order for the team to prepare immediately for departure to Lillehammer, and told Arbel to continue to follow Benaman.

At Oslo Airport the team rented six cars. At that same moment,

Dan Arbel reached Lillehammer and arranged accommodations for the team that was about to arrive. Every room was large enough for two or three combatants. Arbel rented an additional apartment for the team commander and the Mossad executives, Zvi Zamir and Mike Harari, who would be arriving to command the operation.

The rest of the team soon arrived at Lillehammer. They were instructed to tighten surveillance on Salameh and indicate his location to the hit team that would eliminate him. By now, in addition to Sylvia and Abraham Gemer, other combatants sensed that something in the planning of the operation wasn't as it should be. Their cover stories had not been synchronized, and none of them had been properly briefed or trained before they set out. Some of them knew one another from previous missions, but others were unknown quantities. The fact that they didn't all know one another could potentially cause difficulties. For instance, it was totally unclear to the team members how they should behave if something went wrong and, if they were arrested, whether they would be able to stick to their cover stories without contradicting somebody else's.

The resort town of Lillehammer (the name means "mountain ridge") was deep into its afternoon siesta when the Israelis arrived and settled into the living quarters that had been arranged for them. Their first day in Lillehammer was hot and stuffy. All the shops were closed on the main street, apart from a pizzeria and a café. In the summer months, the town of 20,000 inhabitants was almost empty of tourists. Only a few of the hotels and guest rooms in private houses were receiving visitors, since very few tourists bothered to travel 186 kilometers north of Oslo in order to wander through the picturesque streets, photograph the ancient wooden buildings, and visit the local museum. In the winter months, however, Lillehammer's tourist industry attracted more than 600,000 visitors a year. Then the mountains surrounding Lillehammer were covered with snow, attracting both novice and expert skiers, and the town hosted international skiing competitions. In winter Lillehammer awoke from its slumber. The hotels were full to capacity, the restaurants were packed, and the cafés were open at all hours. In contrast, during the summer months nothing much went on.

On July 16, 1973, the Mossad clandestine combatants were practically the only foreigners to be found in Lillehammer. The small number of locals who saw them enter the main street stared curiously at their shiny rental cars. The combatants' confidence in the success of their mission led them to ignore security measures. They didn't even bother to hide their walkie-talkies but used them openly in the street, making Sylvia uneasy about being so closely observed by the residents. This was potentially a very dangerous situation: one of the people watching them might easily be an associate of Ali Hassan Salameh, and even the slightest suspicion might cause the most wanted terrorist to escape from their grasp yet again.

The leader of the team, who was staying in a separate apartment with Harari and Zamir, ordered his combatants to look for Kamal Benaman in the local hotels, restaurants, and cafés. After a prolonged search, they found him having lunch at a small pizzeria in the center of town. They followed him and discovered that he was staying at the Regina, a hotel that was located on one of the side streets off the main road of Lillehammer and was almost empty of visitors. Benaman had booked into the hotel under an assumed name. A few minutes later, this information was conveyed to Zvi Zamir, the director of the Mossad. It raised his spirits immensely, as he was confident that the trap was finally closing on Salameh.

The members of the team took up various positions in the environs of Hotel Regina, walking through the public park, pretending to be shoppers at the small food mart, reading newspapers on a bench in the shade of a tree on the main avenue. They had received photos of Benaman, both clean-shaven and bearded, and they awaited his appearance impatiently.

The next day, Benaman finally left his room. He descended to the hotel restaurant and had breakfast. Afterward, he walked through the main lobby and went out into the street. Again he took safety precautions. He spent an hour or so walking around Lillehammer, lingering by Lake Mjøsa, watching the boats and keeping a wary eye on his surroundings. The combatants took turns in their surveillance of him, making sure to keep their distance, so as not to arouse suspicion.

After sitting by the lake for a while, Benaman walked over to a café with a view of the mountains. He quickly stepped inside and sat at a corner table, far away from the window. A waitress approached him and took his order. Less than an hour later, two men entered the café and joined him at his table. One of them was tall and thin, with black hair and a mustache.

The photograph of Salameh that was distributed to the team

wasn't very clear. The man that appeared in the photo was clean-shaven, and his facial features were indistinct, but that didn't stop the surveillance team from identifying the man with the mustache who had entered the café as Salameh. "There's no doubt about it," whispered one of the combatants. Clearly the mustache on the man in the café was meant to hide his identity.

The three men in the café were deep in discussion. The combatant who had identified Salameh ran to the nearest telephone booth and called the team commander.

"Are you certain that it's him?"

"One hundred percent."

In a state of high excitement, the leader of the team informed Harari of the positive identification, and Harari in turn reported this to Zamir. The operation was approaching its crucial stage. There was no need to obtain the prime minister's approval to shoot Salameh: Golda Meir had given it in advance.

After consulting with Zamir, Harari announced to the team commander that the hit would take place on July 21.

From that moment onward, Benaman was forgotten as though he never existed. Now the focus was exclusively on the man whose description matched that of Ali Salameh. After about half an hour, the man said good-bye to his companions and took his leave. A bicycle was leaning against the café's outside wall. He mounted it and rode for about an hour until he arrived at a tenement providing cheap workers' housing. The man entered the building. Those following him set up a lookout post across the street.

Only late the next morning did the man finally exit the building. He rode his bicycle to the municipal swimming pool, Yorkstad, where he changed into a bathing suit. He jumped into the water. In the large indoor pool were a dozen or so mothers with children and two elderly people. The suspect turned to one of them and began chatting with him.

Marianne Geldinkof quickly rented a bathing suit and also entered the water. She got as close as she could to the men conversing in the center of the pool and overheard them speaking in French, a language she didn't understand. Afterward she emerged from the pool and told her teammates waiting outside that in her opinion the person they were trailing was the wrong man.

Marianne's report gave Sylvia pause. She turned to Arbel and told him that, according to the information that was distributed among the combatants about Salameh, there was no mention of his speaking French.

"Apart from that," she said worriedly, "the photograph is unclear, and I speak as a professional photographer. It would be hard to identify anyone by such a poor photo. We need to double-check the identity of the man we're following. This may well be a case of mistaken identity."

Arbel was also beginning to have misgivings about the man's exact identity, but when Sylvia and he expressed their reservations to the mission commanders, they were waved away. The team leaders were still convinced that they were on the trail of Ali Salameh.

Their confidence didn't manage to calm Sylvia's nerves. She found it hard to believe that Salameh, a man who had been in hiding for years and who generally appeared in disguise surrounded by bodyguards, wouldn't hesitate to ride a bicycle unaccompanied, in broad daylight, through the streets of a small town, where he could easily be watched or followed. She also noticed that the man took no safety precautions before entering the shabby tenement at the end of the street and remaining there all night. It simply didn't make sense.

"That is not the way a senior officer of a terrorist organization would behave if he knew the Mossad was hot on his trail," she said, but nobody listened. Most of her teammates thought she was mistaken. Like the commanders of the operation, they were confident that they were following the right man.

The team commander arrived. Sylvia shared her doubts with him, and he agreed that there were several inconsistencies. He promised to check the details later; but, as fate would have it, he never managed to do so.

While walking around the building that housed the potential victim, the team leader slipped in the dark and fell into a ditch. He felt excruciating pain in his right leg. Leaning on the shoulder of one of the combatants, he returned to his living quarters. The pain became more acute every minute, but he hesitated to call a local doctor for fear that it might jeopardize the operation. He also hesitated to go to the town's small local hospital. He swallowed painkillers, but they didn't help.

In the end he had no choice but to call a doctor, who examined his leg and diagnosed a torn ligament.

"You need hospital treatment as soon as possible," he pronounced.

The team leader understood that he would have to relinquish his post. The option of being hospitalized in a Norwegian hospital was just too dangerous. He consulted his superiors, and they agreed with him. The commander returned to Oslo by train, immediately proceeded to the airport, and got on the first available flight, which was to Rome; from there, he flew directly to Israel. Harari would replace the team commander.

From Ben Gurion Airport, the former team commander went by taxi to Tel Hashomer Hospital. "You arrived here just in time," the doctors told him.

He lay on his bed in the hospital's orthopedic ward in a black mood. His ability to survive had always been one of his most striking character traits. He had survived life-threatening situations, emerging unharmed from the grip of the Nazis in World War II, and now he had been defeated by something as trivial as a torn ligament.

What was supposed to be the greatest mission of his life, the aspiration of every combatant in the Special Operations Unit, would go on without him, and the thought was hard to bear.

Meanwhile, in Lillehammer, the noose was tightening around the neck of the target, but he continued behaving as though he didn't have a care in the world. In the early evening of July 21, a fine summer rain was falling on the town. The passersby on the street walked quickly, protecting themselves from the rain with their umbrellas. The man entered the local cinema with a blonde woman wearing a yellow raincoat. There were only a few dozen people in the audience. One of the clandestine combatants was among them. He was sitting not far away from the couple, observing them eating the snacks that they had purchased at the refreshment counter and intently watching a film about the exploits of the American Air Force in World War II.

Sylvia was part of the surveillance team watching the theater and waiting for the couple to emerge. She was still apprehensive. She couldn't fathom the nonchalant behavior of someone who was purported to be Ali Hassan Salameh. She hadn't seen him turn around even once to see if he was being followed. She watched him striding confidently toward the cinema, holding the arm of his female companion. Shooting him down in the street or in a film theater in such circumstances would be such a simple thing to do. It couldn't be that that hadn't occurred to Ali Salameh. Something strange is going on here, she thought.

When the film ended at 10:15 p.m., the doors opened and the audience started exiting the building. The dark man with the mustache and his companion walked toward the nearest bus stop. They waited a few minutes until the bus arrived and got on. Two surveillance vehicles followed them.

Four stops later, the couple got off. The street was quiet. Flickering television screens could be seen through apartment windows, and in the public park opposite the bus stop some local teenagers could be seen embracing in parked cars.

The couple began crossing Storgten Street when a gray Volvo suddenly blocked their way. Two hit men from the Special Operations Unit emerged from the vehicle. In their thirties, both were former members of crack IDF units who had already participated in missions of major importance to Israel's security and who saw their future in the Mossad. This was not the first time they had been assigned to eliminate wanted terrorists. They approached every mission after having been well trained for it, and they were experienced and level-headed, trusting those who sent them and the justice of their cause.

They both pulled out Beretta revolvers with silencers. Their victim looked down their gun barrels in fear and trembling. "Please," he said in Norwegian, "I beg you not to do this." His cries were drowned out by the shots. The pistols were fired fourteen times, although the shooters took care not to harm the woman. The man sank down, bleeding, on the cobblestones while the Volvo sped away. The woman's screams echoed down the street. Alarmed residents peered from their windows. Someone called the police. The time was 10:47 p.m.

When the police arrived, among the crowd that had gathered were two local teenagers whose clothes were disheveled. The couple told the police that they had been together in the public park and had witnessed the shooting. The boy had also managed to write down the license plate of the getaway car.

Mike Harari's eyes were shining when he heard that the wanted man had been shot and killed. He imagined the huge headlines in the Israeli and international papers announcing the death of Ali Hassan Salameh. For months he had orchestrated the pursuit of perpetrators of Arab terror, but all that shrank into insignificance compared to the greatest operation of them all at Lillehammer. "You did an excellent job," he congratulated the team members, and ordered them to leave town immediately.

The Lillehammer police mustered all its officers. This was the first murder case that they had had to deal with in a very long time, and they were determined to catch the killers. The local police chief told reporters that he assumed the murder was drug-related. The victim had no criminal record, but he was an Arab of Moroccan extraction who had come to Lillehammer, married a local woman, and found employment. But, like many other foreigners, he was probably a drug dealer.

The reporters asked the police to identify him.

"His name is Ahmad Bushiki," the police captain told them.

"Where does he live?"

"Here in Lillehammer."

"What was his profession?"

"As far as we know, he was a waiter."

The Lillehammer police acted quickly. They announced over the radio the number of the car that had been seen driving away from the scene of the shooting. They also began searching for the car's owner.

The morning after the elimination, as soon as the rental car service at the airport opened its doors, Marianne Geldinkof appeared, ready to return the car and pay her bill. Dan Arbel was waiting to return his rental car not far behind her. He was feeling uneasy, since his was the getaway car, and he was praying that nobody had managed to write down the license plate number.

Sitting behind Arbel was a young Norwegian citizen who was also waiting to return a car. He was listening to a radio program on which the announcer was giving details of the getaway car. To his surprise, he saw the same number on the license plates of the vehicle in front of him. He beckoned a policeman who was standing nearby. The policeman approached Arbel and asked for identification. Arbel handed over his Danish passport.

"What are you doing here?" the officer asked.

"I'm a tourist."

"Are you alone?"

Instead of answering in the affirmative, Arbel made a fatal error.

"No, I'm here with my girlfriend."

"Where is she?" asked the policeman.

"She just returned a rental car," he said.

The policeman quickly summoned a patrol vehicle. A few minutes later, Dan and Marianne were both under arrest.

Meanwhile, the rental car containing the two shooters was making its way to Oslo. They had originally been instructed to head for the Swedish border, since it was open around the clock and cars with Norwegian license plates were allowed to pass without a passport check. However, for some reason Harari changed their orders, and they were told to return to Oslo and abandon the car there.

Despite the explicit order to get rid of the guns they had used for the hit, the shooters had left them hidden in the car. Once it was daylight, the traffic on the road to Oslo increased. Suddenly, near the resort town of Hammer, they saw the blinking lights of police cars and a line of vehicles waiting at a barrier that was blocking the road.

The Israeli combatants, startled and puzzled by what was happening, were sure that the barrier had some connection with them. They quickly got out of the car and threw the guns out at the side of the road, preparing to tell the police that they were vacationers, and hoping that nobody had sent ahead an exact description of them.

When it was their turn, the policemen at the barrier approached their car. They checked the men's passports and made a quick search of the vehicle. One of the combatants asked what it was all about, and an officer replied that the German chancellor, Willy Brandt, was staying at a nearby town, so they were taking special security measures. "Have a good journey," the officer said, and opened the barrier for them.

Dan Arbel and Marianne Geldinkof were taken for interrogation immediately after their arrival at the police station. They denied having any connection with the murder but couldn't explain how Arbel's car had been spotted at the exact location where Bushiki had been shot. The police were still convinced that the people they had arrested were from the underworld and that they had arrived in Lillehammer to settle drug-related scores.

They put pressure on Marianne and threatened her.

"I'm not from the underworld," she finally confessed. "I'm an Israeli, and I was sent by the Mossad."

Arbel was put into a dark, narrow cell. He suffered every minute he was in there, feeling choked and finding it hard to breathe. The Norwegian investigator later claimed that this pressure had been effective in breaking down the Israeli's resistance. He promised that if the prisoner told them the truth, he would be transferred to a roomier cell. Arbel told them everything he knew. He also gave the police the addresses of the apartments where the rest of the participants in the operation were staying. A search of Arbel's clothing turned up a piece of paper on which was written the phone number of Yigal Eyal, an attaché at the Israeli Embassy in Oslo.

"What is this?" asked the investigators.

"An emergency telephone number."

In the meantime, seven of the combatants who had stayed behind managed to escape from Lillehammer. Sylvia insisted that her group leave immediately. It was already daylight, and any additional delay would be critical. Finally Sylvia and her companions began their exit, heading for the rental cars that remained at their disposal. "I want to be as far away from here as possible," said Sylvia. But when they opened the door to their apartment, they were shocked to discover that the building was surrounded by police officers pointing weapons at them.

"Hands up!" one of them called in English.

While the team members were being arrested and handcuffed, Mike Harari and Zvi Zamir left their apartment and boarded an express train to Oslo. They, together with seven additional members of the combatant team, managed to return to Israel.

Norwegian police officers who rushed to Yigal Eyal's apartment after finding his phone number in Dan Arbel's clothing discovered two additional team members hiding out there. They were immediately arrested. The next day, Eyal was declared persona non grata by the Norwegian government and was deported to Israel with his family.

7

A Love Story

The arrested members of the Special Operations Unit were transported in separate patrol wagons to Oslo police headquarters, which took over the investigation after it became clear that the killing in Lillehammer was not drug related. From the moment it emerged that representatives of the Mossad had killed Ahmad Bushiki and that this could potentially harm Norwegian-Israeli diplomatic relations, the investigation was given top priority. The Norwegian police recruited its best interrogators and drew a veil of secrecy around the investigation. When Sylvia arrived outside police headquarters, reporters and news photographers attempted to get close to her, thrusting microphones in her face, but the police pushed back anyone blocking her way into the building.

Sylvia was led to an interrogation room, where three police officers were waiting. In a quiet, businesslike way she was told that they already had the detailed testimonies of Marianne Geldinkof and Dan Arbel. "If you talk, it will lighten your sentence," they promised. They told her that her friends had killed the wrong man. If it's true, Sylvia thought to herself, it's not surprising. She remembered the doubts that had plagued her during the mission. "Until your operation in Lillehammer," said one of the interrogators, "we were of the opinion that the Mossad was invincible. It appears that we were mistaken."

They told her that they already knew her real name wasn't Patricia Roxenburg, as stated in her Canadian passport.

"You aren't Canadian, and your real name is Sylvia Rafael," they stated matter-of-factly. "You work for the Mossad."

Sylvia glanced at them coldly and remained silent. They continued to fire questions at her but didn't receive a single reply. She was determined not to say a single word. No threat or promise could induce her to tell them what she knew.

The police officers placed her in isolation in a windowless cell. In the corner was a latrine that smelled strongly of disinfectant. Sylvia had many hours in which to reflect. The respect she had had for her "bosses" had shattered to bits. She recalled questions that had arisen as early as the planning stages, her dissatisfaction with the inclusion of an inexperienced member, the amateurish identification of the man who was purportedly Ali Hassan Salameh, the unnecessary waste of time in the apartment in Lillehammer when it had been imperative to get out of there as quickly as possible. She asked herself how experienced people from the Special Operations Unit could have planned and executed such an abortive mission.

Sylvia assumed that the State of Israel was making a considerable effort to rescue her and her teammates. Thus she was surprised that nobody visited her, neither embassy representatives nor lawyers who could defend her. She didn't know that since her arrest, the Mossad, the Foreign Ministry, and the Foreign Ministry's legal team had been attempting to visit her, but the Norwegian authorities had categorically refused to allow it.

Life in prison became a nightmare. Sylvia's cell was narrow and dark. She couldn't stretch out full-length on the bed because it wasn't long enough. The food they brought her was tasteless. The coffee was cold and muddy. She was forbidden to receive newspapers or books or listen to the radio, and for security reasons she was not allowed out into the exercise yard. Her body ached, and her eyes couldn't get accustomed to the darkness. The total silence got on her nerves.

Sylvia's thoughts for the future focused on the hope that Israel would attempt to end the affair as quickly as possible and would exert heavy diplomatic pressure on the Norwegian authorities to release all the prisoners. Worst of all, she was beginning to have doubts about her future in the Special Operations Unit. Her secret activities, especially the ones that were especially dangerous, had been based on absolute trust, her commanders' belief in her and her faith in the system of which she had been a part. She hadn't joined the Mossad to find adventure or to escape from personal problems. She had done so because of her identification with the Jewish people and her belief in a path she considered to be righteous. She had relied on those who sent her to risk her life and viewed them as a talented, dedicated, and intelligent team, one that would never let chance interfere with their planning. All this faith and trust had suddenly burst like a soap bubble, and she wasn't sure if she would be able to continue serving under people she no longer trusted.

Her thoughts turned to her parents. She knew that the news of her arrest would cause them great pain and anxiety. Their loving care of her when she was a child, the fact that they had allowed her to choose her own path even though it was not what they wanted for her, their loving letters—all these made her feel how strong her connection to them had remained. If only she could explain her behavior to them, alleviate even a small portion of the pain they must be undergoing . . .

During the events in Lillehammer, Ali Salameh was hiding out in an apartment in Denmark disguised as an antiques dealer. Totally occupied with planning the assassination of Israeli diplomats, he was completely unaware of what had gone on in Norway; but Denmark soon proved to be too dangerous for him. His men sensed that they were being followed and that their phones had been tapped. They advised Ali to get out. At first he stubbornly resisted this advice; ultimately, however, he had no choice and made plans to fly to Italy. He instructed his top men in Europe to meet him secretly in Rome and informed them of new plans for terrorist attacks. They, like his men in Denmark, were also of the opinion that the time was wrong for such activities. Too many security services were keeping a watchful eye on aliens of Arab extraction, especially those suspected of belonging to terrorist organizations. Ali decided to return home to Lebanon and wait until the situation calmed down.

His bodyguards accompanied him to the terminal. The day after he arrived in Beirut, the news broke about the murder in Lillehammer. Some of Ali's men speculated that Mossad operatives had been involved in the affair and that they had intended to eliminate their boss but had killed someone else by mistake.

Ali Salameh, Black September's commander of operations, considered this an excellent opportunity to turn the Mossad into a laughingstock. He reported to Arafat about the events in Lillehammer and agreed to be interviewed by any Arab-language paper wishing to do so. He told reporters that the death of Ahmad Bushiki proved that the Mossad was no longer the crack intelligence service it had been in the past. "I know they were after me," he affirmed, "but to this day I don't understand how they got to Norway. I've never been there in my life." In the course of an interview on Radio Lebanon, Salameh boasted, "If the Israelis think they will ever eliminate me, they can think again. They haven't done it up till now, and they won't be any more successful in the future."

While the Mossad commanders bit their fingernails in frustration, Ali appeared to be in an excellent mood. He was photographed grinning broadly, and sent an announcement to all the newspapers that he intended to marry Georgina Rizk. The decision to abandon his wife didn't trouble his conscience in the slightest.

The Beirut-born beauty had waited a long time for this moment. She immediately accepted Ali's proposal, after which her father called him in for a talk. He begged Ali to join his company, leave the path of terror, establish a family, and raise his children in peace and comfort. Ali replied that he could not accept the offer. "I am committed to Palestine," he said. "But the war won't go on forever. When it is over, I will be glad to join your business."

This conversation displeased Georgina's father deeply, but constant pressure on the part of his daughter forced him to agree to the marriage.

The Al Bustan Hotel in Beirut had never in its history seen so many security guards. They surrounded the building, filling the lobby, wandering around the kitchen, and checking each guest at the entrance to the huge ballroom. The security guards were members of Force 17, the elite Fatah unit, and each of them carried a loaded weapon.

Ali had invited reporters and news photographers, as well as television crews and radio announcers, to attend the wedding ceremony, in order to announce to the world that the man at the top of the Mossad's hit list was alive and well, and enjoying his life to the fullest. It was rumored that the bride's father had laid out huge sums of money to pay for the festive event.

Ali and Georgina were photographed smiling and embracing, cutting the wedding cake, kissing Arafat and other Fatah dignitaries. The heads of the Lebanese government, businessmen, and film stars (guests of the bride), along with the heads of terrorist organizations (guests of the groom), stuffed themselves with delicacies, watched a troupe of belly dancers, and complimented the bride, who wore white and held a bouquet of white orchids. She had never looked more radiant.

It appeared that all the high society of Lebanon was present at Georgina and Ali's wedding, but there were three who were not invited: Ali's first wife, Zeinab, and their sons, Hassan and Osama.

Miriam and Ferdinand Rafael, Sylvia's parents, had often asked themselves exactly what their daughter was doing. During her first years in Israel, they had corresponded with her frequently. They read her letters about kibbutz life and about living in Tel Aviv, about her work as a teacher and her impressions of Israel. Once she was recruited to the Special Operations Unit, however, she didn't share much information with them. When she announced that she had been sent to Paris to work for a large commercial company, she didn't reveal her address but gave her parents a registered mail address at a post office in the city. When they asked for her phone number, she answered that she wasn't at home much due to her job, and it probably wouldn't be possible to reach her by phone.

Miriam and Ferdinand didn't understand the mystery surrounding their daughter's life, but they gave her their full support. Over the years, they continued to send letters to her numbered mailbox. She wrote them often about how beautiful Paris was, about books she was reading and plays she had seen, but nothing about her work. When they asked her if she had a serious relationship with a man, she replied, "I'm working so hard that I hardly have time to breathe." She visited them once in South Africa, but even then she had hardly discussed her professional life.

The passing years had affected Ferdinand's health and caused him to be bedridden a good part of the time. He had developed a serious heart condition and was frequently hospitalized. Less than a week after Sylvia was arrested, he had a serious heart attack and was rushed to the emergency room. The heart operation he underwent didn't improve his condition, and he felt that his days were numbered. In his last letter to Sylvia, on his deathbed, he wrote:

My darling daughter,

I am writing this letter from the hospital. Unfortunately, it seems that my heart condition has worsened. It fills me with sorrow that we may never meet again, but even if I cannot be with you as I would like, remember me always as the father who loved you so very much. Please devote attention to your mother, who will need it now more than ever. I pray that you will start a family and bring children into the world to follow in your footsteps. Tell them about me.

Take care of yourself.

Your loving father

Ferdinand Rafael's condition continued to worsen, and the doctors lost all hope for his recovery. Sylvia's mother wanted to summon her daughter urgently to her husband's bedside, but she didn't know where to find her. She contacted the Israeli Embassy in Pretoria and requested that they locate her daughter, who, she said, was working for a commercial firm in Paris. The embassy staff, with the help of the Israeli Foreign Office, discovered that Sylvia was working for the Mossad, but they were ordered not to convey that information to the family. Meanwhile, in Norway, Sylvia, who had not been briefed beforehand about how to behave if she were arrested, continued to deny any connection with Israel at that stage in her interrogation. The Mossad also believed that the disclosure of her true identity must be avoided for the time being.

Ferdinand Rafael was buried while Sylvia was locked up in the detention center; she was totally unaware her father had died. Only on the eve of her trial did a representative of the Israeli Embassy inform her of her father's death, after which her interrogators permitted her to speak to her mother on the phone. She expressed her deep sorrow and revealed to her mother that she was under arrest. Tears rolled down her cheeks throughout the conversation.

"Your father wanted so much to see you before he died," her mother said in a sorrowful voice. "Since you left for Israel, he only saw you once, when you came for that short visit to South Africa. He spoke of you almost every day. We both hoped you would visit us again."

"I couldn't," sobbed Sylvia.

"I really miss you," said her mother.

"I miss you too, Mother."

"Do you need anything?"

"No, thank you."

"Write often."

"I will."

After a four-hour drive north from Oslo, the traveler reaches a small junction that leads to a few remote villages, then a dirt road leading straight into a thick forest. On a sign on a wooden pole at the side of the road is written the name "Schjødt" in black letters and, beneath it, "Private road. No entry."

A car bearing diplomatic plates passed the sign and continued on its way into the forest. Inside, behind the driver, sat Meir Rosen, the legal advisor of the Israeli Foreign Ministry (later to be appointed Israel's ambassador to the United States, and later ambassador to

France), who had arrived in Norway in order to deal with the arrest of the combatant team. By then, all the prisoners had been permitted to confess that they were Israelis.

Rosen was anxious. All his requests to the Norwegian authorities to meet with the prisoners and bring them letters and newspapers from home had been refused. Even a meeting with the Norwegian attorney general hadn't produced results. The Israeli prime minister, the heads of the Foreign Office in Jerusalem, and the commanders of the Mossad all had their hopes pinned on him. He knew that he daren't return to Israel empty-handed.

Rosen's attempts to reach the office of Annæus Schjødt, one of the most prominent attorneys in Norway, in order to convince him to take the case, had been fruitless. Schjødt was vacationing in a remote cabin in the middle of a forest. After a considerable effort, Rosen managed to contact him by phone.

"Is it urgent?" asked the attorney.

"Extremely."

Schjødt invited Rosen to visit him at his cabin.

The vehicle entered the forest and was enveloped in darkness. The driver turned on the headlights and slowed down. A strong smell of leaf mold and pine resin filtered in through the windows. Every now and then, startled reindeer and wildcats dashed across the car's path. Muffled animal sounds could be heard in the distance, and the heat of the day was replaced by a penetrating chill.

After more than an hour, the sun suddenly appeared. The forest was left behind, and a breathtaking panorama came into view: lofty mountains whose peaks seemed to touch the sky, waterfalls, azure lakes, and green valleys. At the heart of these stunning views was located a wooden cabin that looked as though it had emerged from a fairy tale. Next to the hut was a vegetable garden in which lettuce and cabbage were growing. On the veranda facing the mountains sat a tall, gray-haired man of about sixty smoking a pipe. When he saw the car stopping near the hut, he got up and walked toward Meir Rosen, who was emerging from the vehicle. They shook hands. "You must be starving," said Annæus Schjødt. "Please join me for lunch."

They sat down at a table loaded with different kinds of hard and soft cheese, sausages, vegetables, loaves of bread, and yellow country butter. Schjødt invited Rosen's driver to join them. "I escape to this place every four weeks," he said, "in all seasons and in all weather. Nothing can replace quiet, isolation, and a breath of fresh air."

Annæus Schjødt owned a thriving law firm, which was considered among the foremost legal practices in Oslo. The firm employed dozens of lawyers and mainly represented politicians and businessmen. Schjødt, who had accumulated a fortune and considerable real estate, had excellent connections with the government. His father, who had also been an attorney, had represented the prosecution at the trial of Vidkun Quisling, the Norwegian premier who had collaborated with the Nazi invaders in World War II and was subsequently executed for treason.

Schjødt lived in an elegant house on the outskirts of Oslo with his wife and three children, where he would hold receptions that were widely covered in the local press. He was highly respected, even loved, by the press, and was well known in Norway. It was held to his credit that when the Nazis were executing thousands of Norwegians, he had refused to sit back and do nothing, but had escaped to England, where he had served as a fighter pilot in the Royal Air Force, participating in countless bombing missions against the enemy.

At the end of the meal, Rosen and Schjødt closeted themselves in the attorney's study. It was a large room lined with bookcases, in the center of which was an antique writing desk.

"I can imagine why you've come," said the Norwegian. He had read in the newspapers about the arrest of the Mossad clandestine combatants.

"I would be delighted if you would take it upon yourself to defend our detainees," Rosen said hopefully. He didn't expect the prisoners to be released without a trial, and Schjødt was a consummate professional who could surely provide them with the best possible defense.

Schjødt asked for details about each of the detainees.

Finally he said, "My fees are quite steep."

"The State of Israel will foot the bill," Rosen answered quickly. The Mossad had agreed to pay any sum, on condition that the detainees return home safely.

"I'll look into the case upon my return to Oslo," promised the attorney.

Sitting in that remote cabin at the end of the forest, neither Schjødt nor Rosen had any way of knowing if or when the trial would take place. And they couldn't begin to imagine the dramatic, unexpected impact the case would have on the life of the Norwegian attorney.

Sylvia's days in the detention center were long, monotonous, and filled with disturbing thoughts. Sylvia couldn't adjust to being incarcerated, to the darkness, the narrow cell, the food, the isolation. Any attempts to interrogate her had ceased, since she totally refused to cooperate. The only human being she came in contact with was the female prison guard who delivered her meals like clockwork. Although the woman hardly knew any English, Sylvia had tried to engage her in conversation once or twice. Human contact was as vital for Sylvia as the air she breathed, but the guard didn't respond.

Actually, this experience wasn't so different from others Sylvia had undergone during her training as a clandestine combatant. She had been arrested more than once and was forced to adjust to difficult conditions, remaining in isolation for hours; but she had never before been incarcerated for an unlimited period. She had never felt so lonely in her life. Only a short time previously, she had been caught up in the excitement of an operation that was meant to be the biggest and most important of her career. Now her former enthusiasm had been replaced by the fear that she was probably going to be accused of murder.

Her wristwatch had been taken from her when she was arrested, so she had no way of knowing the time or the day of the week or how long she had been under arrest. She only knew that every day, at a fixed time, two female prison guards led her to the showers and waited for her until she was done. That was the only time of day that Sylvia spent in a lighted space. Immediately after her shower, she was returned to her dark cell and locked in as before.

Then one day, miraculously, an electric light came on in her cell. She heard footsteps approaching and the jangling of a key in the lock. The door opened and revealed a prison guard, who said, "You've got a visitor. Come with me."

They walked down long corridors until they reached a small, windowless room. When they entered, Sylvia saw a table and two chairs. On one of them sat a stranger wearing an expensive suit and emanating a faint scent of cologne that was reminiscent of another world outside the prison walls.

The man rose from his chair and shook her hand. He was as tall as she was, and his English was flawless.

"My name is Annæus Schjødt," he began, "and I have been hired by the Israeli government to defend you."

"You have thirty minutes," interjected the prison guard, exiting from the room and leaving them alone.

Sylvia smiled sadly at her visitor and asked him, "Do you think there will be a trial?"

"Unfortunately, yes," her attorney replied. "Norway is a law-abiding country, which is unable to release murder suspects without a trial."

"What are our chances?"

"According to the letter of the law, you are liable to be convicted of murder or as an accessory to murder, which will entail long years of imprisonment. I will do my best to convince the court to impose much lighter sentences on you and your partners."

"How will you do that?"

"I won't do it on my own. I've put together teams of talented lawyers to work with me. Each team will defend a different group of detainees. Irwin Shimron, your former state attorney, will arrive from Israel to assist me. We will claim that Israel has been dragged into a war by the terrorist organizations. Your assignment was to punish the murderers in order to deter further terrorists."

"Do you recommend that I testify?"

"Yes. They know everything already anyhow."

Schjødt took an interest in Sylvia's biography, her family, and details regarding her stay in Norway. His voice was soft and pleasant, and she enjoyed every minute of the conversation.

"Tell me what's happening outside," she asked. "I haven't been allowed to read a newspaper since my arrest."

He informed her that the newspapers had been giving wide coverage to the Lillehammer Affair, that Israel had been exerting pressure to release the detainees, and that there was a suggestion to offer monetary compensation to Bushiki's family. The assumption was that this might soften up the court when the time came to sentence the Israelis.

At the end of their allotted time, Schjødt gathered up his papers and put them into his briefcase.

"It was nice meeting you," he said as they parted. "You are a very unusual woman."

Sylvia was sorry he had seen her dressed in prison uniform.

"I'm not looking my best at the moment," she smiled.

"You look wonderful," he said gallantly as he left.

A few hours later, two prison guards opened her cell door and transferred her to a roomier cell with a window. She was sure that Annæus Schjødt had been instrumental in this. She was now allowed to eat her meals in the communal dining room and take daily walks around the prison yard, where nobody prevented her from having conversations with other women prisoners. One of them asked her the reason for her arrest.

"I'm a call girl," Sylvia joked.

The prisoner looked her up and down, and asked, "Who are your clients?"

"Arabs, mainly," smiled the clandestine combatant of the Special Operations Unit.

Sylvia felt much more comfortable in her new cell. She was still alone, locked up in a detention center and well guarded, but loneliness didn't plague her as it had before. Annæus Schjødt had helped her overcome the worst of her depression and had given her the feeling that she had someone she could depend on. During his frequent visits, he demonstrated much more warmth than might be expected of a cool, formal Norwegian attorney. He knew how to say the right thing and in the correct tone of voice. He cut away her depression like a surgeon removing a malignant growth. After each visit, Sylvia could still feel his warm handshake, while the scent of his cologne remained in her nostrils. She found herself thinking of him often, clinging to his encouraging words, his promises to do everything he could to help her during the trial. She asked herself if she was falling in love with him.

She knew that he was several years older than she was and that he had a wife and family. She was aware that during their meetings he didn't relate to her as a man to an attractive woman, but as a friend coming to her aid in time of need; still, this didn't change her growing feelings for him. She didn't waste time wondering if this love could possibly have a future or if he felt the same way about her. The most important thing was that he had come into her life at its lowest point and he listened to what she had to say and promised his support. She desperately needed to cling to human contact that was warm, pleasant, and sincere, and the attorney supplied just that.

With every passing day, Annæus occupied her thoughts more

and more. At night, her eyes wide open in the darkness, she fantasized about the continuation of their relationship. She believed that they would meet many times more in the detention center in conjunction with the trial. Afterward, she would continue to meet him on a daily basis in the courtroom, and he would probably also visit her later in prison. She found herself repeatedly recalling their first encounter in the visitors' room of the detention center, her pleasure at the attention he paid her, the way he listened to what she said, and his tone of voice. She asked herself continually what he must think of her. What impression had she made on him? Did she appear to him to be a depressive bundle of nerves? Could he see her positive side?

Little did Sylvia know that she also occupied Annæus Schjødt's thoughts. He left the detention center after his visits aware of the fact that Sylvia had aroused emotions in him that he hadn't been prepared for. He had read a lot about her in the newspapers before their first meeting, mainly articles that presented accounts of the operations she had participated in, praising her for her bravery in her struggle against armed terrorists all over Europe. The articles described the hatred and fear she aroused in terrorist leaders in general, and in Ali Hassan Salameh in particular. Schjødt had been expecting to meet a tough, rough-voiced, muscular, hard-faced combatant. Instead he had encountered a radiantly beautiful, softspoken, intelligent woman, who made a powerful impression on him on their very first meeting.

Just as Sylvia had done, Annæus also recalled their encounters in detail. He remembered her tears, her yearning to hear a kind human voice. He admitted to himself that he liked her very much, perhaps even more than that, but developing a relationship with a woman was the last thing he needed, especially one who was a murder suspect and whom he was supposed to defend. He knew that he wouldn't be able to do his job properly if his relationship with Sylvia went beyond what was appropriate between an attorney and his client. When such affairs developed, they generally resulted in scandalous headlines in the gossip columns, broken marriages, and investigations by the Ethics Committee of the Norwegian Bar Association.

He assumed that circumstances would in any case make any relationship between them impossible. Sylvia would remain in the detention center until the end of the trial. After that, she would probably be sent to prison for a few years. He would of course con tinue to meet her, but their encounters would be work related and would take place behind bars.

As he entered the building on Karl Johannes Avenue where his law firm was located, Annæus Schjødt forced himself to shake off such thoughts. After all, he tried to convince himself, this was just another case. In the long run, Sylvia would disappear from his life, and he from hers. He had a wife and children, a reputation, and a satisfying profession. He didn't need to complicate his life with such distractions.

As part of Sylvia's improved conditions, the prohibition on visits by the Israeli Embassy representative in Oslo was lifted, and Vice-Ambassador Eliezer Palmor, who was responsible for looking after the detainees, met with Sylvia and the other prisoners, promising them that everything possible was being done to provide them with a suitable legal defense. He made a list of their requests for things such as toiletries, underwear, books, and newspapers, and announced that the prison authorities would now allow them to send and receive unlimited mail.

Before he left, he handed Sylvia a few English-language newspapers. A prominent headline in one of them screamed, "Lillehammer Suspects to Receive Heavy Sentences." With mounting dread, she read the article: "The spokesman for the prosecution in the upcoming trial of the Lillehammer suspects announced today that according to Norwegian law, they are expected to be sent to prison for a period of no less than ten years."

Sylvia felt the earth give way beneath her. The period after the Lillehammer shooting had not been at all easy, but she had continued to hope that, if and when her case came to trial, the court would not impose a harsh sentence on her. Now she suddenly realized that they might possibly treat her like a common criminal deserving to be severely punished. She was close to forty, a single woman without children. Ten years in prison, even seven years if she were released earlier for good behavior, would eliminate any chance of her marrying and raising a family. Contemplating such a possibility plunged her into deep depression. She crawled into bed and sobbed uncontrollably. The thick walls of her cell stifled her cries. More than ever before, she needed someone to comfort her, a friend she could pour her heart out to, who would give her hope and encouragement. She had no contact with her teammates, who were being held somewhere far away, or with the other prisoners. Even her interrogators no longer took any interest in her.

Her mood rapidly deteriorated. For years no hardship or danger had managed to break her spirit, but her will of iron and her reputation as a tough combatant seemed now to have disappeared without a trace. Indeed, the abortive operation at Lillehammer, her incarceration, and the punishment awaiting her could have easily dispirited people who were a lot stronger than Sylvia.

She called the guard and asked for tranquilizers. The woman replied that she had to consult with her superiors before granting such a request. A while later she returned and told Sylvia, "Only a doctor can prescribe such pills. Do you want me to call him?"

No, Sylvia didn't want a stranger to see her in such an unstable mental condition.

Feeling helpless, she paced around her cell, periodically bursting into tears, wringing her hands nervously, and feeling the will to fight rapidly draining out of her.

Despite the late hour, she could see that it was broad daylight outside. In Norway in summer, the sun shines through most of the night. For that reason, the windows of all the houses in the country are fitted with black curtains in order to block out the light when the residents retire to bed. Sylvia's window also had a curtain, but it didn't manage to darken her cell effectively, which made it difficult for her to fall asleep.

She suddenly had a strong urge to speak with her attorney. He had treated her with such kindness and understanding and had told her she could call on him if she ever needed anything. Now she needed him more than ever; she needed to hear his soothing voice and any encouragement he could give her. He might think that her appealing to him in the middle of the night was unacceptable and refuse to come, but he was the only person she could turn to.

"It's very late," responded the guard, when Sylvia asked her to call Schjødt.

"I'm aware of that."

"Can't it wait until tomorrow?"

"No."

The guard left and returned some time later to tell Sylvia that her request had been approved.

"Do you know how Mr. Schjødt responded?" asked Sylvia apprehensively.

"I don't know," replied the guard. "The duty officer spoke with him."

Less than an hour passed before Annæus appeared. He looked worried when he met her in the visitors' room.

"Why were you crying?" he asked when he saw her red eyes. His presence calmed Sylvia down immediately. He seemed to be an island of sanity, well groomed and elegant, calm and authoritative.

She told him that she had been crying because she felt totally helpless.

"Is that all?" he asked with a smile. He didn't reprimand her for calling him out at such a late hour for no good reason.

"I just had to talk to someone," she admitted. "I felt as though I was losing my mind."

They sat opposite each other. He looked at her with tender, understanding eyes. Then he suddenly got up from his chair, approached her, and hugged her warmly.

"Keep your spirits up," he said softly. "I hope you won't have anything to worry about in court."

Grateful for his kindliness toward her, his vibrant touch, his encouraging promise, Sylvia placed her head on his shoulder like a child seeking refuge in her father's arms.

"Thank you," she mumbled.

In her spacious apartment on Ben Zion Boulevard in Tel Aviv, Judith Nisyhio, the Mossad's director of human resources, finished packing a small suitcase and phoned a taxi to take her to the airport.

A few hours earlier, she had been asked to leave her office and fly urgently to Oslo. She carried a passport under the name of Judith Friedman, her maiden name. She had been asked to visit the prisoners, encourage them, and act as liaison between the Mossad and Eliezer Palmor, the Foreign Ministry representative who was dealing with their case. Palmor met her at the airport. He had imagined that he would be meeting a modern version of Mata Hari, the beautiful German spy who was wrapped in mystery. Instead he met a middle-aged, plump woman wearing glasses and modest attire, who resembled a "good Jewish mother" more than anything else.

Judith Nisyhio had heard a lot about Sylvia, who was fourteen years her junior, but they had never met. Judith had been born in Belgium to an Orthodox Jewish family. Her brother had been active in the Haganah and had smuggled arms for that organization.[1]

Later, in the disguise of a French army officer, he had been instrumental in the illegal immigration of Moroccan Jews.[2] Like her brother, Judith had immigrated to Israel and was a Zionist devoted to the State of Israel; also like him, she had assumed a false identity, posing as a wealthy, non-Jewish Dutch woman who owned a travel agency in Casablanca. Upon returning to Israel, she was recruited to the Mossad and, among other things, was part of the team sent to capture Adolf Eichmann in Argentina. She was responsible for maintaining the apartment where Eichmann was kept from the time of his kidnapping until he was flown to Israel.

In 1962 she was sent by the Mossad to locate Yossele Schuhmacher, a boy who immigrated with his family to Israel from Russia and was transferred to his grandfather's care after his parents fell into financial difficulties. When the parents' situation improved, they asked to have their son back, but the grandfather, an ultra-Orthodox Jew from Mea Shearim,[3] refused, claiming that the parents intended to return the boy to Russia and convert him to Christianity. Yossele disappeared, and his grandfather refused to disclose his whereabouts. On David Ben-Gurion's instructions, the Mossad went into action. It was suspected that the boy was being hidden by the ultra-Orthodox community in Antwerp, Belgium. Due to her Belgian background and her command of the Flemish language, Judith Nisyhio was sent to the Satmer congregation in Antwerp, introducing herself as an ultra-Orthodox woman seeking an arranged marriage. She won the trust of the congregation members and eventually discovered that the boy had been there, but had been smuggled to the United States. A short time later, representatives of the Mossad found Yossele in Brooklyn and returned him to his parents.

"There's a surprise waiting for you," the guard smiled at Sylvia as she opened her cell door. On her way to the visitors' room, Sylvia tried to guess what was in store for her. She thought it was probably her attorney or someone from the Mossad or the Embassy, but it would take more than that to surprise her.

The visitors' room looked more like an ordinary living room than a visitors' room in a detention center. There were a few seating areas, pictures on the walls, and no barriers to isolate the prisoners from their visitors.

To Sylvia's amazement, her mother and one of her brothers were sitting on one of the sofas. Sylvia fell into her mother's arms, tears rolling down her cheeks.

"How did this happen . . . When did you arrive?" she asked.

"We arrived yesterday," said her mother, wiping her eyes with a handkerchief. "We read so much about you in the papers and memorized your letters. We didn't know if we would be allowed to visit you, but we felt that we must come. We booked a hotel room nearby, and luckily our request to visit you was granted right away."

"I'm so happy to see you!" Sylvia cried.

Sylvia's mother told her about her father's last days.

"I was afraid that might happen," said Sylvia softly.

The three of them sat silently for a while, thinking about the father who didn't manage to see his daughter before he died.

"I pray for you to withstand this ordeal," said her mother at last.

"Apparently I'm stronger than I thought."

"You were always a strong girl. You always knew what you wanted."

"I'm so sorry about all the worry I've caused you, Father, my brothers and sisters," said Sylvia. "It is so painful for me that I wasn't with Father at his last moments."

"I was in total shock when I read about your arrest," said her mother. "I knew you were having a hard time, but I was so proud of you. All our friends phoned to commiserate with me, but I told them that I was glad to finally know where you had disappeared to all those years, what you were doing, and for whom. Now I know that you realized your dream, that you risked your life for a cause that was so dear to you. I remember how it all started, with Alex's last request that we do everything to make sure no more Jews would be killed."

"I did my best," said Sylvia. "I worked hard, gave up a comfortable life, children, and a home of my own, and just when I thought I had reached my ultimate goal, I failed."

Her mother murmured words of encouragement, stroked Sylvia lovingly and gave her a present: a package of dried venison "biltong," the South African national snack. Biltong is generally made from beef or lamb, or even elephant, but the best kind is made from venison.

Sylvia impatiently opened the package and chewed on the tough meat. Its taste brought back memories of her childhood in her parents' home.

"People who take action always make mistakes," her mother said, resuming their conversation. "In the end what matters is the sum total, not one detail or another. When you're yourself again, you'll understand how much you've accomplished."

"Thanks for your encouragement, Mother."

"How are you managing here?" asked Sylvia's brother.

"It's not easy, but I have good people on my side. A special representative of the Mossad has arrived, and the vice-ambassador is working hard on my behalf."

"It says in the papers that there will be a trial," added Sylvia's mother.

"It looks like it."

"You'll need a good attorney."

"I have the best one possible."

"Is he encouraging?"

"Yes. He gives me a lot of support. He's a top professional, one of the best in Norway. He's also a very charming man."

"That sounds like there's something going on between you."

"No, Mother, there isn't, but it's enough that he exists. He's there for me when I need him."

"Does the thought of a trial frighten you?"

"Not anymore."

"I hope they don't give you a harsh sentence."

"So do I. They'll probably send me to the women's prison. I've heard that the conditions there are better than they are here."

Sylvia asked about her brothers and sisters in South Africa, how they were and what they were doing.

"Is there anything you need?" asked her mother.

"Your love and support, Mother. I don't need anything else."

Sylvia's mother and brother stayed with her for over an hour. It was the longest visit that she had been allowed since she had arrived at the detention center. For the first time, the guards didn't set a time limit; they understood how important it was for the three of them to be together.

"We intend staying here for a while," said her mother, "so we'll be visiting you often."

"Wonderful!" she answered. "That will help me a lot."

After her mother and brother had left, Sylvia burst into tears. She deeply regretted all the worry she had caused her parents and that she hadn't managed to spend more time with them. The thought of her mother being left a widow so far away caused her deep sorrow.

Oslo was a quiet, uneventful city. Its newspaper editors were forced to turn inconsequential news items into headlines, and the news articles generally dealt with local politics and were of little interest to the average Norwegian. When someone committed a crime, it gained massive coverage, but such events happened very rarely. Against such a background, the Lillehammer Affair and the subsequent arrest of the Mossad operatives caused great excitement in the local press, filling the headlines for days on end. The newspapers did anything they could to obtain new information about the affair. They interviewed almost anyone connected with it: the victim's widow, his employer, Israeli residents of Norway who might have information about the Mossad's operations, representatives of the prosecution, and experts in criminal law. The popular newspaper *Haftenpost* even sent reporters to France and Italy in order to investigate how leaders of Black September and their associates had met their end there. In a special interview, the Norwegian district attorney stated that he intended to present evidence implicating the arrested Mossad operatives in the deaths of these terrorists.

January 1974 was the coldest month of the year. The temperatures plunged below zero, snow piled up on the streets, and the rivers surrounding Oslo froze over. But none of this deterred dozens of local and foreign reporters and several television crews from flocking to the Engineers' Union Building, where the trial of the Lillehammer arrestees was about to begin. The windowless, nondescript building in the city center with only one main door had been chosen for security reasons over the district courthouse, which boasted large glass windows and multiple entrances. The Norwegian security services were aware that a terrorist attack against the defendants was a real possibility, and the Engineers' Union Building afforded a better chance of protecting them.

In the early morning hours on the first day of the trial, reporters wearing fur hats with earflaps, heavy woolen scarves, and coats zipped up to their chins began congregating around the building. At ten o'clock a convoy of seven police cars with dark curtains covering their windows pulled up in front of the building, accompanied by armed guards in two open vehicles, one leading the way and the other bringing up the rear.

The convoy halted, and police officers surrounded the hand-cuffed defendants as they emerged from the vehicles and quickly led them into the building. Other officers kept the crowd of newsmen at bay, so that they only managed to snap a couple of long-range photos.

In the gray, austere union hall, a raised dais had been constructed for the judges, chairs and tables had been arranged for the prosecution and the defense, a special raised bench behind a railing had been set up for the accused, and seating had been provided for media representatives and the general public. Photographers were not allowed to enter the building, so the newspapers had sent artists whose job it was to sketch the proceedings.

Sylvia sat on the defendants' bench together with her comrades and glanced over at her attorney, who sat at the head of a team of lawyers. Annæus Schjødt's eyes met hers for a brief moment only. He sank back into the folds of his black robe, as if to signify that he was there for no other reason than to perform his legal duties. It would be most unfortunate if anyone became aware of his real feelings for Sylvia.

The trial was conducted in Norwegian, but the defendants were allowed to testify in Hebrew and in English. Gyra Piuhansen had been appointed by the court to be a simultaneous translator. She was thirty years old, a slim, energetic woman who had lived in Haifa for several years when her father had served as the pastor of the Protestant church in that city. Her father had established a network of churches and hostels in various cities around the globe, including Haifa, Ashdod, and Jerusalem, whose purpose was to offer a warm welcome to Norwegian seamen and pilgrims.

Finally it was Sylvia's turn to be called to the witness box. She answered the judges' questions in a clear, determined voice. A hush fell over the audience as she testified about her relatives who had been annihilated by the Nazis in the Ukraine in World War II. Men, women, and children, she said, had been murdered for no reason except that they were Jews. The spectators' eyes were riveted on the woman standing tall and focused in the witness box as she told them that in Israel and in Europe innocent people were being killed whose only crime was that they were Israelis and Jews. She emphasized that the murderers were striking secretly, indiscriminately. They were members of extremist terrorist organizations that enjoyed the protection of certain Arab countries. Among other atrocities, they were guilty of the cold-blooded murder of eleven members of the Israeli team at the 1972 Munich Olympics. She emphasized that the citizens of Israel were peace-loving people who hated war and whose only wish was to live a normal life like everybody else, while the terrorist organizations had set as their main goal to disrupt life in Israel and terrorize its residents. "When the situation became intolerable," she said, "when the terrorist attacks became almost a daily occurrence, a group of clandestine combatants decided to put a stop to it. We came to Lillehammer on the trail of the arch-terrorist Ali Hassan Salameh. Our intention was to hurt him and nobody else. Due to a fatal error, and totally unintentionally, an innocent man was killed, and of course we regret this deeply. The people standing trial in this courtroom are not criminals. Our only crime is that we took it upon ourselves to defend our families and our country from imminent danger."

Although he was determined not to show any emotion, Annæus Schjødt watched Sylvia as though hypnotized. The judge and the audience didn't take their eyes off her, either. When she finished speaking, there was a spontaneous burst of applause. The judge called for silence. Later, in a private conversation, he said, "I would be proud if a woman of Sylvia Rafael's caliber was a citizen of my country."

Despite the defense's attempt to exclude the Mossad from the picture, the court ruled that Israeli intelligence had a clear involvement in the Lillehammer Affair, rather than it having been initiated privately by the accused, as they had claimed. Sentences were handed down immediately after the verdict. One of the defendants was released. Marianne Geldinkof was found guilty of being an accessory to an accidental killing and was sentenced to two and a half years in prison. Dan Arbel was found guilty of being an accessory to murder and was sentenced to five years' imprisonment. Abraham Gemer and Sylvia were found guilty of the same crime and were each sentenced to five and a half years. The sentences were harsher than Sylvia had expected. Her hopes that the court would take the defendants' motives into consideration evaporated in an instant.

Two officers directed Sylvia toward a police car. Annæus Schjødt followed her out. He asked permission to speak to her for a moment.

He took Sylvia aside. "It won't be so bad," he said. "I'll submit an appeal to the Supreme Court."

She looked into his eyes.

"Will you find time to visit me in prison?"

"Of course," he said. "I won't abandon you."

The Lillehammer disaster severely damaged the Mossad's reputation, and especially that of the Special Operations Unit. The organization's commanders read the newspaper reports from Lillehammer and the Oslo courtroom with growing consternation. The fiasco turned the tide of public opinion against the Mossad and prompted harsh criticism on the part of the intelligence community. The Mossad never issued statements in response to reports of its activities and kept its counsel on this occasion as well.

Zvi Zamir and Mike Harari, the planners of the Lillehammer operation, refused to discuss the affair, but their faces betrayed their remorse. Harari learned from the media that the Norwegian authorities were demanding his extradition as the person behind the accidental murder of Ahmad Bushiki. Of course there wasn't a chance that Israel would comply with this request, but Harari would never be able to set foot in Norway again.

In the Mossad there was a general feeling of failure that was made worse by the constant taunting of Ali Hassan Salameh. He was in Beirut surrounded by an admiring public, protected by bodyguards, and confident that no harm would come to him. This was his big opportunity to castigate his enemies, and he did so repeatedly and without hesitation.

Salameh assumed that since the Mossad had yet again failed to locate him, they would finally give up the chase. He didn't take one factor into account: Yitzhak Rabin had been elected to replace Golda Meir as prime minister. Rabin, a former chief of staff of the IDF, would prove to be a formidable new opponent. He summoned Yitzhak Hofi, the new Mossad chief, and declared, "One doesn't retreat from the field in the thick of the battle. Don't give up on Salameh. He mustn't be allowed to escape yet again."

Hofi nodded in agreement. He had served in key positions in the Israeli army and was eager to comply with Rabin's request.

The war against Black September was resumed with additional vigor. One by one, Salameh's key men were eliminated, severely limiting the organization's ability to act. Morale was low, operations dwindled, and Ali couldn't prevent rivalries and arguments from breaking out among opposing factions. Still, nothing seemed to tarnish his personal reputation. On the contrary, he was given two additional responsibilities by Yasser Arafat: to be the head of intelligence for Fatah and the commander of Force 17, a special unit whose purpose was, among other things, to ensure the security of the heads of Fatah, especially Arafat himself. Arafat made sure to include Ali in his meetings with Arab heads of state; although he didn't announce it officially, he was obviously grooming Ali to be his heir.

Since Ali had limited his trips abroad and was concentrating most of his activities in Beirut, it became clear to the Mossad that he could only be terminated inside Lebanon.

The Israeli intelligence community began painstakingly collecting every scrap of information regarding Ali's daily routine: where he worked, who his friends were, where he and Georgina were living after their wedding, and the address of his first wife, Zeinab. A list was even made of the restaurants he frequented. It appeared that Ali was spending a lot of his spare time practicing karate, so someone in the Special Operations Unit suggested that he was probably working out at one of Beirut's physical fitness centers. Representatives of the organization in Beirut began locating such places. They became members of a few of them, spending their days at one or the other, lifting weights, sweating on the exercise bicycles, and swimming in the indoor pools. But Ali was nowhere to be seen.

Seven months into the search for Ali's gym, one of the members of the Special Operations Unit entered the sauna of the Hotel International's fitness center. Through the steam, he caught a glimpse of the man that the entire Mossad was searching for. Ali Salameh lay on a wooden bench, naked as the day he was born, while an attendant beat his body with wet branches.

After discovering the location of Ali's health club, the Special Operations Unit went into immediate action. A large explosive charge was smuggled into Beirut, and an explosives expert visited the sauna to determine where the bomb would be placed and the distance from which it could be detonated.

The intention was to set off the explosive charge the moment Ali entered the sauna; but the plan was never put into action, because it would have resulted in the injury or death of too many innocent bystanders.

Bredveitspenal Women's Prison was an hour's bus ride from central Oslo, on the outskirts of a suburb inhabited mainly by factory hands and middle-class office workers. Formerly a school, the three-story building was surrounded by a high fence in the center of which was a large iron gate. There were no sentry towers or patrols around the fence. One guard sat at the gate, and when he wasn't there, someone could be summoned to open it by ringing an electric bell.

It wasn't easy to obtain a place at Bredveitspenal. Sylvia had to undergo a series of psychological tests before being declared suitable to be an inmate there. Every woman who was sentenced to imprisonment in Oslo hoped to be sent to Bredveitspenal. On her arrival, Sylvia was led to a large private apartment with a view of a thick forest. The apartment had its own shower. On the table in the center of the room was a freshly baked cake that had been placed there by the prison administration as a welcome gift to the new inmate.

One of Sylvia's first visitors was Judith Nisyhio, the Mossad representative.

"Is there anything we can do for you?" Judith asked.

"There is only one thing I want," Sylvia replied. "That you make every effort to close accounts with Ali Salameh. I can no longer do it, so now it's up to you."

Judith Nisyhio promised to convey Sylvia's message to the commanders of the Special Operations Unit immediately upon her return to Israel.

Sylvia was pleasantly surprised by conditions in the prison. Although she had expected an improvement compared to the detention center, the transfer to the women's prison proved to be a total reversal. She had a three-room apartment, whose only resemblance to a prison cell was the bars on the windows. The treatment she received was friendly and considerate. The prison warden, Karen Petersen, resembled a house mother more than a jailer. She devoted personal attention to each prisoner, offering assistance when necessary, lending a listening ear, and acting as a kind of social worker.

The prisoners lived in roomy, clean, and well-kept quarters, filled with the light that poured in through the large windows. The bars didn't disturb the feeling of home that the prison imparted to its inhabitants. They were allowed to wear ordinary clothing and could choose from a variety of enrichment courses, including language learning, art, history, child education, and psychology, among other subjects. Sylvia chose to study psychology. Nurit Golan, an Israeli student who was studying Norwegian literature on a scholarship at Oslo University, was hired by Eliezer Palmor to tutor Sylvia and

Marianne in Hebrew twice a week. Nurit quickly realized that the two women were less interested in the lessons than in the hour of pleasant conversation that broke up their daily routine. The tutoring was done one on one, since even as prisoners together the two women hadn't taken to each other. Once a week, all the prisoners saw a psychologist named Leo Eitinger, a Holocaust survivor.

After a few months of good behavior, the two Israeli prisoners were allowed to spend an afternoon at a dental clinic in Oslo accompanied by the prison social worker. In order to fulfill requirements toward a Bachelor of Arts degree at Tel Aviv University, Abraham Gemer was given permission to leave his prison unguarded in order to study in the Oslo University library. Even when he needed an orthopedic operation and had to be hospitalized, he did so unguarded.

Sylvia was permitted to send and receive an unlimited number of letters, which were not subject to censorship on the part of the prison authorities. She was also allowed to receive visitors who were not relatives or official representatives. One of these was the author and playwright Ephraim Kishon, who was in Oslo with his wife for the screening of his film *The Policeman* on Norwegian television. Sylvia never forgot that heartwarming visit.

She asked to receive guitar lessons and showed a real aptitude for the instrument. She was soon playing well enough to accompany the prison chorus in singing popular Norwegian folk songs. She soon added some Israeli songs to their repertoire. Annæus Schjødt visited Sylvia almost daily. When she knew he was about to arrive, she would be especially careful about her appearance. When the weather allowed, they would sit on a bench in the well-tended garden and talk for hours. In winter, they would sit by the fire in the prison's large visitors' room. Schjødt always brought Sylvia a box of her favorite chocolates, and when she was given the opportunity to spend a few hours in town, he would invite her to a good restaurant or a popular café.

Sylvia greatly enjoyed Annæus's visits; he was not only an attentive companion, but also an intelligent man of the world. Their conversations ranged over a wide variety of subjects, and Sylvia felt more strongly than ever that she had finally found a man she could love and respect.

Neither of them ever mentioned his wife or children. Sylvia respected the fact that he had a family and didn't encourage him to disrupt it for her sake. His friendship was too important for her to jeopardize by her making unreasonable demands. "I would marry him today," she once told the prison warden, "but he hasn't asked me, and I won't suggest it."

"Give him time . . . he will," the warden assured her. "I've seen how his eyes shine when he looks at you."

A few months after she was sent to prison, Sylvia received a surprising letter from Hadas and Shmuel Zamir, members of Kibbutz Ramat Hakovesh. They informed her that her younger brother, David, had been a volunteer in the kibbutz for a year and had told them about her fascinating life. It had been decided by the general meeting of the kibbutz to adopt her as an honorary member. Hadas, a special education teacher, was in charge of coordinating activities on Sylvia's behalf. She sent her letters written by the kibbutz members and pictures drawn for her by the kindergarten children. She sent photos of the Festival of the First Fruits, the Passover Seder, and various cultural events. "We would be delighted if you would come here after your release," Hadas wrote. "We would provide you with a house and do everything in our power to spoil you as much as possible. Your presence in Ramat Hakovesh would be a great honor."

Sylvia was deeply touched by this gesture and began regularly corresponding with Hadas and Shmuel. She distributed among the prison inhabitants the crate of oranges they sent her at the height of the picking season. She smiled to herself while peeling one of the oranges, remembering how her instructor at the School for Special Operations had taught her how to do so without arousing suspicion.

Sylvia pasted all the letters and drawings she received from the kibbutz in a special album. None of the kibbutz members ever asked her questions about her activities in the Mossad. They were aware that she would never answer such questions.

In addition to the correspondence with Ramat Hakovesh, Sylvia was swamped with encouraging letters sent by Israeli citizens and Jews all over the world. She received many letters from the relatives of those who had been killed or injured in terrorist attacks. They sent her parcels with various sweets as well as clothing. She received marriage proposals from at least half a dozen men.

She answered all the letters in English in her own handwriting. She corresponded constantly with her mother and her brothers and sisters, and in her letters she described prison life: her conditions, her daily routine, the other prisoners, and the prison staff.

She repeatedly begged their forgiveness: "I can only imagine the grief I have caused you, but you needn't worry about me. You know that I behaved as I did out of conviction. As a Jew and a Zionist, I was duty-bound to do so. I took a mission upon myself, and I am at peace with my decision. The conditions in prison are excellent, and there's a good chance that I will be released sooner than expected."

Sylvia also wrote to Abraham Gemer, who had been her friend and colleague for so many years, and asked her teacher, Nurit, to make sure he received her letter:

> To Abraham, my teacher and mentor:
>
> You must understand how I feel after the whole dreadful affair. It seems that my time in prison will be quite comfortable and that they won't be too tough on me. But I can't stop turning over in my mind what happened, and the more I think about it, the more convinced I am that the unfortunate events in Lillehammer could have been avoided. Something in me broke after Lillehammer . . . it eroded my desire to continue serving with the people I respected so highly. My heroes had appeared to be men of absolute integrity, but suddenly I saw them in a different light. What a pity . . .

After Abraham had finished reading the letter, he asked Nurit to tell Sylvia that he completely understood what she was feeling.

A few days later a letter arrived for her from Tel Aviv. It was unsigned, but it was obviously from one of the Mossad commanders. In the envelope was a poem dedicated to her:

> Like a huge vacuum cleaner
> The Mossad sucks in
> A variety of people
> But only the best remain—
>
> An impressive array of women,
> An excellent choice of men,
> All of them top-grade clandestine combatants
> And—above all—loyal to the end.

They're determined to succeed
In reaching every target.
They are skilled in tracking them down
Even on the darkest night.

Among their ranks was a woman
Who was beautiful, clever, and wise,
But she had one defect,
That stood out above the rest:

She considered all of us to be
Absolutely perfect.
She viewed us as being
God's messengers on earth.

So please inform her loud and clear
That all of us, whether on land or on sea,
And as talented as we may be
Are only human, after all.

Please explain that we haven't descended from Heaven,
That we all have faults
And not a trace of wings
And that we too can err . . .

The Supreme Court of Norway rejected the appeals made on behalf of the prisoners, and their sentences were not rescinded. The Norwegian authorities, however, had in fact no intention of incarcerating the Israeli prisoners for the full term of their sentences. Government ministers, police authorities, and wardens were all sympathetic with their cause, but it was important that they appear to uphold the law. The Norwegians were full of pride that, despite diplomatic pressure from Israel, the suspects had been tried and convicted. Justice had been done, and now it no longer mattered how long they actually remained in prison.

Thus, one after another, as a result of Israel's continuing efforts on their behalf, those accused of the Lillehammer killing were granted early release and sent home. Not a single newspaper was critical of the government's decision. After all, these weren't hardened criminals, but clandestine combatants whose motives were understandable and whose ideology was easily identified with.

Eventually, Sylvia Rafael and Abraham Gemer, who had received the most severe sentences, found themselves the last of their fellow combatants to remain in prison. Although there had been no official announcement as yet, rumor had it that they were soon to be released. The expected decision aroused a wave of speculation among journalists, who competed with one another to collect every scrap of information regarding it. Annæus Schjødt told Sylvia that he expected to receive news of her release at any moment.

Sylvia's life in prison couldn't have been more comfortable, but she was still denied personal freedom. She was gradually given more days off and was allowed to spend them unguarded. She received time off to go shopping for clothes and cosmetics or just take a walk around town. She was careful to watch her weight by not ordering whipped-cream cakes with her coffee when she was invited out by Annæus to a café or restaurant.

Sylvia waited anxiously for news of her release. She would have loved to stay on in Oslo with Annæus, but she knew that this was impossible, as the prisoners would not be allowed to remain in Norway after their release. All those released before her had undergone the same process: a hurried departure from prison and direct transport to a plane that was waiting on an airport runway to take off for Israel. After their arrival, after a short time spent with their families, they were whisked off for debriefing at the Mossad, in an attempt to finally close the Lillehammer file.

Sylvia's love affair with Annæus was still a well-kept secret. Nobody else knew anything about it, not even the attorney's closest friends, who had indeed noticed that his relationship with his wife had become distant of late. She had always joined him at official events, but now no longer did so. Their friends and family assumed that they were going through some kind of temporary crisis.

Eliezer Palmor, the Israeli vice-ambassador in Oslo, faithfully continued to fulfill the role of liaison with the Lillehammer prisoners. He visited Sylvia frequently, bearing newspapers and books from Israel as well as up-to-date reports regarding the efforts being made toward her release. Before Passover, Palmor appealed to the prison authorities and asked that Sylvia and Abraham Gemer be allowed to celebrate the holiday with his own family. He promised to put them up at his residence and return them to prison on time. Three days before Passover eve, the request was granted, and they were given eight days off.

They were taken in an embassy car to Palmor's house, where they were each provided with a room. It was the two Israelis' first opportunity to discuss the Lillehammer fiasco. The events had obviously taken their toll on Abraham. He grimly enumerated the causes of the failure, accusing the commanders of the Special Operations Unit of faulty planning and execution, which had irreparably injured its reputation and that of the Mossad as a whole. He complained that the arrested team members had been forced to pay a high price for blunders that were no fault of their own. Sylvia agreed with him completely.

On Passover eve, some of Palmor's prominent Jewish friends were invited to the Passover Seder, along with embassy employees and Annæus Schjødt.[4] They sat around a table covered with a pure white cloth and laden with festive dishes that had been especially flown in from Israel. Eliezer Palmor conducted the Seder in the traditional manner. As was customary, each of those present was asked to read a portion of the Haggadah,[5] and Sylvia read a passage in Hebrew that stated, "Next year we will be freed from slavery," just as her father had declared at their family Seders at home in South Africa. Annæus, who was sitting beside her, joined in as they enumerated the Ten Plagues of Egypt. Later they ate a traditional meal and sang holiday songs, accompanied by Sylvia on the guitar.

Palmor's youngest daughter, nine-year-old Emmy, was wandering among the guests and suddenly burst into the kitchen, where her mother was preparing coffee and cake.

"Have you noticed?" she asked her mother excitedly.

"Have I noticed what?" Shoshana asked in surprise.

"Annæus and Sylvia. Something's going on between them."

"What do you mean, Emmy?"

"I heard her call him 'my Viking.' The whole time they keep looking at each other so tenderly, whispering together, laughing, and looking so happy. They're in love, Mommy . . ."

Spring arrived. The sun appeared among the clouds, birdsong could be heard again from the budding tree branches, and the snowdrifts slowly melted. In Eliezer Palmor's office at the Israeli Embassy, the telephone rang. The director of the Norwegian attorney general's office asked to see him immediately but didn't reveal the purpose of the meeting.

Palmor waited anxiously for the Norwegian's arrival. It wasn't an everyday occurrence for such a dignitary to visit the embassy. Once he arrived, the visitor entered Palmor's office and hurriedly closed the door behind him.

"What I'm about to tell you," said the director, "must remain a carefully guarded secret for the time being. I implore you not to reveal it to a soul, not even to the embassy staff."

"I promise," said Palmor in surprise.

"Well," the director said in a celebratory tone, "we decided to-day to release Rafael and Gemer, the two remaining prisoners."

Palmor had known that this was bound to happen eventually. Even so, he hadn't imagined that he would be so deeply touched when the time actually arrived.

"Secrecy is essential," said the director. "We fear that a terrorist group might jeopardize their safety."

"Four prisoners have already been released," commented Palmor, "and they got away unharmed."

"Rafael and Gemer are a different story, my friend. They were the only ones accused of being accessories to murder after the court decided that they had played a central role in the Lillehammer kill-ing. We are convinced that if news of their release gets out, they are liable to be the victims of a terrorist attack before they even reach the airport."

He emphasized yet again that nobody was to know the exact time of their release, not even the prison authorities. The director of the attorney general's office then told Palmor the details of a plan that had received the approval of the Norwegian security authori-ties. According to this plan, Palmor would appeal to the authorities of the prisons where Sylvia and Abraham were incarcerated and request that they be given two days off in order to participate in a large dinner party in honor of his wife's birthday. "The request will probably be granted," said the Norwegian.

Palmor made the request a short time later, and it was imme-diately approved. Palmor suggested to Sylvia that she pack a case with a few things that she might want to take with her, and when she heard this, she immediately guessed that the birthday party was a ruse to get her out of prison and onto a plane to Israel. Her heart was pounding and her hands shaking with excitement as she packed her belongings, picked up her guitar, and took her leave of the prison warden and her staff, who didn't understand why she was acting so emotional. "You'll be back in two days' time," they reminded Sylvia.

She didn't answer, but only smiled faintly.

"Do you know something that you're not telling us?" the director demanded.

"I don't know a thing," said Sylvia truthfully.

She got into Palmor's car, which was waiting outside the gate. As they drove off, she turned around and glanced at the prison for the last time. She had been imprisoned for almost two years, first at the detention center, and then at the prison. During that period, one factor had helped her retain her optimism for the future: the growing love between herself and her attorney.

On the way, they collected Abraham Gemer, who had also guessed that the birthday party was no more than a cover story. He had also packed his things and brought along a radio that he had acquired while in prison. They both asked Palmor if they had guessed correctly, but received no reply.

That evening Annæus Schjødt arrived at Palmor's apartment. He had already been informed about what was about to occur.

He and Sylvia spent a long time together alone in one of the rooms. He told her that he had already informed his wife about her and that he was initiating divorce proceedings. "Unfortunately, she reacted quite badly," he said. For the first time they discussed their future together, and he promised to marry her as soon as he was free.

Early the next morning, police officers knocked on Palmor's door. They transported Sylvia, Abraham, and Palmor to a police car that was carefully guarded by a vehicle full of armed police officers. The streets of Oslo were still empty, the windows were tightly shuttered, the shops hadn't yet opened, and there was hardly any traffic on the road leading to the airport.

For security reasons, the three of them were to be flown first to Zurich. As the plane took off from Oslo, Sylvia looked out of the window at the city receding below her and hoped that she would soon return, marry her beloved, and spend the rest of her life there with him. These thoughts partially compensated for the mental anguish she had suffered since Lillehammer.

After a short stopover in Zurich, Sylvia and Abraham boarded an El Al plane and took off for Israel carrying Israeli passports.

"Patricia Roxenburg" had ceased to exist, and Sylvia Rafael reverted back to her true identity.

The report that the last of the Lillehammer detainees had been released was made public only after Sylvia and Abraham had left Norway, but then it became front-page news. Only authorized persons—close relatives and representatives of the Special Operations Unit of the Mossad—were allowed to await their arrival at Ben Gurion Airport. After the plane touched down, Yael and Michal, Abraham Gemer's daughters, ran toward him and fell into his arms, as did his wife, Dina. His son, Amit, who had been born after his imprisonment, stood at the sidelines, hesitating to approach the strange man. When his father turned to give him a hug, he exclaimed in surprise: "I didn't know Daddy had blue eyes." From the airport the family went off to a hotel in southern Israel for a restful vacation.

A car from Kibbutz Ramat Hakovesh collected Sylvia and transported her to Hadas and Shmuel Zamir's home. That evening the kibbutz held a celebratory dinner in her honor, which was attended by a large number of guests, including several newspaper reporters and photographers. A few weeks later Moti Kfir, the commander of the School for Special Operations, invited Sylvia to his home for dinner. The governor of Gaza, Yitzhak Segev, took her on an excursion to Mount Sinai and its environs.[6]

A month after her return, Sylvia was called for debriefing at Mossad headquarters. The directors of the Mossad received her warmly, expressing their deep regret for what had occurred in Lillehammer. Although they didn't trouble her with unnecessary questions, she felt compelled to say, "It is important for me to testify regarding the events at Lillehammer, and I insist that my testimony be examined by the committee investigating the affair." They wrote down her request and invited her to return to work for the Mossad in an executive capacity. She turned down the offer and didn't need to explain the reasons why. When it came time for her to leave, one of the Mossad commanders accompanied her to her car.

"We haven't forgotten Salameh," he told her. "We'll eventually track him down."

Meanwhile, Annæus Schjødt was back in Oslo, working on Sylvia's being allowed to return to Norway. He hadn't anticipated that there would be any problem with this, but he soon discovered that he was mistaken. The government authorities promised to discuss his request, but they made it clear that the matter was delicate and that there was no guarantee of a positive outcome.

A leak in the Norwegian Foreign Office prompted an article in the *Dagenblat* newspaper about Sylvia's intention to return to Oslo. This disclosure aroused a widespread response. Editorials and letters to the editor fell into two categories: support of Sylvia's return and objections to it. Those opposed claimed that it was unacceptable to permit an "Israeli terrorist" to return to the scene of her crime. A reader by the name of Jansen Schumann wrote to the *National* newspaper, "Norway mustn't allow criminals to live within its borders, especially those who are pursued by various terrorist organizations. We mustn't create a situation in which blood flows through our streets again. Ms. Rafael must be informed that she is unwelcome here."

Public opinion fired the first shots, but the politicians finished the job. A short time later, the Norwegian government gave its official reply: Sylvia would not be awarded an entry visa.

Annæus didn't give up. He inundated government offices and law courts with appeals against the decision, but his efforts were again unsuccessful. He finally gathered together all his influential friends and convinced them to take up the cause. Even Annæus's wife, although he was involved in divorce proceedings against her, and the widow of the murdered waiter, Ahmad Bushiki, joined in the campaign to return Sylvia to Norway.

Annæus flew to Israel and arrived at Kibbutz Ramat Hakovesh. Sylvia greeted him joyfully. The hugged passionately, and Annæus told her that he had decided to remain with her in Israel until such time as the Norwegian government changed its decision.

The days passed slowly. With Annæus's encouragement, a committee had been established in Oslo to act on Sylvia's behalf. The committee met with members of parliament and newspaper editors, publishing supportive articles in the press and appearing on national television.

The members of Ramat Hakovesh did whatever they could to make the couple feel at home. Sylvia and Annæus weren't about to be parasites, however, and demanded to be of some use. Sylvia was put to work in the orange groves, while Annæus found himself feeding the chickens and collecting eggs in the poultry runs. The news finally arrived from Norway that Annæus's divorce was final, so at last there was nothing to prevent him from marrying the woman he loved.

A few months later, the wedding ceremony took place in the Rafael home in South Africa.

Annæus continued working on Sylvia's return to Norway. He sent letters to the Norwegian prime minister and foreign minister, in which he asserted that he and Sylvia were legally married and that nothing was more natural than for them to live together in his native country. He quoted passages from the verdict, which expressed sympathy with Sylvia's motives for participating in the Lillehammer operation, and also stated that Sylvia had cut off all connections with the Mossad. A few newspapers were impressed by these claims, demanding that the Norwegian government reconsider its decision. The headline "The Norwegian Government Is Anti-Love" appeared in the weekly *Ag*.

Nevertheless, efforts to rescind the Norwegian government's decision dragged on for another year. Both Prime Minister Yitzhak Rabin and his successor, Menachem Begin, exerted pressure on the Norwegians on Sylvia's behalf.

And then suddenly, in 1977, Annæus received an official letter from the Norwegian attorney general's office announcing that after renewed deliberations it had been decided to allow Annæus's new wife to return to Oslo.

Sylvia's life as the wife of a famous attorney fell into a pleasant routine. She was the life and soul of the parties and receptions that were held in their home for friends and well-known personages. Her beauty, intelligence, and conversational skills—and especially her reputation as a courageous clandestine combatant—won her many admirers, men and women alike. News of her activities constantly appeared in the newspapers. Publishers offered her large sums in exchange for exclusive rights to tell her life story, and television stations begged her to award them interviews about the Mossad's activities. She politely turned them all down.

Sylvia became totally involved in this new chapter of her life and in her great love for her husband. She was finally free to come and go as she liked, no longer needing to hide behind a cover story or to worry that she was being followed. She took long walks, went on shopping sprees, was photographed by the press, and agreed to participate in festive occasions at the Israeli Embassy in Oslo. Only one thing spoiled her mood: Ali Hassan Salameh continued to carry on with his terrorist activities. The Mossad had still not managed to stop him.

What Sylvia didn't know was that Ali himself was tracking her down. His plan to kill Sylvia in Oslo was ready for execution. Everything was in place: the hit team, arms, ammunition, and escape routes from the city. But despite the secrecy of Ali's plan, a security leak caused it to reach the wrong ears. One of the six members of the hit team turned out to be a double agent who was working simultaneously for the Israelis and for Ali Salameh. Before leaving for Oslo, he contacted his Israeli case officer and informed him of the murder plan. The case officer passed on the information to his superiors.

The Mossad immediately appealed to the Norwegian security services, which went into action. They discovered that Ali's team had already reached Oslo. Its members were staying in three separate hotels, planning to collect the weapons waiting for them in a left-luggage compartment in the railway station and then to set up an ambush near Sylvia's home.

A Mossad representative met with Sylvia and informed her of the plot against her life. She was totally shocked to hear about it; the possibility that Ali Salameh would send his men to eliminate her never crossed her mind. She was now a Norwegian citizen, married to a prominent attorney. She had made her permanent home in Oslo, and she spoke fluent Norwegian almost without a trace of a foreign accent.

When the plan to eliminate Sylvia was revealed to the Norwegian authorities, they posted twenty-four-hour protection around her house. They insisted that she remain at home until such time as the matter had been dealt with. On the instructions of the Israeli Foreign Ministry in Jerusalem, the Israeli ambassador in Oslo requested an urgent meeting with the Norwegian prime minister, Edward Nordley, to make him aware of the information that had been received by the Mossad. The prime minister knew that the Mossad would never pass on unreliable information, so he accepted that there really was a plan to murder Sylvia Rafael. His face reddened in anger. "I'll take care of this personally," he said.

After the ambassador had left his office, the prime minister asked to be connected with Yasser Arafat in Beirut. The Fatah leader was surprised to receive the call from Oslo. He had never met the Norwegian premier and couldn't imagine why that prominent statesman was calling him.

"Mr. Arafat," began the Norwegian leader without preamble, "we have been informed by a reliable source that your organization has sent a team to Oslo with the intention of murdering Mrs. Sylvia Rafael-Schjødt."

"I have no idea what you're talking about," said Arafat. In fact, he knew every detail of the assassination plan and had personally approved it.

The prime minister ignored his response. Arafat was obviously not telling the truth.

"I would like to make it clear to you, sir," he said in a serious tone, "that Mrs. Rafael-Schjødt is a Norwegian citizen. I would like you to promise me here and now that you will recall your people from Oslo this very day. I also want your solemn oath that nobody from your organization will ever lay a finger on that woman."

Arafat realized that there was no point in further denying his involvement. He tried to play for time.

"I'll check with my associates to see if there is any basis for the rumor you mention," he said evasively.

"I'm prepared to wait on the line," insisted the prime minister. "I asked for your guarantee, Mr. Arafat, and I want it now."

Arafat understood that the game was up. He knew that if he continued to annoy the Norwegians, they were capable of taking action detrimental to the Palestinians: they could arrest the six members of the hit team, banish Fatah representatives from Oslo, deport Arab students studying in Norway, and prevent others from entering the country.

"All right," Arafat said finally. "On the assumption that the team you're talking about really exists, I will make every effort to withdraw them from Oslo."

"I also asked you to promise that you will never harm the woman in question."

"I guarantee that she will not be harmed."

"Thank you, Mr. Arafat."

Ali Salameh heard from the Fatah leader about his conversation with the Norwegian premier and realized that he would not be able to carry out his plan of revenge. The woman who, together with other clandestine combatants, had chased him tirelessly was now out of bounds, having been given iron-clad protection. Ali seethed with rage, but came to the conclusion that there was nothing to be done. He angrily instructed the hit team to return home immediately.

As time passed, the noose around Ali Hassan Salameh's neck tightened. The disclosure of the plan to eliminate Sylvia brought home to him how closely the Israelis were following him, and how primed they were for action. It became clearer than ever to him that the Mossad wouldn't leave him alone as long as he walked the earth.

His lust for life was stronger than ever, especially since he had married Georgina and had a child with her. More than anything, he needed to find an insurance policy that would deter the Israelis and allow him to stay alive. He searched for an authority that had influence over the Mossad and would force it to relinquish the plan to eliminate him. There was only one power that might succeed in this: the United States of America.

As usual, Ali planned his next move carefully and cleverly. He wanted to approach the Americans in the context of a situation in which they felt that he was indispensable to them and that without his help they were liable to suffer serious consequences. He convinced Arafat that it was worthwhile to secretly cooperate with the Americans, since only they could help the PLO restrain the extreme elements in the organization and avoid Arafat's being deposed as its leader. "We will send them inaccurate information," he suggested, "and in return they will promise their protection whenever we need it." Arafat bought the idea.

All that remained was to convince the Americans that it was in their interest to form such an alliance. Ali put together a plan that he felt sure the Americans would welcome with open arms. On June 16, 1976, a team of men who were loyal to Ali ambushed a convoy of automobiles carrying the new American ambassador to Lebanon, Francis Malroy, to his first meeting with the Lebanese president, Elias Sarkis. A few minutes before the convoy reached its destination, its way was blocked by a truck from which shots were fired at the passengers. At the same moment, Ali's men attacked the ambassador's car, killing his bodyguards and kidnapping him, together with the embassy's economic attaché and his Lebanese driver, to an unknown hiding place. The Lebanese security forces, which initiated a widespread manhunt in pursuit of the attackers, didn't manage to turn up a single clue. The next day the bodies of the kidnapped men were discovered in a deserted area of southern Beirut.

Upon Ali Salameh's instigation, the Fatah leadership announced that they had had no part in the kidnapping and the murders. They accused extreme factions of the organization of being responsible. The Beirut police arrested a few suspects, but they were quickly released.

The Americans, greatly perturbed by the Lebanese incident, were glad when Ali secretly approached the CIA in Beirut and offered his help in wiping out the extreme factions of the PLO in return for American know-how and weaponry. He also disclosed to American intelligence agents that the Russians planned to kidnap a CIA agent, Charles Waterman, who was then quickly surrounded with bodyguards and instructed to avoid traveling to potentially dangerous parts of Lebanon.

One day, after a night out with Georgina at a local nightclub, Ali was hit by two bullets fired at him at close range by attackers who escaped from the scene. He was rushed to the hospital, where it became clear that, luckily for him, his wounds were superficial. After a few days, Arafat announced that the attack had been perpetrated by one of the factions opposing him. No suspects were arrested.

The Americans invited Ali to recuperate in the United States. He traveled there with Georgina. For the first time since he had become a terrorist, he was not apprehensive, confident that the Americans were providing him with bullet-proof protection.

It was 1978. Heavily armed British security forces surrounded the London Hilton, where an international conference against terror was being held. Representatives of intelligence services and security organizations from around the world had convened to discuss ways to combat the terrorism that now threatened so many countries. They analyzed the developmental processes of terrorist movements in Europe and Asia, expressed growing concern that terror would strike in the United States as well, and raised suggestions for making the war against terror more effective in combating the growing menace.

Two top executives from the Mossad were also present. They had arrived in order to listen to what others had to say and to voice their predictions regarding trends in world terror. In their presentation, they pointed out that terrorist activity had been born in the

Middle East, where so many Muslims were being recruited to fight a "Holy War" against Israel and her allies. Al-Qaeda had yet to be established, but the Mossad representatives raised the speculation that an upsurge in terrorist activity would soon give rise to an extremist terrorist framework that would put any past activities in the shade.

Representatives of the CIA shook hands with the Mossad delegates and complimented them on their eye-opening comments. They didn't mention their alliance with Ali Hassan Salameh, but the Mossad already knew about it. In an informal encounter between Israelis and Americans in the hotel bar, one of the Mossad men expressed concern regarding the strong ties between Ali and the CIA. The Israelis expected the Americans to mention that Ali was cooperating with them and that they did not want anything unexpected to happen to him.

The Americans did indeed hint in that direction.

"What would you say," one of them asked the Mossad men, "if we were to ask you to put aside any plans regarding that man?"

"We would agree to pass on your request to our superiors, but we wouldn't be able to promise anything."

"Isn't it about time you called a truce?"

"Maybe so, but Ali Salameh has a lot to answer for."

The Americans had expected a different answer.

"Why is it so hard for you to forgive and forget?" one of them asked.

"If you want the honest truth," said the Israeli, "the Lord forgives . . . we don't."

Preparations for formulating a plan that would finally neutralize Ali Salameh went into high gear. After lengthy deliberations, the Special Operations Unit of the Mossad finally developed a plan of operation that was capable of success, but the unit needed to find the right people to carry it out. It was decided to place most of the responsibility on the shoulders of what seemed on the surface to be an unusual candidate. She was a determined young Jewish girl whose father was a British engineer and whose mother was a Czech theater actress who had escaped from Prague to England at the outbreak of World War II and later appeared on the London stage. The recruit had grown up in the family home in a fashionable area of the English capital, attended a private school, and later studied geography at London University. She was an average student, but she loved participating in sports competitions and traveling long distances in her Morris Mini car. She spent a few years with relatives in Australia and then transferred to the Hebrew University in Jerusalem, where she met a headhunter from the Mossad. The young British girl enthusiastically accepted his offer of possible recruitment to the Special Operations Unit. After months of tests and investigations, she was accepted into the organization.

She arrived in England on a new passport, rented an apartment, and, as instructed by her case officer, avoided any contact with friends and family. For three months she remained shut up in her apartment to avoid being spotted in the street, as she anxiously awaited the Mossad's instructions.

Word finally arrived. She packed her things and flew to Germany. At the Mossad's command, she signed up to study botany and biology at the University of Frankfurt and, in order to give credibility to her cover story, set up a branch of a Swiss charity association that aided needy children all over the world. She spent most of her free time working toward this goal. She recruited German volunteers, initiated charity functions, sent letters of thanks to the newspapers from children who had been helped by donations, and paid herself a small salary out of the proceeds.

While she was in Germany, she carried out some routine assignments for the Mossad, but these didn't exactly fire her with enthusiasm. She felt that she was capable of contributing much more, but she didn't know when she would be asked to do so. Her case officer didn't divulge information about any future plans for her—until the day he told her she would be flying to Beirut. When she heard the details of the mission, her face lit up. This was exactly the operation she had been waiting for.

Through the heavy raindrops beating on the window of the plane that was coming in to land, the tenements of Beirut appeared blurred and distorted. The sea was gray and stormy, and the sandy beach bordered by the promenade looked abandoned and dreary.

The dark-haired passenger of average height waiting in line at the passport control with the other passengers appeared calm and self-confident. Her dowdy clothes indicated that she wasn't particularly well-off, and she was wearing glasses with thick lenses.

The border control officer opened her British passport. The last exit stamp was from Frankfurt airport.

"What were you doing in Frankfurt?" asked the clerk politely.

She told him about the charity association and showed him advertisements in the papers and photos of benefit functions.

The passport officer had instructions to call security if a passenger aroused the slightest suspicion. Foreigners visiting Lebanon were liable to cause trouble, but the passenger from Germany appeared to be simply a junior clerk from some dreary office. He asked her a few routine questions, just so that he could claim to have done his job properly.

"What do you intend doing here?"

"I'm interested in helping needy children in Lebanon."

"You'll have plenty to do, especially with the refugee children."

"I know," she answered.

He stamped her passport with the entry date of November 1, 1978.

"You should have come in summer," the clerk commented. "Winters here are cold and unpleasant."

She nodded her head.

"I'll remember that for next time," she said with an attempt at a smile.

She collected her suitcase at the baggage carousel. The customs officers didn't bother checking it, but even if they had, they wouldn't have found anything. Who would have suspected that her hair dryer concealed a sophisticated remote-control device that could detonate a powerful explosive charge?

She went by cab to the Meridian Hotel, where she had reserved a room in advance. The next day she walked over to a real estate agent's office near the hotel, routinely checking whether she was being followed.

The agent filled in a form stating name, passport number, family status, and type of apartment required: three furnished rooms on Verdun Street that could serve as an office and living quarters. She went out with him in his car to search for a suitable apartment.

"You have expensive tastes," the real estate agent commented. "Verdun is one of the most fashionable streets in the city. Almost every building has a doorman and a well-appointed lobby. The residents are members of parliament, government officials, writers, and artists. It's a very pleasant, quiet area."

He showed her an apartment on the sixth floor of an elegant apartment building. She examined it quickly and said that it didn't

suit her. In fact she had nothing against the apartment, except that it
was in the wrong place.

There were two more empty flats on Verdun Street. She visited
them and finally chose one located on the eighth floor of the building. The flat had spacious rooms furnished in good taste and a large
balcony with a view of the building across the street. She noticed
that the shutters on the fourth floor of that building were drawn
tight, but she knew who lived there: the man who was the real reason for her arrival in Beirut.

She went out onto the balcony facing the street.

"This is the quietest street in central Beirut," the agent said, urg-
ing her to make up her mind. "You won't find a quieter one."

She didn't need much time to decide.

"I'll take it," she said. The rent was a bit higher than she had
expected, but she didn't bargain. She paid the agent's fee in cash,
along with a two-month advance on the rent, signed the lease, and
was given the keys. An hour later her suitcase arrived.

The new occupant had regular habits. She would leave her apartment every morning, buy a paper and milk and rolls for breakfast.
Afterward she would drive in her hired Datsun automobile to visit
refugee camps in order to estimate the amount of funds they required. Upon returning from the camps, she would shut herself up
in her apartment and make phone calls connected with relief work.
When she met her neighbors on the stairs, she importuned them to
contribute to the charity. Only a few of them did so.

In the evening the lights in her apartment were always on. She
wasn't interested in enjoying the city's nightlife; instead, she stayed
home, listening to music on the radio and staring out the window at
the building opposite. If the weather was dry, she would sit on her
balcony. She didn't receive any letters or parcels.

She had another occupation that her neighbors were unaware of.
From her window she checked the timetable of two vehicles, one a
Land Rover and the other a Chevrolet, which would regularly stop
outside the house opposite to collect a passenger and make their
way to Fatah headquarters and back. The vehicles arrived at exactly
the same hour every day: 9:30 a.m. on the way to headquarters and
5:15 p.m. on the way back. She had a clear view of the man who
was being picked up. She recognized him from photographs that
she had been shown before her trip to Beirut. It was Ali Hassan Salameh. It was he who occupied the fourth floor of the building oppo-

site her apartment. By means of an electronic communication device that had been especially developed for the operation, she reported this timetable to the Special Operations Unit.

She remained in the apartment on Verdun Street for several weeks. Simultaneously, careful preparations were being made in Israel for the last stages of the operation. According to plan, a man landed at Beirut airport on a flight from Zurich. He carried a British passport and presented himself as a businessman. He registered at a hotel on the Corniche, the promenade along the sea, and rented a Volkswagen. He parked the car in the hotel's underground garage. The day after his arrival, another man arrived in Beirut on a flight from Canada, introducing himself as an agent of an international corporation that manufactured cutlery. He booked in at another hotel on the Corniche, and also rented a car. In the middle of the night, he got into his car and drove to a deserted stretch of beach near Beirut. A short time later, IDF soldiers landed there with rubber boats loaded with explosives. The charges were quickly loaded into the man's car, the rubber boats returned to the sea, and the man drove to the underground garage where his British colleague had parked his car. The garage was almost empty, providing ideal conditions for undercover activity.

The two so-called businessmen, members of the Special Operations Unit of the Mossad, transferred the explosive charges to the Volkswagen and prepared them for use, as they had been trained to do in Israel. Afterward they drove the car to Verdun Street and parked it carefully outside Ali Hassan Salameh's building. The men of Black September had learned their lesson from the Mossad's attacks against the organization's commanders. No senior member would dare enter his car before it was thoroughly checked by bodyguards. For that reason, the Mossad had decided to place the explosives in a car that would be parked next to the victim's vehicle, not inside the vehicle itself.

From the window of her apartment, the woman clandestine combatant watched nervously as the Volkswagen drew up. She saw the driver emerge and walk away with firm steps, disappearing down the street.

Everything was ready for action—the death trap, the hand that would press the remote button, the getaway cars for the perpetrators of the attack.

That night she found it hard to sleep. She knew that there was no guarantee of success. The smallest change in the victim's plans, a faulty connection in the explosive device, a malfunction of the remote control—any one of these could be critical. So much planning, so many people, so many dangers were involved in this mission. The Mossad and the entire Israeli intelligence community were all depending on her at this moment.

She stood at her window as a cold day dawned in mid-January 1979. The street was deserted. Not a soul could be seen on the sidewalks, and there was no traffic on the street. The shops were still shut. She packed her few belongings into her suitcase and placed it in the trunk of her car. She didn't want to leave anything for the last minute.

She was shaken to observe that Ali didn't leave his house that morning. She had seen him return the evening before, and she had never seen him remain at home until so late in the day. She waited anxiously for the arrival of the vehicles that were supposed to collect him.

Ali Hassan Salameh was upstairs eating lunch with his wife, Georgina. She was in the final stages of her second pregnancy and had no appetite. He was on his way to a congress of the Palestinian Council in Damascus, which was held every six months. He told his wife that he would return the next day.

"Be careful," she said.

Ali just smiled. "Damascus is the safest place on earth for me," he said reassuringly.

At 3:45 p.m. Ali's security men arrived to take him to the airport. He kissed his wife good-bye. "I'll miss you," he said.

"I'll miss you, too," she whispered. "*Alla ma'akh.* God be with you."

Ali got into the Chevrolet. His bodyguards took up their positions in the Land Rover. The rented Volkswagen loaded with explosives was parked a couple of yards away.

The moment had come.

Peering down at the street from behind the curtain that covered her window, the woman combatant pressed the button on the remote control device.

A huge explosion blew the Volkswagen carrying the explosive charges to pieces and instantly shattered all the windows of the adjacent buildings. The Chevrolet went up in flames, and Ali Hassan Salameh was mortally wounded. The time was 3:55 p.m.

When she heard the explosion, Georgina ran out onto the balcony. She saw the smoke rising from her husband's car and let out an unearthly scream. She knew in her heart that Ali was lost to her forever.

Verdun Street filled with people moving toward the site of the explosion. Ambulances and police cars arrived, their sirens shrieking.

The combatant left the apartment, got into her car, and made her way through the excited crowds. She drove to the Hotel Meridian, entered the lobby, and sank into a soft leather armchair. She had a few hours to spare before she was scheduled to meet her fellow team members on the seacoast. She drank coffee and read the newspaper. Scenes from the site of the explosion flashed on the television screen in front of her. The camera followed a stretcher carrying Ali Hassan Salameh's body.

After it became dark, she drove her car southward to a deserted beach. The two men who had prepared the explosives were already there waiting. They were all picked up shortly afterward by an Israeli Navy vessel.

The port of Haifa was covered in darkness when the three disembarked. The night air was chilly, and a light rain was falling. A transport vehicle of the Special Operations Unit collected the arrivals and headed for Tel Aviv. Their mission was complete.

There was still one matter that demanded attention. The Israeli government sent a representative to the son of Ahmad Bushiki, the man who had been mistakenly shot in Lillehammer, to discuss the amount of damages that would be paid to the family. The son finally agreed to accept the sum of $400,000 and to cancel his plans to take legal action against the State of Israel.

Sylvia read about Ali Hassan Salameh's death in the morning paper, while drinking coffee in the dining room of the house she and Annæus had bought near her family home in the town of Graaff-Reinet, South Africa. They had moved there after Annæus retired. Sylvia had originally suggested that they settle in Israel, but such a plan had too many drawbacks. Annæus didn't know Hebrew and wasn't sure if he could adjust to life in Israel. In addition, Sylvia's family was pressuring them to move to South Africa. Her mother wrote that after years of separation the family expected Sylvia to finally return to its bosom. "I pray for the chance to spend time with you before I die," she wrote. Sylvia was very moved by this letter. "I would so love to make it up to my mother for disappearing from her life for so many years," she told her husband. Annæus understood her feelings and told her that he was prepared to retire and spend the rest of his days with Sylvia in South Africa.

The sun lit up the breakfast table and the well-tended garden outside the window. Sylvia continued reading the report about Ali Hassan Salameh's elimination in Beirut. The paper speculated about who was responsible for the incident, but Sylvia didn't doubt for a moment that the Mossad was involved.

"Read this," she said to Annæus, who was sitting with her at the breakfast table. "It's a particularly interesting article."

He read it carefully and smiled. "It seems that we have come full circle," he said.

"I'm thrilled that justice has finally been done."

"Do you regret not having participated?"

"Of course."

Annæus parted from her with a kiss and drove off to buy some books in the town center. When he returned home, he was surprised to find Sylvia lying in bed with her eyes closed. This was unexpected, since they were invited to lunch with friends and she should already have been dressed and ready to go.

He stroked her face gently. It was burning with fever.

Sylvia opened her eyes.

"I'm sorry, Annæus," she whispered. "I think I must be ill."

He suggested calling a doctor, but she objected.

"I just have a bad cold," she said. "It will pass."

But when her temperature hadn't gone down after two days and her stomach started to ache, she agreed to call a doctor. He examined her thoroughly.

"I haven't found anything," he told her, "but you should go to the hospital for tests. They will be able to diagnose you properly."

Annæus drove her to the hospital and sat beside her while the doctors took blood and examined her heart, blood pressure, and reflexes. During the more complicated tests, he waited anxiously outside the door.

The results arrived twenty-four hours later, and they came as a shock.

Sylvia and Annæus sat in the office of the hospital director. His face was sad as he said, "I'm sorry that I don't have better news for you."

Sylvia went pale, and Annæus held her arm tightly as the doctor informed them that Sylvia had cancer.

"Is it curable?" asked her husband.

"We'll do everything we can to return your wife to good health. We may have to operate, but maybe not. In any case, chemotherapy will be necessary, and . . ."

Sylvia and Annæus didn't hear the rest. Stunned, they sat there holding hands. At one blow, fate had shattered their hopes of a long, happy life together.

"I'll turn the world upside down for you," promised Annæus. "I'll get the best doctors, the newest medicines. We'll fight this thing together until we overcome it."

"Are you sure we'll succeed?" asked Sylvia with a shiver.

"Of course," her husband smiled at her gently. "You know that we're both born fighters."

The best doctors were brought in to treat Sylvia, but it was too late. The cancer had spread throughout her body and had metastasized, causing her bouts of severe pain. She didn't know how bad her condition was because the doctors didn't tell her the whole truth.

"I'm not sure the treatments are helping me," she said one day to her husband.

Annæus was also slowly losing his optimism. His eyes followed his wife as she lost weight, her hair fell out, her face lengthened, and its bone structure became more prominent.

In order to cheer her up, Annæus took her on a round-the-world cruise. They occupied a stateroom on the upper deck of a pleasure cruiser, sailed around the Caribbean and down the Yangtze River in China, and docked in Venice, Naples, and Casablanca. Sylvia made an effort to act normally and to appear cheerful. She didn't reveal how much pain she was in, secretly swallowing tranquilizers and painkillers. She skipped around the dance floor, swam in the pool, gambled in the casino. She had the feeling that this cruise was sounding the final chord of her life.

"I don't know how to thank you," she said to Annæus on the final evening of the cruise, while they both stood on deck watching the sunset, "for all the happiness you've given me."

He embraced her and cried in his heart. He understood that she was beginning her good-byes.

After the cruise, Sylvia resumed treatment. A few years went by.

The doctors managed to put her into remission, but the cancer eventually reappeared, stronger than ever.

Sylvia and Annæus took a last trip to Norway to say good-bye to friends in Oslo and to Israel to part from Sylvia's friends in Ramat Hakovesh and the Special Operations Unit. Sylvia, wearing a wig and sitting in a wheelchair, pretended to be in a great mood without a care in the world, but she couldn't hide the truth. She hugged and kissed dozens of friends at the kibbutz. "I would really like to end my life in Israel," she said, "but I owe my family so much. I cut myself off from them when I was young, and we hadn't met for many years, so I owe them whatever time I have left." Before she left Ramat Hakovesh, Hadas and Shmuel presented her with a photo album and parted from her in tears. They all understood that they would never meet again.

From Israel Sylvia and Annæus flew back to South Africa, which was to be her final destination. They spent their days together attempting to make the best of whatever time remained. They spoke about the past and the present, but avoided discussing the future.

The last letter she sent to Aviva, a friend from the Mossad, was written with Sylvia's characteristic humor:

"Cancer has its advantages and its disadvantages. It's very possible that I'll die bald, but thanks to being ill, I've taken off all those unwanted pounds; my figure has never been better. Another advantage: I have three wigs and I look great in all of them."

On February 8, 2005, at the age of sixty-eight, Sylvia lost consciousness. She was rushed to the hospital and died the next morning.

In her will, she asked to be buried in the cemetery at Ramat Hakovesh. The inscription on her marble headstone was decided upon by her friends at the Special Operations Unit:

I loved my country with all my heart and soul
And when my time came, I was buried in its soil . . .

The Mossad's insignia was engraved next to the inscription.

Sylvia was buried in the military section of the kibbutz cemetery, on a small hill surrounded by orange groves, near the graves of those who had fought in the 1948 War of Independence to ensure the survival of the Jewish people in its land. Sylvia had continued their heritage, striving toward the same goal.

The location of her final resting place symbolized her life to perfection. It overlooked the kibbutz she loved, which was an integral part of the country to which she had devoted most of her life and for which she had braved considerable dangers, the kibbutz that had made such an eloquent gesture by allowing a non-Jewish woman who was not a member to be buried in its soil. To the east was a view of the minarets of Tira, the nearby Arab village. Arab cities and populations had formed the backdrop of so many of the operations in which she had taken part, both in enemy territory and in pursuit of Palestinian terrorist organizations. How symbolic, then, was her final resting place: to the west, green fields and singing birds and the intoxicating smell of citrus fruits in flower; and to the east, the muezzin's call to prayer wafting on the breeze.

At the funeral the eulogies were read by her husband and the heads of the Mossad. Mike Harari said, "You were an empress of royal blood, a remarkable clandestine combatant, a loyal emissary of the people of Israel. Your motivation to succeed was truly remarkable, and on more than one occasion, you endangered your life to perform the impossible. Sylvia, you will be sorely missed by all of us."

Surrounding the grave with bowed heads and moist eyes were friends and fellow combatants, representatives of the Mossad. Many of them had known her personally and had shared dangerous operations with her, learning to appreciate her devotion, her love of life, and her ability to handle any situation, no matter how difficult. Only Abraham Gemer—the instructor who had been her first instructor and was later to be her case officer in Paris and a fellow member of the team in Lillehammer, the man to whom she was closest of all—was absent from the funeral. News of her death had reached him at the rehabilitation center where he was hospitalized. His wife, who had known Sylvia, said at the funeral that her husband had shed tears when he heard about the death of his protégé.

At the end of the ceremony, Sylvia's husband approached Moti Kfir, the director of the School for Special Operations, and they both reminisced about Sylvia. "I hope that one day a book will be written about her," said Annæus.

After the ceremony, the mourners made their way to a photographic exhibition in Sylvia's memory that was being held at the kibbutz's cultural center. There were photographs that she had taken in her early years in Israel as a volunteer, those she had taken in Arab countries under the false identity of Patricia Roxenburg, others of her friends from the kibbutz and the husband who had nursed her through her last days. In most of the photographs she appeared smiling, happy, and at peace with the difficult task she had taken upon herself so willingly.

A Personal Afterword

Moti Kfir

No story ever truly ends, and no account of a person's life can be all-inclusive. Did we manage in this book to portray Sylvia Rafael in all her many facets? Do the events described here portray who she truly was? Not necessarily.

During my years of working in the Mossad, friends often expressed curiosity about the secret operator, seeking to understand what makes such a person stand out from others. In recent years some of our greatest heroes have been revealed through the media, books, and films: Eli Cohen, Wolfgang Lotz, Baruch Mizrahi, Ya'akova Cohen, Max Bennett, and now Sylvia Rafael.

Are their lives better understood now than they were before? Are their motivations, their life decisions, and the path that led them to become what they were any clearer today? I doubt it.

I am not an expert on the human psyche. All I am able to do is describe a sequence of events, leaving it to the readers to interpret these events as they will.

Heroism is always a major actor on the stage of history, but when we meet a person who is destined to be called a "hero," even though he or she never intended to be one, we encounter a human being first and foremost. Have they achieved greater self-realization than other individuals? Not necessarily. Do they and those that sent them—who have often become myths in their own right—belong to a special category? Could their parents and teachers have predicted what turn their lives would take? I doubt it. True dramas are a combination of actions, decisions, constraints, challenges, and sleepless nights. I was lucky enough to meet and work with people who featured in such dramas. None of them resembled another. Some were Spartan introverts who went through life observing rather than acting. They had superlative powers of observation and, after years of experience, were able to size up people and situations quickly and accurately. Such people felt comfortable far from the public eye, never seeking fame or recognition. They didn't consider their lives to be the slightest bit extraordinary.

Sylvia was cut from a different cloth. Even when she was living in the shadows she stood out, like a leading actress on the stage of life, relishing all its pleasures, always pushing forward, like someone who realizes that her time is limited and that she still has so much to accomplish. Her high intelligence made her brilliant at problem solving. She had wisdom and extensive knowledge in a large number of fields. She could get close to, and win the trust of, a wide variety of people. She had a restless curiosity, resourcefulness in times of stress, and a strong sense of belonging to a people and being part of its history. Even though she wasn't Jewish according to law, she identified deeply with and felt totally committed to the Jewish people and its future. She never asked, "Why me?" She knew why. As a volunteer, she was ready to make any sacrifice and chose to take part in an impossible mission that brought out the very best in her.

Only a part of what Sylvia was could be told here. All the rest will come to light in the fullness of time.

This book is dedicated to the memory of Sylvia Rafael—the woman and the clandestine combatant—and to all the other combatants, past and present, wherever they are.

I would like to express my sincere gratitude to Ram Oren, who has succeeded, in this book and in others, to describe the great historical dramas that enrich our lives as a series of events that can be understood and appreciated by a wide audience.

To my wife, Nira, for being there, then and now.

To my parents, Bella and Yehuda Karpov, who always asked me about the nature of my work and who are now finally able to know something about it.

To my daughters, Shirley and Efrat, for the love, patience, and tolerance they have shown, despite the many days when I was away from home and couldn't tell them the reasons why.

To Yoske Yariv, my commander and friend, who demonstrated to me that intelligence work is both an art and a craft.

To my friends, for giving me constant support and encouragement.

To Or, Tal, May, Gal, and Omer, my grandchildren, in hopes that this book serves them as a testimony and a heritage.

To Fate, which decreed that I would be part of such an exciting enterprise.

"If it were all to happen again, I would not wish it to be any different" (Alexander Penn).

Moti Kfir held a number of senior positions in the Special Operations Unit of the Mossad, serving among other things as the director of the School for Special Operations. He was awarded a doctorate in history by the Paris Sorbonne.

Notes

1. A Murder Plot

1. For a full description of this event, see chapter 5.
2. The Givati Brigade was founded in December 1947. At the start of the 1948 War of Independence, the brigade was charged with operations in the central region of Israel. As the war entered its second stage, Givati became the 5th Brigade and was moved to the south. One battalion fought on the Jerusalem front. When Israel declared independence, Givati consisted of five battalions. A sixth battalion was founded on May 30, 1948. It was converted into a reserve brigade in 1956.

2. An Unexpected Visitor

1. "Boer" is the Dutch and Afrikaans word for farmer, which came to denote the descendants of the Dutch-speaking settlers of the eastern Cape frontier in Southern Africa during the eighteenth century.
2. "Muftis" are Muslim religious leaders, similar to bishops; they are often (as here) political leaders as well.
3. Mandatory Palestine was a geopolitical entity under British administration, carved out of Ottoman Southern Syria after World War I. The British civil administration in Palestine operated from 1920 until 1948. This administration was formalized with the League of Nations' consent in 1923 under the British Mandate for Palestine.
4. Following the outbreak of disturbances at the end of 1947, the road between Tel Aviv and Jewish Jerusalem became increasingly difficult for Jewish vehicles. Ambushes by Palestinian Arab irregulars became more frequent and more sophisticated. In January 1948 the number of trucks supplying Jewish Jerusalem had fallen to thirty. By March the daily average number of trucks reaching Jerusalem was six. The intention of the besieging forces was to isolate the 100,000 Jewish residents of the city from the rest of the Jewish inhabitants of Palestine. In particular, the Arab forces tried to cut off the road to Jerusalem from the coastal plain, where the majority of the Jewish population resided. The Arabs blocked access to Jerusalem at Latrun and Bab al-Wad, a narrow valley surrounded by Arab villages on hills on both sides. The breaking of the siege on Jerusalem and the annexation of the captured areas to the Jewish state became primary goals for the Israelis in the 1948 War of Independence.
5. For information on Masada, see chapter 3. The Siege of Jerusalem

in the year 70 was the decisive event of the First Jewish-Roman War. The Roman army, led by the future emperor Titus, besieged and conquered the city of Jerusalem, which had been occupied by its Jewish defenders in 66. The siege ended with the sacking of the city and the destruction of its famous Second Temple. The destruction of both the First and Second Temples is still mourned annually as the Jewish fast of Tisha B'Av. The Arch of Titus, celebrating the Roman sack of Jerusalem and the Temple, still stands in Rome.

6. The Battle of Tel Hai in the Upper Galilee was fought in March 1920 and is perceived by some scholars to be the first armed engagement of the Arab-Israeli conflict. Shiite Arab militia, accompanied by Bedouin from a nearby village, attacked the Jewish agricultural settlement of Tel Hai. Eight Jews were killed, including Joseph Trumpeldor, a hero of World War I and commander of the Jewish defenders of Tel Hai, who was shot in the hand and stomach, and died while being evacuated to Kfar Giladi that evening. The battle is considered to have been decisive in determining the border between Palestine and Lebanon, making the Upper Galilee part of Mandatory Palestine. A national monument depicting a defiant lion was erected in memory of Trumpeldor and his seven comrades. The city of Kiryat Shemona (literally "Town of the Eight") was named after them. Today Tel Hai is home to a large regional college offering bachelor's and postgraduate degrees in a variety of disciplines.

7. The United Nations Partition Plan for Palestine was meant to lead to the creation of two separate independent Arab and Jewish states and the Special International Regime for the City of Jerusalem. On November 29, 1947, the General Assembly adopted a resolution recommending the adoption and implementation of the plan as Resolution 181. The plan was accepted by the leaders of the Jewish community in Palestine through the Jewish Agency, but was rejected by leaders of the Arab community, including the Palestinian Arab Higher Committee, who were supported in their rejection by the states of the Arab League. The Arab leadership both inside and outside of Palestine opposed partition and claimed all of Palestine. Immediately after adoption of Resolution 181 by the General Assembly, civil war broke out. The partition plan was not implemented.

8. Egged Israel Transport Cooperative Society Ltd., a cooperative owned by its members, is the largest transit bus company in Israel. Egged's intercity bus routes reach most cities, towns, kibbutzim, and moshavim in Israel and the West Bank, and the company operates urban city buses throughout the country. Petah Tikva was founded in 1878 by religious pioneers from Europe. It was the first modern Jewish agricultural settlement in Ottoman Palestine (hence its nickname "Mother of the Moshavot") and has since grown to become one of Israel's most populous urban centers.

9. In 1947 a civil war broke out in Mandatory Palestine between Jewish Yishuv forces and Palestinian Arab forces in response to the U.N. Partition Plan. An alliance of Arab states intervened on the Palestinian side, turning

the civil war into a war between sovereign states. The fighting took place mostly on the former territory of the British Mandate and for a short time also in the Sinai Peninsula and southern Lebanon.

10. Herod was born in 74 BC, the son of a prominent family in Idumea, now part of modern-day Jordan. He converted to Judaism and adopted Jewish customs. He supported King Hyrcanus II (a Hasmonean king descended from the Macabees), who appointed him governor of the Galilee. With the support of the Romans, who had conquered Judea in 63 BC, Herod was eventually crowned king of Judea, despite the strong objections of observant and nationalist Jews. He was a great lover of Graeco-Roman culture and was nicknamed "the Great" due to his colossal building projects, which included Caesarea, Antipatris, and the renovation of the Temple in Jerusalem. The Western (Wailing) Wall still stands today as a reminder of the Temple's magnificent proportions.

11. The Haganah ("The Defense") was a Jewish paramilitary organization that was active from 1920 to 1948 and later became the core of the Israel Defense Forces. Etzel is the common Israeli name for *Irgun Tzvai-Leumi*, or Irgun, an organization that was active in Mandatory Palestine from 1931 to 1948. Lehi (Combatants for the Freedom of Israel), commonly referred to in English as the Stern Gang, was a militant Zionist group founded during the British Mandate of Palestine. The avowed aim of both Etzel and Lehi was to forcibly evict the British authorities from Palestine and to allow unrestricted immigration of Jews and the formation of a Jewish state. They were incorporated into the Israel Defense Forces after David Ben-Gurion declared the founding of the State of Israel in 1948.

12. Nathan Alterman (1910–1970) was an Israeli poet, playwright, journalist, and translator who—though never holding any elected office—was highly influential in Socialist Zionist politics, both before and after the establishment of the State of Israel. His poem "The Silver Platter" is read out at Memorial Day ceremonies every year. Its title is based on a famous saying attributed to Chaim Weizmann, the first president of Israel: "The state will not be given to the Jewish people on a silver platter."

"Bab al-Wad" is a song commemorating the fierce fighting between the Jordanian Arab Legion and Jewish convoys on the way to blockaded Jerusalem during the 1948 Arab-Israeli War. On April 20, the Arabs recaptured the heights around Sha'ar HaGai (Bab al-Wad), closing the Tel Aviv road. The Palmach 10th Brigade (under the command of Lt. Col. Yitzhak Rabin, future prime minister of Israel) managed to capture the area, but the rest of the Jerusalem road remained under Arab control. In order to bypass the road, the so-called Burma Road was constructed (named after the World War II road into China). After the 1967 Arab-Israeli War, when the Latrun area was captured, the main Tel-Aviv–Jerusalem highway was once again constructed through Sha'ar HaGai. To this day, rusted armored cars that were destroyed during the 1948 war line the route to commemorate the battles.

Haim Gouri (born October 9, 1923) is an Israeli poet, novelist, journalist, and documentary filmmaker. During the 1948 Arab-Israeli War he was a deputy company commander in the Palmach's Negev Brigade. "The Friendship Song" was the late Yitzhak Rabin's favorite song and is sung every year at ceremonies commemorating his assassination in 1995.

13. The Hashemite Kingdom of Jordan is an Arab kingdom on the East Bank of the River Jordan, consisting roughly of the historic region of Transjordan. Jordan borders Saudi Arabia to the south and east, Iraq to the northeast, Syria to the north, and Israel to the west, sharing control of the Dead Sea with the latter. The desert kingdom emerged out of the post–World War I division of the Middle East by Britain and France. In 1946 Jordan became an independent sovereign state officially known as the Hashemite Kingdom of Transjordan. After capturing the West Bank area during the 1948–49 war with Israel, Abdullah I took the title King of Jordan and Palestine, and he officially changed the country's name to the Hashemite Kingdom of Jordan in April 1949.

14. Husseini was killed while personally reconnoitering an area of Qastal Hill that was shrouded by fog in the early hours of April 8, 1948. His forces later captured Qastal from the Haganah, which had occupied the village at the start of Operation Nachshon six days earlier with a force of about 100 men. They retreated to the Jewish settlement of Motza. Palmach troops recaptured the village on the night of April 8–9, losing eighteen men in the attack; most of the houses were blown up, and the hill became a command post. Husseini's death was a factor in the loss of morale among his forces.

15. Kibbutz Artzi (literally, "Nationwide Kibbutz") is a kibbutz movement associated with Hashomer Hatzair, a Socialist-Zionist youth organization. It was founded on April 1, 1927, and had 85 kibbutzim and 28,000 members in 1998.

16. Hashomer Hatzair (The Youth Guard) is a Socialist-Zionist youth movement that was founded in 1913 in Galicia, Austria-Hungary. It is the oldest Zionist youth movement still in existence. Initially Marxist-Zionist in orientation, it was influenced by the ideas of Ber Borochov, Gustav Wyneken, and Robert Baden-Powell, as well as by the German Wandervogel movement. Members of Hashomer Hatzair believed that the liberation of Jewish youth could be accomplished by *aliyah* (immigration) to Palestine and living in kibbutzim. After World War I, the movement spread to Jewish communities throughout the world as a scouting movement.

17. An *ulpan* is an institute, or school, for the intensive study of Hebrew. *Ulpan* is a Hebrew word meaning studio, or teaching, instruction. The *ulpan* is designed to teach adult immigrants to Israel the basic language skills of conversation, writing, and comprehension. Most *ulpanim* also provide instruction in the fundamentals of Israeli culture, history, and geography. The primary purpose of the *ulpan* is to help new citizens become integrated as quickly and as easily as possible into the social, cultural, and economic life of their new country.

18. Degania Alef, a kibbutz in northern Israel that falls under the jurisdiction of the Emek HaYarden Regional Council, was the first kibbutz established by Jewish Zionist pioneers in Palestine, which was then under Ottoman rule. It was founded on October 29, 1910, by ten men and two women. Degania Bet was established to the south in 1920. On May 20, 1948, during the Battles of the Kinarot Valley, Degania Alef and Degania Bet repelled a Syrian attack.

19. The Dead Sea Works, part of the Fertilizers Division of Israel Chemicals Ltd., is an Israeli potash plant in Sodom, on the sourthern basin of the Dead Sea coast of Israel. It is the world's fourth largest producer and supplier of potash products. The company also makes magnesium chloride, industrial salts, de-icers, bath salts, table salt, and raw materials for the cosmetics industry, and has customers in over sixty countries.

3. Night in an Arab Village

1. Titus Flavius Josephus (37–ca. 100) was a first-century Roman-Jewish historian and hagiographer who was born in Jerusalem—then part of Roman Judea—to a father of priestly descent and a mother who claimed royal ancestry. His most important works were *The Jewish War* (ca. 75) and *Antiquities of the Jews* (ca. 94). *The Jewish War* recounts the Jewish revolt against Roman occupation (66–70). *Antiquities of the Jews* recounts the history of the world from a Jewish perspective for an ostensibly Roman audience. These works provide valuable insight into first-century Judaism and the background of early Christianity.

2. The Mista'arvim, or Arab Department, of the Palmach performed covert operations and espionage missions against Arab militias, which frequently attacked Jewish settlements before 1948. It was the basis for founding the Mista'arvim units of the Israeli Defense Forces and the Israeli Border Police. These are counterterrorism units in which soldiers are specifically trained to disguise themselves as Arabs in order to kill or capture wanted terrorists. They are also commonly known as the Arab Platoons.

3. Ness Ziona is an Israeli town that was founded in 1883 by settlers from Russia at a time when Palestine was part of the Ottoman Empire.

4. Armed militias known as *fedayeen* emerged from militant elements among the Arab Palestinians. The *fedayeen* made an effort to infiltrate territory in Israel in order to strike targets in the aftermath of the 1948 Arab-Israeli War. Members of these groups were largely based within the refugee communities living in the Gaza Strip (then controlled by Egypt) and the West Bank (then controlled by Jordan) or in neighboring Lebanon and Syria.

5. Reuven Rubin (1893–1974) was a Romanian-born Israeli painter and Israel's first ambassador to Romania. His pleasant landscapes of Israeli scenes, notably olive trees, the red roofs of the agricultural settlements, and workers in the fields are very popular to this day.

4. Arrest and Investigation

1. The Hebrew Reali School in Haifa, Israel, is one of the country's oldest private schools. It numbers among its alumni Ezer Weizmann, the late president of Israel, and many other famous individuals, especially among the military.

2. The relationship between the Moroccan royal house and the Jews had traditionally been a cordial one. However, in the 1950s, after the State of Israel was established, Morocco's increasing identification with the Arab world, and pressure on Jewish educational institutions to arabize and conform culturally, added to the fears of Moroccan Jews. As a result, emigration to Israel jumped from 8,171 persons in 1954 to 24,994 in 1955, increasing further in 1956. Between 1956 and 1961, emigration from Morocco to Israel was prohibited by law; clandestine emigration continued, and a further 18,000 Jews left Morocco. On January 10, 1961, a boat carrying Jews attempting to flee the country sank off the northern coast of Morocco; the negative publicity associated with this prompted King Muhammad V to allow Jewish emigration, and over the three following years, more than 70,000 Moroccan Jews left the country. By 1967, only 50,000 Jews remained in Morocco.

5. Imprisoned in a Refugee Camp

1. Umm Kulthum (1898–1975) was an internationally famous Egyptian singer, songwriter, and film actress from the 1930s to the 1970s. More than three decades after her death in 1975, she is still widely regarded as the greatest female singer in Arabic music history.

2. For a detailed account of this operation, see chapter 6.

3. The *hamsa* is a palm-shaped amulet popular throughout the Middle East and North Africa, and a design commonly used in jewelry and wall hangings. Depicting the open right hand, the *hamsa* is an image recognized and used as a sign of protection in many societies throughout history, as it is believed to provide defense against the evil eye. The symbol predates Christianity and Islam. In Islam, it is also known as the Hand of Fatima, so named to commemorate Muhammad's daughter Fatima Zahra. Levantine Christians call it the Hand of Mary, for the mother of Jesus.

7. A Love Story

1. As noted earlier (chapter 2, note 11), the Haganah was a Jewish paramilitary organization that was active before 1948.

2. See chapter 4, note 2, on the Moroccan Jewish emigration.

3. Mea Shearim is an isolated neighborhood in the heart of Jerusalem. With its overwhelmingly ultra-Orthodox population, the streets retain the flavor of an East European settlement of the eighteenth century. Life re-

volves around strict adherence to Jewish law, prayer, and the study of Jewish texts. Traditions in dress may include black frock coats and black or fur-trimmed hats for men and long-sleeved, modest clothing for women. Strict dress regulations are enforced for visitors, and on the Sabbath they are asked to refrain from driving, smoking, and using mobile phones or cameras.

4. The Passover Seder ("order, arrangement") is a Jewish ritual feast that marks the beginning of the Jewish holiday of Passover. It is generally celebrated in late March or early April. The Seder is performed by a community or by multiple generations of a family, and involves a retelling of the story of the liberation of the Israelites from slavery in ancient Egypt. This story is in the Book of Exodus. The Seder itself is based on the Biblical verse commanding Jews to retell the story of the Exodus from Egypt: "You shall tell your child on that day, saying, 'It is because of what the LORD did for me when I came out of Egypt'" (Exodus 13:8). Seder customs include drinking four cups of wine, eating matzoth, partaking of symbolic foods placed on the Seder plate, and reclining in celebration of freedom. The Seder is performed in much the same way by Jews all over the world.

5. Traditionally, families and friends gather on Passover evening to read the text of the Haggadah, an ancient work derived from the Mishnah (Pesahim 10). The Haggadah contains the narrative of the Israelite exodus from Egypt, special blessings and rituals, commentaries from the Talmud, and special Passover songs.

6. Mount Sinai (also called Mount Moses or Mount Horeb) is a high granite mountain (7,497 feet) in southern Sinai believed to be the place where Moses received the Torah from God. There is a dispute about which mountain really is the one, but it is traditionally believed to be the one next to the peak upon which the St. Catherine Monastery was built.

Index

CPSIA information can be obtained at www.ICGtesting.com
Printed in the USA
LVOW12*0419220914

405207LV00001B/51/P